Software Engineering

Software Engineering
Architecture-Driven Software Development

Richard F. Schmidt

AMSTERDAM • BOSTON • HEIDELBERG • LONDON
NEW YORK • OXFORD • PARIS • SAN DIEGO
SAN FRANCISCO • SINGAPORE • SYDNEY • TOKYO

Morgan Kaufmann is an imprint of Elsevier

Acquiring Editor: Todd Green
Editorial Project Manager: Lindsay Lawrence
Project Manager: Priya Kumaraguruparan
Designer: Mark Rogers

Morgan Kaufmann is an imprint of Elsevier
225 Wyman Street, Waltham, MA, 02451, USA

Library of Congress Cataloging-in-Publication Data
Schmidt, Richard, 1956-
  Software engineering: architecture-driven software development / Richard Schmidt.
    pages cm
  Includes bibliographical references and index.
  ISBN 978-0-12-407768-3
  1. Software engineering. 2. Software architecture. 3. Computer software—Development. I. Title.
  QA76.758.S364 2013
  005.1—dc23   2013000589

British Library Cataloguing-in-Publication Data
A catalogue record for this book is available from the British Library

Printed and bound by CPI Group (UK) Ltd, Croydon, CR0 4YY

Transferred to digital print 2012

For information on all MK publications visit our website at www.mkp.com

Contents

SECTION 3   STAGES OF SOFTWARE ENGINEERING APPLICATION

A Note from the Author

Several controversial subjects are raised by the material presented within the book. These provocative topics address the scope of "software engineering" and are central to the author's motivation for publishing this material. If the Software Engineering discipline was well established and proven to achieve successful results, then there would be no need to publish and promote this material. However, this is not the case. The success rate of projects within the software industry has hovered around 30% for the past two decades. The failure of these projects can be associated with two primary symptoms which can be observed in almost every software development project and methodology. The first symptom involves an almost complete misconception of what a software product design is and how to develop a complete design description. The second symptom involves the lack of a standard set of software engineering principles and practices which establish an appropriate scope for a software engineering discipline.

The material presented in this book provides a comprehensive set of practices which are integrated and tightly coupled. However, this material deviates with popular "best practices" which have been encouraged due to the lack of a flawless way to design software. Some of my comments may seem critical; when suggesting an approach to fix a flawed system, criticism is inevitable. The intent is to stimulate the software community into a broad dialog by which a crucial set of software engineering principles and practices can be established.

I hope that the reader can set aside his or her personal opinions concerning mainstream concepts on software engineering. Do not let these controversial topics divert your attention from the fundamental line of reasoning being discussed. This book offers a rigorous, disciplined approach to the engineering of software products. It is time for the software community at large to take action to improve its dismal performance. I hope that this material will prove beneficial to future generations of professional software engineers.

Richard Schmidt
April 15, 2013

Preface

The purpose of this book is to provide comprehensive treatment of the software engineering discipline. The material presents software engineering principles and practices that are based on systems engineering. This book provides a detailed explanation of the essential software engineering philosophy, which emphasizes a disciplined approach to designing software products. To accomplish this, Section 1, Software Engineering Fundamentals, discusses the software development framework and project constructs within which software engineering is performed. Section 2, Software Engineering Practices, presents six technical conventions that convey a philosophy for harnessing computing technologies, applying scientific principles and invoking ingenuity to architect (i.e., design) the structure of software products. Section 3, Stages of Software Engineering Application, discusses the role a software engineering team undertakes within a software development project to establish and control the software product architecture. Each stage of a typical software development project is discussed with a focus on how a software engineering team collaborates with other technical and project-related organizations to influence the architectural design and implementation of software products. These sections clarify the practices, principles, tasks, and artifacts associated with a disciplined approach to software engineering.

The fundamental concepts this material is based on were derived from systems engineering practices to achieve the objectives identified in Table 1. These objectives are achieved by applying a set of principles and practices derived from the systems engineering discipline that have been successfully applied for over 50 years to develop complex systems. The emphasis is on the establishment of a complete software architecture, which enables each element of the product to be specified for fabrication, assembly, integration, and testing (FAIT). Applying these practices to the field of software engineering provides the basis for resolving the challenges listed in Table 1.

Current practices for software analysis and design stem from computer programming languages and the logical constructs by which the languages process data. This has driven software design methodologies, such as object-oriented design, that were not formulated to handle the complexity of advanced software products. By adapting systems engineering practices, this book presents a comprehensive approach to *designing* a software product by establishing rigorous software engineering principles and practices. These software engineering practices are clearly articulated to ensure that there is no uncertainty concerning their importance and applicability to software development. These practices are applied during a walkthrough of the software development process to control, revise, and manage the software architecture throughout a typical software development project context. The contents of this book are aligned with the Software Engineering Body of Knowledge[1] (SWEBOK) key process areas identified in Table 2. This alignment

---

[1] Institute of Electrical and Electronics Engineers (IEEE) Computer Society, *http://www.computer.org/portal/web/swebok*.

Table 1 Software Engineering Challenges and Objectives	
Software Engineering Challenge	**Objectives**
Design must take place before coding	Know what you are building before you begin to improve cost and scheduling accuracy Reduce product complexity with design detail and precision Cost, schedule, and risk control
Delivering the software technical data package	Complete design diagrams, drawings, and specifications for software implementation (construction)
Allocate requirements among elements of the design configuration	Requirements for decomposition and allocation among software components and units Requirements traceability
Integrated product and process development (IPPD)	Concurrent design and development of product sustainment capabilities Life-cycle costs control
Preparing a software integration strategy	Planned software component integration developed during architectural design activities Efficient software implementation planning
Controlling software complexity	Reduce software maintenance/support costs Efficient, user-friendly interactions
Enabling change assimilation	Stakeholder/user satisfaction Product competitiveness
Trade-off analysis	Cost and schedule control Design optimization Product evolution/incremental release stability Increased probability of project success
Preplanned product improvement	Delayed functionality to later releases to permit on-time product delivery

with the SWEBOK demonstrates how the topics addressed in the book are arranged and associated with the topics addressed by the SWEBOK. However, the SWEBOK is based on current software development practices and does not embrace the systems engineering practices in a rigorous, technical manner.

Book outline and subject matter

The following provides a brief overview of the content of each section and chapter of this book. The sections arrange the material into three coherent topics intended to permit readers to increase their knowledge and understanding of the principles (Section 1), practices (Section 2), and application of software engineering (Section 3). By adapting systems engineering practices to the field of software engineering,

Table 2 SWEBOK Key Process Areas

Key Process Areas	Book Coverage

Software requirements knowledge areas	Section 1
	    Chapter 3
	Section 2
	    Chapter 7
	    Chapter 9
	Section 3
	    Chapter 17

Software design knowledge area	Section 1
	    Chapter 3
	    Chapter 6
	Section 2
	    Chapter 10
	    Chapter 11
	    Chapter 12
	    Chapter 13
	    Chapter 14
	Section 3
	    Chapter 18

Software construction knowledge area	Section 3 Chapter 19

Software testing knowledge area	Section 3
	    Chapter 19
	    Chapter 20

Software maintenance knowledge area	Section 1
	    Chapter 5
	Section 3
	    Chapter 17
	    Chapter 18
	    Chapter 19
	    Chapter 20

Software configuration management knowledge area	Section 2
	    Chapter 9
	    Chapter 16
	Section 3
	    Chapter 20, configuration audits addressed (FCA/PCA)

Software engineering management knowledge area	Section 1
	    Chapter 4
	Section 2
	    Chapter 9
	    Chapter 16, project and technical plans addressed; work packages addressed
	    Section 3, project and technical plans addressed; work packages addressed

Software engineering process knowledge area	Section 2 Section 3

(Continued)

Table 2 SWEBOK Key Process Areas (*Continued*)

Key Process Areas	Book Coverage

Software engineering methods knowledge area	Section 2
	  Chapter 13, Software Design Synthesis
	  Practice object-oriented methods addressed, as applicable
	  Chapter 14, modeling and prototyping addressed

Software quality knowledge area	Section 3, identifies software quality assurance tasks within test and evaluation subsections

this material is intended to provide an innovative, disciplined, and technically demanding approach to developing software products.

Section 1: Software engineering fundamentals

This section discusses the basic principles associated with software engineering and their execution within a software development venue. The fundamental principles, practices, and doctrine are presented to establish software engineering as a professional discipline. Software product characteristics and software development strategies are discussed to stress the challenges confronting software development projects. Software engineering, as an organizational entity, bridges the notable differences in outlook and perception that exist among technical and project management specialists. Therefore, this section addresses the integration of software engineering practices with project management responsibilities and other software development roles.

Chapter 1: Introduction to Software Engineering. This chapter provides an overview of software engineering concepts, principles, and practices that are necessary to cope with the challenges of designing and developing complex software products. Software engineering practices and tools are investigated and their relationships to project management mechanisms are identified.

Chapter 2: Generic Software Development Framework. This chapter discusses the progression of software development activities describing how the software product is defined, designed, and implemented. This chapter tracks a typical software development effort through a series of sequential stages of development separated by project milestones and reviews. The discussion addresses the relationship between the software technical and project management realms of control.

Chapter 3: Software Architecture. This chapter identifies the composition of the software architecture in terms of the software product, computing environment, and post-development processes that enable product sustainment. It relates the generation of architecture design representations, models, and documentation to technical and project-related mechanisms necessary to keep the software development effort within budget and on track for scheduled delivery. Techniques for establishing the software requirement specifications are discussed, and functional and physical architectures are aligned with the stages of software development. This chapter discusses how the software product architecture provides the structural foundation for software implementation (programmatic design, coding, integration, and testing), as well as product life-cycle support.

Chapter 4: Understanding the Software Project Environment. This chapter acquaints readers with the software product characteristics that cause software development to be convoluted and incomprehensible. It addresses the software product complexity challenges and relates those to the project constructs and practices proven to facilitate successful software development endeavors. The discussion provides insight that will help reduce project impediments, upheaval, cancellations, and failures.

Chapter 5: Software Integrated Product and Process Development (IPPD). This chapter presents the philosophy of IPPD and its impacts on project scope and post-development considerations. It attempts to substantiate the need for a well-conceived and structured software architecture to ensure that the product's useful life is extended as a result of engineering attention to life-cycle concerns during development. The simultaneous engineering of software post-development processes is examined to show how early architectural decisions can affect life-cycle and ownership costs.

Chapter 6: Impediments to Software Design. This chapter examines the underlying characteristics of software that cause its "design" praxis to be unconventional and more difficult to fathom. It investigates the characteristics of software as a design and construction material that challenges conventional engineering scrutiny. This chapter presents the software engineering principles that govern the design of software products. Finally, this chapter introduces the software design chasm to contrive a resolution which permits software products to be engineered and designed.

Section 2: Software engineering practices

This section identifies the six practices that contribute to the profession of software engineering: (1) software requirements analysis, (2) functional analysis and allocation, (3) software design synthesis, (4) software analysis, (5) software verification and validation, and (6) software control. Each practice is characterized by a number of tasks that every software engineering professional should comprehend. These practices establish a coherent set of tasks focused on the design and elaboration of *the* software product architecture.

Chapter 7: Understanding Software Requirements. This chapter presents an approach to developing software requirement specifications that are derived from stakeholder needs and expectations and contribute to determining the scope of the software development effort. Software specifications drive the definition of the software architecture, but should not infer any architectural design scheme. Software requirements serve as the point of departure for deriving the software functional and physical architectures. The architecture is engineered by formulating a functional architecture and configuring the physical architecture. Every element of the architecture must be specified and traceable back to the software specifications. The relationships among software requirements, software engineering tasks, and project and technical plans are examined.

Chapter 8: Software Requirements Analysis Practice. This chapter identifies the specific tasks that must be selectively applied to establish the software product and post-development process specifications. This practice involves the allocation of performance quotas among lower-level functional and structural elements of the software architecture. This practice begins with the effort to solicit stakeholder needs and expectations and concludes with establishing a software product requirement baseline.

Chapter 9: Software Requirements Management. This chapter discusses the importance of controlling the software architecture in a proactive manner to facilitate the assessment of proposed changes. Software requirement management tools and practices are considered that enable a software engineering team to perform pragmatic appraisals of the change impact to the software architecture and the latitude of project resources to accommodate a desired alteration. The intent is to equip the development team to react judiciously to authorized changes and to assimilate modifications into the software architecture while not disrupting project scope, plans, or progression toward a successful conclusion.

Chapter 10: Formulating the Functional Architecture. This chapter discusses the nature of the functional architecture and how it is developed by decomposing specified requirements into successive layers of functional elements. Each functional element is specified in an approach of continual refinement that culminates when a function is recognized to be uncomplicated and for which an implementation can be realized. The functional architecture provides a logical and coherent representation of the software product's behavior in response to stimulus, events, or conditions that arise within the computing environment.

Chapter 11: Functional Analysis and Allocation Practice. This chapter identifies the specific tasks that must be considered to ensure that a complete, consistent, and traceable functional architecture is fashioned. Analysis is performed to understand the operational and software product behaviors by examining, decomposing, classifying, and specifying the top-level functions derived from requirement specifications. Performance requirements are allocated among contributing functions to establish measures of effectiveness and performance for lower-level functional elements.

Chapter 12: Configuring the Physical Architecture. This chapter describes the purpose and strategy for arranging and specifying the software product's physical architecture. The physical architecture identifies the foundational building-blocks for software unit design, coding, and testing. The software integration strategy is developed to identify the product structure and prescribes how the software units and components are to be incrementally combined, integrated, and tested to form the complete software product.

Chapter 13: Software Design Synthesis Practice. This chapter identifies the specific tasks that must be considered to ensure that a complete, consistent, and traceable physical architecture is generated. Design synthesis is a proven systems engineering practice for transitioning from a pure functional representation of a product to a physical configuration. It involves a "make-or-buy" trade-off that corresponds to a software "implement-or-reuse" decision.

Chapter 14: Software Analysis Practice. This chapter identifies the specific tasks that must be performed to conduct design-alternative trade-off analyses and risk assessments. Architectural design decisions must be made with sufficient insight to restrain growth in application complexity and software life-cycle costs. The tasks associated with conducting a trade-off analysis and risk assessment are described to provide a basis for understanding the nature of architectural design decisions and their impact on the software development effort.

Chapter 15: Software Verification and Validation Practice. This chapter identifies the specific tasks that must be performed to ensure that the elements of the software architecture remain consistent and aligned with authorized change proposals and requests. Verification tasks must be performed to ensure that the software implementation and test and evaluation efforts are synchronized with the software architecture specifications and design documentation.

Chapter 16: Software Control Practice. This chapter identifies the specific tasks that must be selectively applied to ensure the software product architecture reflects the current design concepts and incorporates authorized change proposals, requests, and design decisions. Requirements traceability must be embedded within the software architecture and associated documentation so that the technical team can promptly and efficiently respond to decisions of the change control boards. In addition, it is necessary for authorized change proposals and requests to be reflected in project and technical plans, schedule, budgets, and work-package descriptions.

Section 3: Stages of software engineering application

This section discusses the roles and responsibilities assigned to technical organizations throughout a software development project. The participation of technical organizations in a software engineering integrated product team (IPT) is stressed.

Chapter 17: Software Requirements Definition. This chapter identifies the manner by which the software requirement specifications are generated by the software engineering IPT. The contributions of participating organizational representatives are identified as the requirements for the software product, and post-development processes are established.

Chapter 18: Software Architecture Definition. This chapter identifies the manner by which the software functional and physical architectures are defined during the preliminary and detailed architecture stages. These stages focus on an IPPD approach to facilitate the establishment of the software implementation, testing, and post-development process infrastructures necessary to facilitate the fulfillment project objectives.

Chapter 19: Software Implementation. This chapter identifies the tasks to be performed by the software implementation organization to programmatically design, code, and test software units and conduct software integration and testing. During this phase the post-development processes are implemented concurrently to support acceptance testing and the deployment readiness review.

Chapter 20: Software Acceptance Testing. This chapter identifies the tasks to be performed by the software test and evaluation organization during the conduct of software product acceptance testing. The roles of the participating organizational representatives are identified as they monitor acceptance testing, react to test failures and respond to software problem reports resulting from acceptance testing. In addition, the post-development processes must be qualified to confirm that they are ready to support software product distribution, training, and sustainment operations.

Software Engineering Fundamentals

This section provides an overview of the software engineering discipline to acquaint readers with the lexicon used to describe software engineering principles, practices, and tasks. Fundamentally, software is a unique material from which software products are crafted. The distinctive characteristics of software as a fabrication material represent an enigma to software professional. The challenges associated with engineering and designing software products is investigated to diminish the confusion surrounding the various approaches to software engineering. Software engineering's fundamental doctrine is established to provide a set of principles and practices against which the software engineering discipline can be founded.

Foremost, this section introduces a lexicon for discussing the application of sound software engineering techniques. The terminology inherent in this lexicon coalesce accepted nomenclatures from a variety of professions, particularly systems engineering, project management, and configuration management. This lexicon is intended to combat the myriad of illegitimate terms thrown about the software communities that enhance the confusion and difficulty associated with establishing distribution, training, operations, support, and disposal. The principles of systems engineering include:

1. A system represents a complex, human-made product that involves hardware, software, and human operators to work effectively. The system or product must be understood in terms of its complete set of life-cycle processes, which impact the feasibility of potential design solutions.
2. A product is a combination of interrelated parts organized into a complex whole.
3. A product is human-made (designed, manufactured, tested, operated, and sustained) for a specific, sometimes generalized, purpose. This eliminates "natural" or "biological" systems from consideration as a system of interest.
4. The effectiveness of the product in operation is a result of the application of system thinking, which attempts at understanding how parts influence, cooperate, and collaborate with one another within a collective whole. This necessitates understanding the effects of the operational environment on the performance of the product and its constituent parts.
5. A product involves a hierarchical arrangement of smaller, less complex components and parts. The design of a complex product cannot be derived without decomposing the problem space into manageable problems for which one or more technical solutions can be discriminated.
6. The system architecture represents the complete set of product life-cycle requirements and the product functional and physical configurations that provide its technical description.
7. The product is realized when the individual parts or components are fabricated (or procured), assembled, integrated, and tested.

These systems engineering principles can be easily adapted to a software product. The computing environment provides the hardware component and represents the major element of the operational environment. The software product is the focus of the software engineering effort, and it must be designed to be operated by end users. The set of software life-cycle processes differs slightly since software is not manufactured or fabricated, and its methods of replication, distribution, and training may vary significantly from a system-based product that involves hardware.

The practices associated with systems engineering were established in the early 1940s and have been proven to resolve large, complex system or product design challenges. These practices involve:

- Requirements analysis
- Functional analysis and allocation
- Design synthesis
- Systems analysis
- Verification and validation
- Control

These six practices, and their adaptation to apply to the engineering of software products, is the main focus of this book. Section 2 provides the detailed definition of these practices as they apply to software engineering. The titles of these practices have been modified slightly to distinguish them from the systems engineering practices. This enables the same practices to be applied while acknowledging the difference in their application to solve a different design problem.

Summary

The chapters in this section provide a framework within which the software engineering principles and practices are founded. The vocabulary used to present these software engineering principles and practices has been carefully chosen to avoid confusion. However, the language quagmire that exists in the software industry coupled with potential conflicts in other engineering disciplines may impair the applicability of the precise terms used to express these software engineering concepts. For the sake of comprehending this manuscript, accept the terms used within the book as a means of expressing underlying philosophies. Once they have served their usefulness, the terms themselves may be discarded and replaced with more pleasing words and expressions.

Software development should be conducted in a project context. This establishes a relationship between the technical endeavor to design, implement, and test a software product, and management and control mechanisms intended to ensure that project expenditures, resources, and schedule milestones are satisfied. This highlights the fact that all products must be designed to be manufactured and supported throughout their life cycle to achieve established cost and schedule objectives. Terms like *design-to-cost*, *design-to-support*, and *life-cycle costs* denote that a product has a perceived value, and the engineering of the product must ensure that its value, as expressed in purchase price, operational costs, etc., is in line with the benefits it offers its customers and stakeholders. Therefore, architectural design decisions must account for the impact a design solution bears on project resources, as well as the customer or consumer.

Architectural decisions will ultimately have the most substantial impact on software development costs, as well as the effectiveness of the product throughout its life cycle. Software is easy to modify, thereby stakeholders believe that there are low costs to adding new features, functionality, or improved user interface mechanisms. Architectural decisions affect the structure of the software product that facilitates its ability to be modified, extended, and enhanced. Therefore, it is essential to understand what a software architecture looks like, how it is developed, and how it is analyzed to facilitate shrewder design decisions. Architectural decisions establish a structural framework for the software product that makes it resilient to elementary changes. This resilience enables the software product to evolve during the software development effort, as well as throughout its operational life cycle.

Furthermore, software engineering must embrace an integrated product and process (IPPD) philosophy. IPPD development addresses the consideration of software life-cycle complications during the engineering of the product. It encourages the use of integrated product teams to ensure that an array of software technical disciplines is involved in architectural decision making. This ensures that a more robust structural framework is established upon which to base the product realization. In addition, IPPD emphasizes the concurrent establishment of post-development processes and infrastructure. The software replication, distribution, training, and sustainment processes must be available when the product is ready to be deployed.

The central theme of this manuscript is to present architectural-driven development. This is fundamental to the software engineering paradigm that emphasizes the importance of designing the complete software product before initiating the software implementation activity (programmatic design, code, integration, and testing). Software implementation represents the manufacturing of a software product, while software replication represents the software production process. Manufacturing is to produce something into a finished product using raw materials. Mass production is the manufacturing of carbon copies of a finished product on a large industrial scale. Software implementation involves the programmatic design, coding, and testing of software units, modules, routines, objects, etc. These software units represent the "raw material" utilized in the manufacturing of a software product. These software units must be identified and specified to establish the physical architecture. Then, these structural units must be assembled, integrated, and tested in a manner that results in a complete software configuration item. This approach executes the FAIT (fabrication, assembly, integration, and testing) convention used by international standards[4] on systems engineering.

Finally, this section presents the impediments to the design of software products due to software's nonmaterial nature. It presents the software design chasm as an illustration characterizing the difficulty associated with defining an architectural framework for the structural configuration of a software product. It presents the software engineering principles and practices that vanquish this dilemma and provides a rigorous, disciplined approach to designing the software architecture.

---

[4]ISO/IES 26702:2007, IEEE Standard for Application and Management of the Systems Engineering Process, and IEEE 1220–2005, IEEE Standard for Application and Management of the Systems Engineering Process.

Introduction to Software Engineering

1

CHAPTER OUTLINE

This chapter provides an overview of software engineering as a discipline critical to software product development. Software engineering, as described in this book, utilizes proven practices and techniques derived from the systems engineering discipline. These systems engineering methods and tools have been adapted to address the challenges plaguing the software development industry. The resulting software engineering practices provide a more regimented approach to the development of software products.

Systems engineering practitioners have developed a set of principles and practices that enable complex products to be designed and developed within a project framework. Many of the challenges encountered by the systems engineering community have been resolved through years of rigorous research, trial-and-error, and lessons learned from past failures. The software development challenges that are targeted to be resolved by adopting these proven systems engineering practices include:

1. Establishing the structure of complex products.
2. Managing interfaces with external systems or products.
3. Minimizing and mitigating risks to project success.
4. Making informed decisions by considering design alternatives and performing trade-off analyses.
5. Evaluating change requests and proposals in a formal manner, which enables the adoption of changes and maintains the scope of work to be performed within established budgets and timelines.

1.1 Specifying software requirements

Establishing the requirements for a software product is a significant undertaking and directs the course of action for the remaining software development effort. Traditionally, requirements specifications address the overall product under development and its external interfaces. However, an important practice employed by most engineering disciplines is the specification of requirements for every element of the product architecture or design. Therefore, there are significant implications with this practice that demand that the complete software architecture be formulated, including a specification for each element of the software product and associated post-development sustainment processes.

The software requirements specifications for the product guide the definition of the product architecture, software implementation, and software test and evaluation efforts. Requirements that are nonessential, overspecified, or introduce unacceptable risks place the project in jeopardy of being unsuccessful. This represents a situation where the software development team may attempt to do too much with too little. Projects are constrained by the amount of resources available to produce a product. Project budget and schedule objectives must be the primary focus when establishing product requirements. This is complicated by a number of competing factors that impede the formulation of a requirements baseline, including:

1. Multiple stakeholders each with their own insular desires associated with the software product.
2. Competition and the desire for a larger share of the marketplace.
3. The need to establish the software development infrastructure, environments (architecting, implementation, and testing), staffing, etc., which facilitate the pursuit of project objectives.
4. The simultaneous development and establishment of post-development software sustainment processes to maintain the product throughout its life expectancy.
5. Enterprise goals for return on investment and enhanced reputation within its industry.

Every software product is intended to serve a purpose and the software requirements should represent those product features and performance factors that enable the product to serve its purpose. Software products may support a business process, control the operation of a system or process, support data gathering and analysis activities, guide work productivity by automating mundane tasks, or provide some entertainment relevance. Thus, there exists a significant cost-benefit motivation for every software development undertaking that must be appreciated. Caution must be taken when establishing software requirements that broaden the scope of the development effort beyond the means of the project to achieve its objectives. Improperly extending the software product scope sets the development effort on a path destined for failure. Every requirement implies a level of effort necessary to devise a suitable solution. Managing the scope of the software engineering undertaking is essential to the success of each and every development project.

1.2 **Software architecture**

Software products are a combination of software routines, procedures, modules, or objects that provide some functionality. Software, as a substance for developing products, does not exhibit physical characteristics. Software is actually a language that is transformed into electrical currents within a processing unit that permits mathematical calculations. Software commands are translated, which permits data manipulations or, for the sake of being precise, functions that represent a basic operation of a computer yielding a single result when invoked. Therefore, it is essential that the software product be designed to address the full set of functional behaviors that must be exhibited by the final product. The software architecture represents the decomposition of requirements into the functions and subfunctions that are necessary to provide the specified behavior and performance characteristics. Software architecture refers to the art and science of designing and implementing software products. It involves three partitions: 1) the product requirements; 2) the functional architecture, which exhibits functional, performance and resource utilization characteristics; and 3) the physical architecture which establishes the software product structural configuration and relationships among structural elements.

The software architecture is analogous to the set of engineering drawings and diagrams for a building. The construction of the building does not begin until the set of drawings and diagrams have been drafted; are shown to conform to established Uniform Building, Mechanical and Plumbing, and National Electrical codes; and have been approved by the authorized regulatory agency. Similarly, the implementation (the design, coding, and testing of modules, etc.) of a software product should not begin until the software architecture is complete, can be shown to be consistent with the software requirements, and has been authorized by the project lead to enter into the implementation stage of development. It is not advisable to begin "construction" without understanding the full scope of the engineering responsibility.

The software architecture establishes a complete design framework for a software product that has been rigorously explored, refined, and scoped to be implementable within established budget and schedule provisions. The term *design* is defined in the *Encarta Dictionary* as "to make a detailed plan of the form or structure of something, emphasizing features such as its appearance, convenience, and efficient functioning." This definition identifies four important elements that are examined here as they apply to the software architecture:

1. *Detailed plan of the form or structure of something:* The term *plan* implies a set of engineering drawings depicting the various perspectives of a product's form or structure. The software architecture provides several types of design diagrams, drawings, or views to represent the unambiguous structure and behaviors of the software product. These views are necessary to communicate the architectural concepts to members of the software development team and other stakeholders.

2. *Appearance:* The mechanism by which the user or operator can observe, interact, and control software operations. Typical user interface elements involve sounds, notification lights, windows or forms, dialog boxes, and report formats. The appearance of the software product may be casual for consumer products or may require advanced human–machine interface designs aided by human factors specialists.
3. *Convenience:* The usability of the software product in terms of simplicity of maneuvering between and among features to control processes, data entry, data retrieval, data manipulation, and report generation.
4. *Efficient functioning:* This addresses the action or use for which the software product is designed; its performance or the manner in which it functions, operates, or behaves; and the utilization of computing resources. The software architecture must be designed to make the best use of available computing environment resources, such as processing speed, data transfer rates, memory, data storage, and communications bandwidth.

Clearly, the definition and design of a software product architecture demands a rigorous approach, as well as techniques for capturing and expressing architectural design characteristics. Software engineering involves several design challenges that involve computing technology, software components, human factors engineering, as well as interfaces with other systems or software applications. The software architecture involves:

- The set of requirement specifications derived by interactions with the software product stakeholders.
- Functional representations of the software behaviors and interactions among users, operators, and external systems.
- The physical or structural arrangement of software "building blocks" and the strategy for combining these software elements into a single, integrated product.

1.3 Integrated product and process development

IPPD is an organizational technique that provides a systematic approach to product development. IPPD is focused on improving product quality through timely collaboration of relevant stakeholders throughout product development to better satisfy stakeholder needs. A basic tenant of IPPD is to involve all technical disciplines at the beginning of the development process to ensure that requirements are properly gathered, understood, and specified. The intent of IPPD is to encourage developers to consider all aspects of the product life cycle to ensure that the product architecture is resilient to changes in operational and technological conditions. The IPPD philosophy ensures that all technical and management organizations are represented by participating members of the software engineering integrated product team (SWE-IPT).

Requirements are developed initially at the software product level, then successively at lower levels as the requirements are decomposed and flowed down throughout the software product architecture. This is different from a traditional software development approach where software analysts perform the requirements definition work and pass the requirements along to product design, implementation, test and evaluation, and post-development process engineers. This results in a loss of understanding caused by asynchronous communications. The general approach for executing IPPD is to form multidisciplinary teams for all products and post-development processes to address technical issues, balance requirements, and help integrate the various teams. Participation by technical and management groups will vary throughout the product life cycle as the work transitions throughout the phases of software development.

1.4 Integrated product teams

The use of IPTs is a mechanism for ensuring that stakeholders, project management, and technical organizations are represented throughout the software development effort. A SWE-IPT involves representatives from the various stakeholder communities and software development technical and management organizations. Figure 1.1 depicts the representation associated with several software development IPTs. The suggested software development IPTs are defined as:

1. *Software engineering IPT:* Represents the primary organizational entity responsible for defining and controlling the software architecture, integrating technical plans and schedules, conducting architectural trade studies and analyses, and monitoring software development progress and risks.

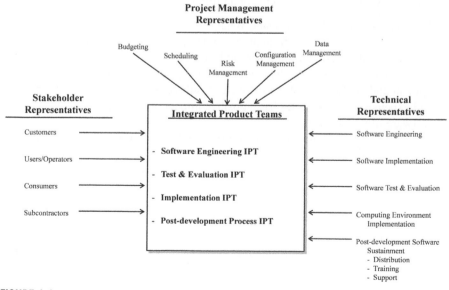

FIGURE 1.1

Software integrated product team representatives.

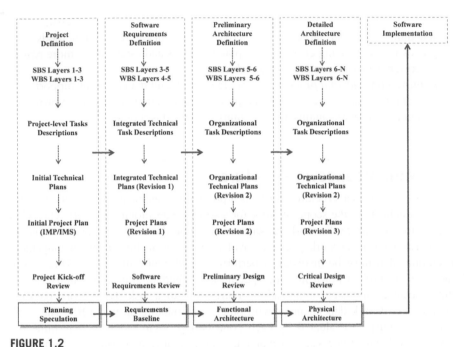

FIGURE 1.2

The evolution of the WBS.

work allocated for their specification, implementation, and testing. The challenge here is that the software architecture and resulting SBS morph over time as architectural design decisions are made. Architectural decisions may affect the software requirements and functional and/or physical definitions. Figure 1.2 shows the evolution of the SBS as the software architecture is defined and refined. With each refinement of the software architecture, the work definitions and resource estimates should become increasingly accurate and maintained within the scope of initial project speculation.

The flow of software development stages follows a typical project sequence of time-phased, incremental steps. The initial phase of development addresses the product requirements. This is followed by a stage of design that establishes a functional architecture that establishes *what* the software product must accomplish to enable each operational data processing transaction. The third stage, detailed architecture definition, transforms the functional representation into a structural configuration (physical architecture) that provides the elemental specifications and guidance for software implementation. These three stages provide the detailed architectural information, specifications, diagrams, and drawings to permit the product to be implemented (fabricated, assembled, integrated, and tested). During these first three stages of development, the software breakdown structure evolves in depth (number of layers of decomposition) and in detail (technical accuracy). The software architecture, as it evolves, provides the structural information necessary to establish the SBS. As a result of each stage of development the software architecture evolves to provide a more comprehensive and accurate description of the software product. This permits the estimated work remaining to implement and test the product to be increasingly accurate. The definition and evolution of the software architecture leads to an evolution of the SBS, WBS, and technical and organizational plans and schedules.

1.7 Specification and documentation trees

The specification tree identifies the requirement specifications that must be prepared to guide the design and testing for the software product and every element of the product configuration. For a software product, the specification tree will identify the requirement specifications associated with each software configuration item, software external interfaces, and the computing environment. In addition, each of the post-development processes (e.g., replication, distribution, training, and support) should have a process specification prepared. The specification tree is a project management tool where the required specifications are identified as formal deliverables for the project.

The documentation tree is a technical management tool that addresses the related specifications, design documents, drawings, and diagrams that are necessary to be generated in support of the software development effort. It provides a complete view of the set of documentation necessary to document the software product and post-development sustainment processes. The documentation tree should include all of the technical documentation, including technical plans, software architecture descriptions, software development folders, test procedures, installation guides, and user manuals.

The SBS and specification and documentation trees are useful tools for understanding the actual progress of the software development effort and the readiness of the product to transition to operations and sustainment. The SBS and documentation tree are also critical in determining the full impact of proposed changes and their impact on the software development effort.

1.8 Integrated master plan and schedule

The IMP is an event-driven project plan that documents the significant accomplishments to be achieved and associates each accomplishment to a key program event. The IMS is a time-based schedule containing the networked, detailed tasks necessary to ensure successful project execution. The IMS is traceable to the integrated master plan, the WBS, and the statement of work or project directive. The IMS is used to verify progress toward meeting program objectives, and to integrate scheduled program activities with the organizational and integrated technical plans.

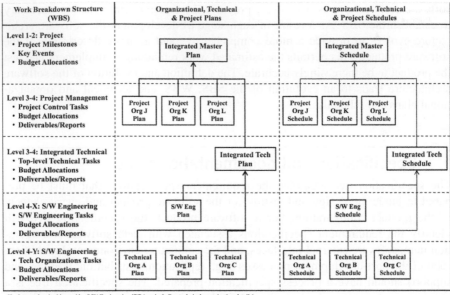

FIGURE 1.3

Hierarchy of organizational, technical, and project plans and schedules.

The WBS provides the basis for constructing project and technical plans and schedules. There is a hierarchy of plans and schedules prepared by the various project organizations. Figure 1.3 portrays a general hierarchy that associates the layers of the WBS with the various organizational, technical, and project plans and schedules. As the project, systems architecture, and WBS evolve in definition and clarity, the details of organizational, technical, and project plans can be expanded. The integrated technical plan is developed by integrating technical organizational plans with the systems engineering plan. The IMP and IMS incorporate and summarize the project and integrated technical plans and schedules.

The hierarchical development of these plans and schedules provides a separation of concern so that the project management and technical organizations can address their roles and responsibilities within the overall project context. Determining the full impact of proposed changes on the project effort will require that all of these plans and schedules are considered and the work packages revised to provide a basis for incorporating a change into the project workflow.

1.9 Reviews and audits

A typical software development project is defined by a series of phases of time during which the product is defined, designed, implemented and tested. Each phase of

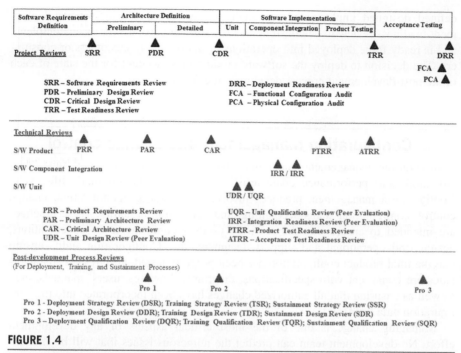

Software Requirements Definition	Architecture Definition		Software Implementation			Acceptance Testing
	Preliminary	Detailed	Unit	Component Integration	Product Testing	

Project Reviews

SRR   PDR   CDR   TRR   DRR   FCA   PCA

SRR – Software Requirements Review
PDR – Preliminary Design Review
CDR – Critical Design Review
TRR – Test Readiness Review

DRR – Deployment Readiness Review
FCA – Functional Configuration Audit
PCA – Physical Configuration Audit

Technical Reviews

S/W Product   PRR   PAR   CAR   PTRR   ATRR

S/W Component Integration   IRR / IRR

S/W Unit   UDR / UQR

PRR – Product Requirements Review
PAR – Preliminary Architecture Review
CAR – Critical Architecture Review
UDR – Unit Design Review (Peer Evaluation)

UQR – Unit Qualification Review (Peer Evaluation)
IRR - Integration Readiness Review (Peer Evaluation)
PTRR – Product Test Readiness Review
ATRR – Acceptance Test Readiness Review

Post-development Process Reviews
(For Deployment, Training, and Sustainment Processes)

Pro 1   Pro 2   Pro 3

Pro 1 - Deployment Strategy Review (DSR); Training Strategy Review (TSR); Sustainment Strategy Review (SSR)
Pro 2 – Deployment Design Review (DDR); Training Design Review (TDR); Sustainment Design Review (SDR)
Pro 3 – Deployment Qualification Review (DQR); Training Qualification Review (TQR); Sustainment Qualification Review (SQR)

FIGURE 1.4

Series of project and technical reviews and audits.

activities concludes with a formal review of the product development status, and involves most of the stakeholders. It is necessary to conduct technical reviews of the software architecture, implementation, and test status to ensure that the technical organizations are prepared for project reviews. In addition, the IPPD philosophy broadens the number and scope of these reviews to address the definition and status of the software post-development processes. Figure 1.4 provides a conceptual schedule of technical reviews that support formal project reviews. Section 3 provides a detailed agenda for each formal review that addresses the project and product status, key architectural decisions, proposed changes under review, and the plans for the next stage of software development.

Technical reviews address the software product under development while the post-development reviews address the development of post-development processes. Technical reviews address the state of the evolving software requirements and functional and physical architectures. The development effort then transitions to focus on software implementation, which involves a series of technical reviews to assess the adequacy of software programmatic designs, integration, and testing activities. The main difference between project and technical reviews is the level of formality and participation. Technical reviews do not involve project management or stakeholder participation.

The post-development process reviews address the status of distribution, training, and support process definition and implementation. These processes must be defined, designed, implemented, and qualified prior to the software product deployment readiness review to demonstrate that the software product has been completed and is ready to be deployed into operations or distributed to customers or consumers. The decision to deploy the software product must account for the state of each of the post-development process development efforts.

1.10 Configuration management and change control

Configuration management maintains the coherent alignment of functional, structural, and performance characteristics throughout the product's life cycle. Configuration management practices involve configuration identification, change control, configuration status accounting, and configuration audits. These practices are intended to ensure that the software product conforms to its specifications, design, and operational and support documentation. Configuration audits ensure that the final product configuration has been properly tested, all physical characteristics are consistent with specifications, diagrams, drawings, users' manuals, etc., as well as ensuring that all authorized changes have been incorporated into the configuration data (artifacts).

Managing change is one of the most critical aspects of any development effort. No development team can predict the numerous issues that will be encountered throughout a software development effort. The term *develop* has several meanings, including to change and become larger, stronger, or more impressive; and to become apparent and thus resolve a question or clarify a situation. This implies that the problem space is not understood well enough at the inception of a project to accurately define a plan or schedule that will not vary from its original account. When considering change control, the following underlying facts must be acknowledged:

- Projects are established to develop a software product and are driven by cost and schedule objectives and resource constraints.
- Project planning establishes a roadmap that the project will initially proceed to execute. As the development effort analyzes the problem space and solution alternatives, project plans and schedule definitions must be revised to correctly reflect the new understanding of the project outlook.
- Project management involves numerous control mechanisms for achieving established project objectives including budgets, resource allocations, and risk tracking.
- The software architecture provides the technical framework for establishing the product structural configuration. This product configuration will evolve as more detail is derived as a result of analysis, investigation, modeling, and prototyping.
- As the product configuration is meticulously detailed the product and WBSs must be extended to provide the basis for revising technical plans, schedules, and key milestone accomplishment criteria.

- Cost and schedule objectives compel a project to make progress toward its conclusion. External forces, such as customer and stakeholder needs and expectations, computing technology, competition, and market conditions, apply pressure for the project to divert from established plans.

These assertions suggest that project management and software engineering practices should be established in a manner that governs these diametrically opposed forces. The goal-driven nature of a development project is focused on developing and delivering a quality software product in a timely and cost-effective manner. This warrants a strategy envisioned to insulate the project from sources of change. The nature of the marketplace suggests that the software development project must be cognizant of the ever-changing conditions occurring in the environment that will ultimately determine the acceptability and success of the software product. The enterprise invests in the project by providing the people, facilities, tools and equipment, and resources necessary for the project to be conducted. Because of its investment, the enterprise desires to recognize a profit from the software product, or it may aspire to improve its reputation within its industry as a reliable software development organization.

To properly cope with the dynamic forces of change, the central software engineering philosophy must support a technical approach that facilitates the following principles:

1. Change is inevitable! It is necessary to be able to distinguish which changes are beneficial to adopt and which changes should be resisted or delayed until future versions of the product.
2. Changes that are adopted must be able to be incorporated into the planning, budgeting, and product configuration with a minimal amount of rework or schedule interruption.
3. Every change represents a form of rework, unless the change is a totally new requirement that does not interact with any other element within the software architecture. However, even such an isolated change will require the project plans and schedules to be updated to incorporate the revised work scope into work packages.
4. Change affects the software architecture involving the software product or the computing environment within which it is intended to operate. Change analysis should be performed to understand the perceived impact caused by a change to support a project determination to adopt the change. Depending on the state of the software development effort, the amount of rework involved with incorporating a change will vary significantly. In some instances, a change may require reperforming work that has already been accomplished. The scope of a change can be determined by assessing the number of elements and interfaces within the software architecture that are affected. This will provide an indication as to the amount of existing design and implementation work that must be redone. Review of the specification and documentation tree will support the change impact determination.

5. Before a change is adopted, the scope of the work package adjustments must be understood to ensure that project cost and schedule objectives remain achievable. The software engineering IPT must ensure that the impact of the proposed change is thoroughly understood to support a cost-benefit analysis of adopting the change.

6. Change impact analysis should be sufficiently detailed to permit the authorized change to be assimilated into the software architecture, technical plans, and schedules without introducing additional risks to the success of the project.

The desire for a change may arise from sources external to the project, such as customers, competition, or advances in computing technology, or from sources within the technical team arising from an improved understanding of the architectural solution. These internally proposed change requests may represent opportunities to improve the solution or may identify modifications necessary to resolve existing architectural deficiencies. These changes stemming from architectural deficiencies should dominate the technical change control board's attention since these adjustments must be conducted within the existing scope of the technical effort.

Changes that arise from external sources represent unfunded change proposals that are typically outside the scope of the current project in terms of the funding and resources associated with the current work plan. Change proposals that impact the scope of the planned technical effort must be authorized by the project's change control board to ensure that all stakeholders understand the cost and benefits associated with the change authorization. Therefore, the term *change request* will be used to refer to a change that does not change the funding or schedule profile of the project, while *change proposal* will refer to a change that impacts the scope of the planned effort. A change proposal must be accompanied by funding or schedule relief before the project should consider authorizing the proposed change.

1.11 Trade-off analysis

There are numerous approaches for conducting technical, project, and business analyses of a situation to gather information to aid decision-making. Cost-benefit analysis (CBA) is a systematic process for calculating and evaluating the costs and benefits of a proposed action. This analysis serves two purposes: (1) to determine if the action is a sound, feasible, and viable undertaking, and (2) to compare it with alternate approaches to accomplishing the same purpose. It involves comparing the total expected cost of each alternative against the expected benefits to determine whether the benefits outweigh the costs and by how much. This technique is useful for project-level decisions since they must ultimately be addressed in a monetary measure of utility. However, technical decisions require techniques that deal with situations where design factors, such as performance or computing resource utilization, do not lend themselves to financially based consequences.

Trade-off analysis provides an approach to architectural problem solving and decision making accompanied by uncertainty. In many situations, technical alternatives

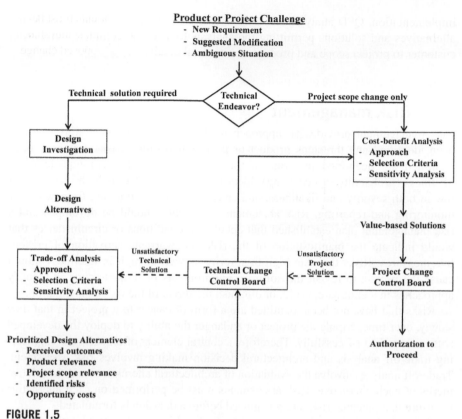

FIGURE 1.5

Project and technical decision-making domains.

must be evaluated in terms of their relative merits to product performance, acceptability, and success within the marketplace. Ultimately, the implementation of an architectural solution must be quantified in cost-benefit terms if the solution affects the scope of the project. Software engineering involves situations where the technical or design challenge is within the established scope of the project. The aim is to make the best architectural decisions despite uncertainty and unpredictable outcomes. Figure 1.5 provides an illustration relating the use of trade-off and cost-benefit analysis within the technical and project domains of a development project.

Because trade-off analysis deals with uncertainty and sometimes unquantifiable outcomes, innovative approaches have been developed to facilitate the evaluation of merits of design alternatives. Quality function deployment (QFD) is a popular technique that has been used widely within the automotive and electronics industries worldwide. QFD utilizes a matrix to arrange and correlate what the customer wants (voice of the customer) against how a product can be designed to meet customer wants. QFD, when used appropriately, may increase the cross-functional integration within organizations, especially between marketing, engineering, and software implementation. QFD analysis can also be cascaded to address lower-level design alternatives and solutions permitting the analysis to span the complete range from customer to project scope and product architectural details.

1.12 Risk management

Risk management provides an approach to dealing with an uncertainty that has been identified and threatens product or project feasibility. Risks that have been identified are quantified in terms of their severity (potential consequence) and likeliness (probability of occurring). Identified risks are rated as high, medium, or low in both severity and likeliness, and entered into a risk tracking framework for monitoring and reporting. Risk abatement approaches should be developed and a risk management plan established that details the conditions or circumstances that would indicate the manifestation of the risk and warrants activation of preventive measures. Risks that rate high in severity as well as high in likeliness should cause the project to revisit the software requirements or project scope to identify approaches that eliminate, avoid, or diminish the threat of the risk manifestation.

Risks that have not been identified are a form of cancer to a project in that they slowly, over time, cripple the project or endanger the ability to deploy the developed software product successfully. Therefore, a central element of all software engineering trade-off analysis and architectural decision making involves risk assessment. Trade-off analyses involve the evaluation of architectural alternatives and the relative merits of each alternative. Risk assessments must be performed on each alternative to ensure that potential risks are recognized before a decision is formulated.

Software development is a very complex undertaking and is littered with potential hazards. Risk identification involves discovering, defining, describing, documenting, and communicating risks before they adversely affect project fitness. An important aspect of risk identification is to capture as many risks as possible. During the risk identification activity, all possible risks should be considered. Risk identification is a form of brainstorming that is best accomplished when the approach is unrestrained or unstructured. Not all risks will be acted on and, once more details are gathered about each risk, a decision can be made concerning the handling of unavoidable risks. It is important to search the realm of what could happen, considering events or architectural characteristics that have a potential for instigating challenging situations.

1.13 Modeling and simulation

Many engineering disciplines utilize modeling and simulation techniques to support design experimentation and analysis. Computer technology has provided an undemanding means for constructing these models and eliminated the tedious use of initial product articles as test subjects. The manufacturing industries now utilize sophisticated computer-generated models or virtual prototypes to support design evaluation with significant success and cost savings. However, this concept of a virtual prototype does not translate well into the software development community.

The software industry has embraced the prototyping concept as a means of achieving timely and incremental deliveries of the software product. Many software development strategies have adopted a prototyping philosophy. These methodologies have deliberately introduced a calculated diversion into their software development approach. By prototyping the software product, software personnel are permitted to do what they do best—programming. By the time the prototype has reached a certain state of completeness, the majority of the time and labor available to the software development project has been consumed. This travesty belies the appearance of developing an "evolutionary prototype" that eventually must be acknowledged to be the deliverable software product. (It looks like the product, was developed by the project, therefore it must be the product!) This practice avoids the exertion of engineering rigor necessary to establish a stable architecture upon which the software product can be sustained and evolved. As the prototype is evolved by adding additional functionality, the fragility of the underlying architecture is destined to fracture. This *is not* a legitimate or justifiable software engineering practice.

Prototypes are, by definition, a sample or model built to test a concept or to behave as a design entity.[4] Prototypes mimic or imitate a design entity in an attempt to allow engineers and designers the ability to explore design alternatives, test theories, and confirm engineering expectations. Prototypes serve to enable the specification of the product rather than basing the specifications on a theoretical or contemplated engineering solution. Software prototyping is fundamentally an oxymoron and, as such, is an unprofessional contradiction devised to permit software personnel to focus on coding rather than architecting the software product.

Software prototyping does serve a purpose in software engineering if used ethically and sparingly. Prototyping the graphical user interface (GUI) is an example of a proper use of a software prototype. The GUI test article can be exposed to human test subjects to gather human–machine interface data that can be used to refine the GUI specification and design motif. Software prototypes should be undertaken prudently to ensure that the information gathered (benefits of prototyping) merits the investment in the prototyping development. That's right! Prototyping is a form of development and the software prototype must be properly scoped, specified, designed, and implemented before it can be used to gather engineering data or user feedback. This suggests that many of the rigorous and meticulous practices associated with implementing the software product may be disregarded to reduce the cost of prototype development. However, this lack of rigor relegates the software prototype to a disposable mockup. Fundamentally, no software code developed under prototyping conditions should be utilized within a deliverable software product.

The different treatments of prototypes by traditional engineering disciplines and the software community should be examined prior to adopting a software prototyping strategy. Table 1.3 provides a comparison of the use of prototyping by traditional

---

[4] See *http://en.wikipedia.org/wiki/Prototype*.

Table 1.3 Comparison of Prototyping Strategies

Traditional Engineering	Software Practices	Disadvantages[*]
Proof of concept prototype is used to test some aspect of the intended design without attempting to exactly simulate the visual appearance, choice of materials, or intended manufacturing process.	Rapid prototyping refers to the creation of a model that will eventually be discarded rather than becoming part of the final delivered software.	Working prototypes continually are tweaked, enhanced, and incorporated into the final product.
Form study prototype allows designers to explore the basic size, look, and feel of a product without simulating the actual function or exact visual appearance of the product.	Evolutionary prototyping constructs a very robust prototype in a structured manner and constantly refines it.	Evolutionary prototyping acknowledges that the requirements are not well understood and pays attention only to those that are well comprehended.
Visual prototype will capture the intended design aesthetic and simulate the appearance, color, and surface textures of the intended product but will not actually embody the function(s) of the final product.	The final product is built as separate prototypes and the separate prototypes are merged in an overall design.	Overall software architecture does not exist and product performance cannot be ascertained until the prototypes are integrated and tested.
The full-scale prototype and the ultimate test of concept is the engineers' final check for design flaws and allows last-minute improvements to be made before larger production runs are ordered.		The focus on a limited prototype can distract developers from properly analyzing the complete project. This can lead to overlooking better solutions, preparation of incomplete specifications, or the conversion of limited prototypes into poorly engineered final projects that are hard to maintain.
User experience model invites active human interaction and is primarily used to assess how potential users interact with various elements, motions, and actions of a design concept.		Prototyping is supposed to be done quickly. Developers may try to develop a prototype that is too complex. Users can vacillate over details of the prototype, holding up the development team and impeding development progress.

[*]*See* http://en.wikipedia.org/wiki/Software_prototyping.

engineering and by popular software methodologies. Traditional engineering disciplines utilize prototypes to support experimentation and data collection to confirm some critical feature of a product design. The prototype is not considered a production-ready model, but is used to work through design challenges and explore important design concepts.

The software industry is challenged by prototyping since its products do not have any discernible physical characteristics that would prevent their inclusion in the ultimate product. Once software code is written and demonstrated to function properly, it is difficult to discard the prototype and spend additional effort on the design, development, and testing of the production-quality software product. Software prototypes are not often constructed utilizing the rigors of software design and coding standards. This makes them inadequate to be included in the final, deliverable product, and will increase the effort associated with software support and incremental development. Software engineers are not inclined to value the lessons learned from prototypes and to spend additional effort reconstructing the software component through design, coding, and testing. The working prototype may be "cleaned-up" to conform to design and coding standards, but its architecture may prohibit future modifications or enhancements. Ultimately, the software product may have to undergo a complete rearchitecting to overhaul design limitations and obstacles stemming from an unstable structural framework resulting from prototyping efforts.

The remaining chapters in this section address the software development environment within which software engineering is applied. These topics include a generic development project framework, software architecture, how to contend with project complexity, and the integrated product and process development approach. Chapter 6 examines the material challenges that cause the engineering of software products to be more perplexing than mechanical, electrical, aeronautical, automotive, thermal, or chemical-based systems. In addition, Chapter 6 presents an overview of software engineering principles and practices.

Generic Software Development Framework

2

CHAPTER OUTLINE

Software Engineering.
© 2013 Published by Elsevier Inc. All rights reserved.

29

Throughout this book a generic software development framework is utilized to identify and consider compelling software engineering propositions. Without this framework, software engineering cannot be understood or expressed since it operates within a project environment undertaking a software development objective. This suggests that the practice of software engineering is *always* carried out within a software development project environment. It is not possible to discuss software engineering without broaching the topics of software development or project management. This implies that software engineering is closely related and integral to software project management. However, because it represents a technical discipline, software engineering must emphasize the techniques employed to design, implement, and maintain software products. Therefore, the discipline of software engineering must stress the nature of this technical burden while accentuating its affiliation with software project management or a larger system development project management framework. Fundamentally, software engineering represents the supervisory function that bridges the technical effort with the project management domain.

This chapter establishes the vernacular that will be utilized to convey the principles and practices that form a software engineering branch of knowledge. Several dominant concepts are revealed and examined to initiate our investigation of software engineering. These concepts address fundamental observations concerning what is a software product, how software is fashioned in a project context, and how some of the basic management tools are utilized to organize, monitor, and keep a software development project directed toward successful completion. It is important to comprehend these concepts because the software engineering philosophy and principles are dependent on this foundation and will be expressed utilizing this lexicon. Even the term *software* has a specific meaning that is similar to, but more influential than, the term *product*. Therefore, every technical term or expression used throughout this book has a specific connotation, and the use of one term over another designates a precise meaning.

The expression of a generic software development framework is predicated on understanding the term *software*. Similar to the word *system*, *software* has been overburdened with connotations to the point that its value as a means to communicate has been lost. Therefore, the term *software* will be examined so that its use throughout this material will be apparent. The software development framework is discussed to provide a frame of reference within which software engineering techniques and practices can be investigated. When *software development* is mentioned it should invoke a project representation with several increments of time separated by project milestones and reviews. Software development shares both a project and a product creation connotation. The development of a software product must progress through several natural stages of evolution. The software development process involves a series of development stages through which the software product progresses. These basic stages of software development are requirements, design, implementation, and testing.

Development process $\rightarrow$ Project stages $\rightarrow$ Product stages of development

2.1 **Software breakdown structure**

To truly grasp the meaning or nature of a software product its structure must be understood. Software, as a product, should not be thought of as a sequence of lines of code that provides instructions to a computer processor or data processing systems. Lines of code represent the medium by which software products are implemented, much like a house is constructed by lumber, bricks, pipes, and wire. A house is a product that must be architected and designed before it is built. Software is a revolutionary form of product since its medium is electronic in nature. This makes software intangible, meaning it "cannot be touched."[1] This does not eliminate the need for a software product to be designed, implemented, and tested before it is made available for deployment or operation. Using a house again as a point of reference, the house design is generated by an "architect" trained in the planning, design, and oversight of the construction of buildings. The architect understands the engineering challenges associated with the construction of a house, and utilizes certain materials in its design to accommodate the structural and natural forces that bear on the structure. Upon the completion of the engineering drawings, the architect prepares a "bill of materials," which is a list of the raw materials and building products, and the quantities of each needed to build the house.

Most human-made products are comprised of multiple assemblies, components, or parts. The bill of material for a house provides an itemized list of supplies and building products needed for the house to be constructed. Therefore, it is reasonable to apply this concept to a software product. However, because software is intangible, it is intimately associated with the particular computing environment or data processing system it is designed to perform with. Therefore, it is not possible to distinguish a software product from its computing environment, as depicted in Figure 2.1. As the software breakdown is expanded it will provide a basis for discussing the software development framework.

The concern of software engineering is the further composition of the software product. There have been many terms used to identify the building blocks or elements that comprise software products, including *function*, *procedure*, *routine*, *subroutine*, *application*, and *object*. These terms stem from the individual or

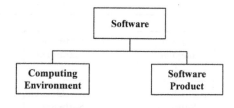

FIGURE 2.1

First layer of a software breakdown.

---

[1] See *http://en.wikipedia.org/wiki/Computer_software*.

teams who produced the computer languages and compliers who translate code into machine-executable instructions. To discuss the software breakdown it is necessary to utilize terms that do not carry superfluous connotations. The terms must indicate a relative position within the product hierarchy or structural configuration. This will be facilitated by the use of *component* and *unit*. Component infers a part, ingredient, or constituent forming a part of something larger. More importantly, per the *Encarta Dictionary*, component is used to define an assembly as "a set of components before they are put together to make a finished product." From this it can be inferred that a software component represents an element of the software breakdown structure (SBS) from which the final product is assembled. Component also is flexible enough to accommodate its use to represent several layers of assembly, as illustrated in Figure 2.2.

This structural concept works well with the exception that it implies a never-ending hierarchy of components. Therefore, it is necessary to establish a software building block that will terminate the hierarchy. For this, the term *unit* will be used. A software unit represents the basic element or part of a software product from which initial software components will be assembled. The *Encarta Dictionary* defines unit as "an individual or discrete part or element into which something can be divided, especially for analysis." Thus, a software unit represents a discrete element of the SBS from which a software component can be assembled. Figure 2.3 depicts an example of a SBS.

Throughout the material presented in this book the terms *component* and *unit* will refer to the position or station the software element has relative to the hierarchy of software elements. A software unit is the basic building block and does not involve any decomposition or further breakdown. A software component represents

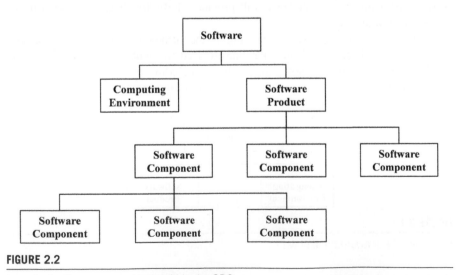

FIGURE 2.2

Layers of software components within the SBS.

an element that is comprised of two or more software units and/or components, as depicted in Figure 2.3.

The challenge presented by this breakdown view is why there is a need to differentiate the term *software* from *software product*. Is the association with the computing environment significant enough to transmit the meaning associated with the terms *product, component,* and *unit*? This is better explained by examining the concept behind software development. Just like the architect addresses the design of a house, there are other aspects of the construction effort beyond the design of the house itself. Things that must be considered involve positioning the structure of the house onto a plot of land, access to a street, a source electrical power, water, and sewage. These peripheral factors affect the design of the house and its structure and must be integral to the overall architectural aptitude and exactness.

The peripheral factors that must be addressed during software development involve how the software product will be sustained after the product is released, delivered, installed, and deployed. The systems engineering branch of knowledge has formulated an integrated product and process development concept to address the concurrent engineering of the product and life-cycle sustainment concepts. When this paradigm is applied to software it captures the peripheral factors associated with the post-development processes. Just like software development can be referred to as a development process, software product distribution, user operational training, and product support and maintenance can be regarded as processes. The inclusion of the integrated product and process development (IPPD) concept within the SBS results in a software hierarchy identified by Figure 2.4.

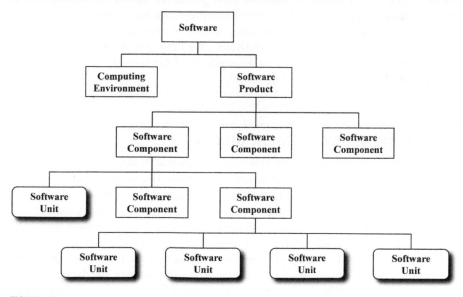

FIGURE 2.3

Layers of software components and units within the software breakdown structure.

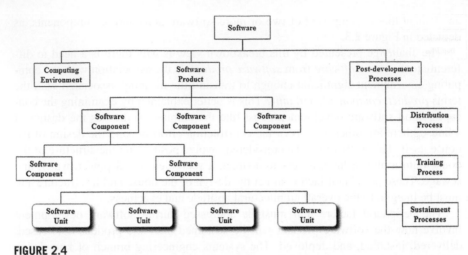

FIGURE 2.4

Full software breakdown structure.

Each of the post-development processes represents a significant endeavor to define, design, implement, and establish the requisite facilities, computing environment, networks, etc. needed to enable the deployment of the software product after the development effort has been concluded. These processes must be developed in a timely manner to ensure that they are available when the software product is ready for deployment. The effort to establish these processes should be situated within the software development effort as subordinate projects since members of their staff will be required to participate in the software engineering integrated product team (SWE-IPT) to contribute their perspectives to the definition of the software product. This will necessitate inclusion of these efforts within the software development planning, budgeting, and scheduling tasks.

2.2 Software development process

Software development has always followed a sequence of stages once it emerged from the laboratory environment of advanced research. The most fundamental set of stages involves requirements, design, coding, and testing. This simplistic representation of software development aligns with most project management approaches and has been adapted over time as the size, complexity, and costs associated with software products has increased. Alignment of software development with these project management and IPPD principles generates a framework, with a series of stages, milestones, and reviews intended to accommodate software as a standalone product or as a product embedded within a system. Figure 2.5 depicts a conceptual framework for software development projects. It is conceptual in that it deviates from established literature by identifying software technical reviews that are necessary to prepare for the project review. Technical and project-level reviews are strategic points

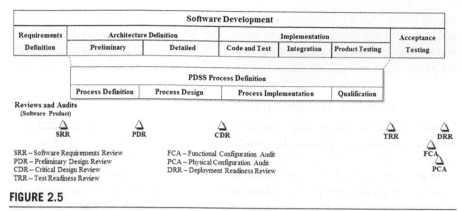

FIGURE 2.5

Conceptual software development framework.

in the development effort where it is constructive to review the evolving product definition with important stakeholders. Milestones represent a significant achievement in the development of a new software product and permit the investors to determine the values in proceeding with the next development stage. These software development stages, reviews, and audits are described in the following sections.

2.2.1 Requirements definition stage

During this development stage the project team interacts with all stakeholders to gather, analyze, and prioritize a set of needs and expectations concerning the software product to be developed. Requirements specifications are prepared to document the agreed-to set of product functions, features, and characteristics that shall be present when the product is delivered. An initial set of requirements for the post-development software sustainment (PDSS) processes may be captured within the product specification or as one or more related specifications.

2.2.1.1 Product requirements review

The product requirements review (PRR) is a technical review of the software product requirement specifications with participation of the software technical and management staff. The purpose is to ensure that the software product requirements are sufficiently specified and collectively complete and achievable within established software development resources. The PRR is necessary to ensure that the software requirement specifications and technical plans and schedules position the software development effort for successful execution. The PRR should be conducted in preparation for the project-level software requirements review.

2.2.1.2 Software requirements review

The software requirements review (SRR) is a project-level review with stakeholders and project management representatives to review the software requirement specifications, and gather feedback on the requirements, product qualification requirements (testing, analysis, inspection, and demonstration), PDSS concepts, and plans for the next development stage. The SRR is determined to be complete when all action items or comments generated by the review have been satisfactorily resolved.

2.2.2 Preliminary architecture definition stage

During this development stage the SWE-IPT establishes the functional architecture for the software product by conducting functional analysis and allocation. Alternative functional designs should be evaluated and compared utilizing the software analysis approach for performing risk assessments and trade-off analysis. The models, design documentation, and initial data dictionary should be prepared. The PDSS processes should be defined and their requirements documented in one or more process specifications.

2.2.2.1 Preliminary architecture review

The preliminary architecture review (PAR) is a technical review of the evolving software architecture that is intended to ensure that the architectural solution is ready for the preliminary design review. The emphasis is on the functional architecture and initial structural configuration of the software product. This technical review involves the software development team and key stakeholders for the purpose of evaluating the preliminary architecture definition to ensure that it adequately satisfies the software requirements and stakeholder needs, and is uncomplicated (noncomplex) and can be implemented within established software development resources.

2.2.2.2 Deployment strategy review

The deployment strategy review is a technical review of the software deployment approach to product replication, packaging, distribution, and installation and setup, as necessary. This strategic review identifies the preferred approach(es) to software replication and distribution and the business process concepts for these post-development processes. The review should address the infrastructure items that would be necessary to enable the processes and support staff required for their operation. An initial requirement specification for each business process should be reviewed and baselined upon the completion of the review.

2.2.2.3 Training strategy review

The training strategy review is a technical review of the software training approach to end-user training and education on the operation of the software product. This strategic review identifies the preferred approach(es) to software training and education and the business process concepts for this post-development process. The review should address the infrastructure items that would be necessary to enable the process and support staff required for their operation. An initial requirement specification for the software product training process should be reviewed and baselined upon the completion of the review.

2.2.2.4 Sustainment strategy review

The sustainment strategy review is a technical review of the software sustainment approach to customer and software support for the software product. This strategic review identifies the preferred approach(es) to customer and software support and the business process concepts for these post-development processes. The review should address the infrastructure items that would be necessary to enable the process and support staff required for their operation. An initial requirement specification for software customer and software support processes should be reviewed and baselined upon the completion of the review.

2.2.2.5 Preliminary design review

The preliminary design review (PDR) is a project-level review with stakeholders and project management representatives to review the software functional architecture, and gather feedback on the functional definitions, performance allocations, behaviors, data definitions, functional specifications, and plans for the next development stage. The PDSS process specification(s) may be reviewed at the product PDR or at a separate review with a more limited set of stakeholder representatives. The PDR is determined to be complete when all of the accepted action items or comments generated by the review have been satisfactorily resolved.

2.2.3 Critical architecture definition stage

During this development stage the SWE-IPT establishes the physical architecture for the software product by conducting software design synthesis. Alternative structural designs should be evaluated and compared utilizing the software analysis approach for performing risk assessments and trade-off analysis. The PDSS processes should be designed and documented during this stage. Process models should be generated to verify the capacity of each process to handle anticipated demand.

2.2.3.1 Detailed architecture review

The detailed architecture review (DAR) is a technical review of the complete software architecture that is intended to ensure that the architectural solution is ready for the preliminary design review. The emphasis is on the physical architecture that establishes the structural configuration of the software product. This technical review involves the software development team and key stakeholders for the purpose of evaluating the detailed architecture definition to ensure that it adequately satisfies the software requirements and stakeholder needs, and is uncomplicated (noncomplex) and can be implemented within established software development resources.

2.2.3.2 Deployment design review

The deployment design review is a technical review of the software deployment process design and implementation plan. The review should specify the infrastructure items and staffing necessary to enable the process. The process specifications and design documentation should be baselined and the deployment process organization authorized to execute the implementation plan upon final approval.

2.2.3.3 Training design review

The training design review is a technical review of the software training process design and implementation plan. The review should specify the infrastructure items and staffing necessary to enable the process. The process specifications and design documentation should be baselined and the training process organization authorized to execute the implementation plan upon final approval.

2.2.3.4 Sustainment design review

The sustainment design review is a technical review of the software sustainment process design and implementation plan. The review should specify the infrastructure items and staffing necessary to enable the customer and software support processes. The process specifications and design documentation should be baselined and the sustainment process organization authorized to execute the implementation plan upon final approval.

2.2.3.5 Critical design review

The critical design review (CDR) is a project-level review with stakeholders and project management representatives to review the software physical architecture and gather feedback on the functional definitions, performance allocations, behaviors, data definitions, functional specifications, and plans for the next development stage. The PDSS designs may be reviewed at the product CDR or at a separate review with a more limited set of stakeholder representatives. The CDR is determined to be complete when all of the accepted action items or comments generated by the review have been satisfactorily resolved.

2.2.4 Software unit code and testing stage

During this development stage the software implementation team prepares the unit designs and conducts peer reviews with the implementation IPT. Upon acceptance by the peer review, unit designs are then coded and tested against the structural unit specifications. Tested units should be reviewed by the implementation IPT, and upon acceptance, finished units should be made available for component integration and testing.

2.2.4.1 Unit design review (peer evaluation)

Each implementation unit should undergo a unit design review to evaluate its design to ensure compliance with the structural unit specification. The review should be conducted by a senior member of the software implementation team with a representative from the SWE-IPT in attendance.

2.2.4.2 Unit qualification review (peer evaluation)

Each implementation unit should undergo a unit qualification review to assess its operational behaviors under test conditions and its satisfaction of the structural unit specification. The review should be conducted by a senior member of the software implementation team with a representative from the SWE-IPT in attendance.

2.2.5 Software component integration and testing stage

During this development stage the software implementation team executes the component integration strategy. Integrated components are then tested against structural component specifications and peer reviews should be conducted with the implementation IPT to review the results of integration testing. Upon acceptance by the peer review, integrated components should be made available for further integration efforts, as required by the component integration strategy, until the software elements are completely assembled and integrated into one or more software configuration items.

2.2.5.1 Integration readiness review (peer evaluation)

Each implementation component should undergo an integration readiness review to (1) ensure that every implementation unit or component to be involved in the integration has satisfactorily passed the qualification review, (2) evaluate the integration approach, and (3) evaluate the component integration test procedures. The review should be conducted by a senior member of the software implementation team with a representative from the SWE-IPT in attendance.

2.2.5.2 Product testing readiness review

With the product testing readiness review, the software implementation team should present the status of the software product implementation to provide evidence of its readiness to begin the product testing stage of software implementation. Representatives of the SWE-IPT should be present to ensure that the software product integration testing has been completed and the software test procedures and environment are in a ready-state to support product testing.

2.2.6 Product testing stage

During this development stage the finished product should be exercised using the acceptance test procedures. The test environment used for product testing should be consistent with the acceptance test environment to ensure that unknown defects or failures will not arise during acceptance testing. Upon successful completion of product testing, the product configuration item and its associated documentation should be prepared for the functional and physical configuration audits.

2.2.6.1 Acceptance testing readiness review

The acceptance testing readiness review is a technical review with technical stakeholders and software development management representatives to review the results of software product testing and the status of software problem reports stemming from identified deficiencies. The SWE-IPT makes a recommendation to the software development manager concerning the readiness of the software product to enter the acceptance testing development stage.

2.2.6.2 Testing readiness review

The testing readiness review is a project-level review with stakeholders and project management representatives to review the results of software dry-run testing and the status of software problem reports stemming from identified deficiencies. The SWE-IPT makes a recommendation to the project manager concerning the readiness of the software product to enter the acceptance testing stage.

2.2.7 Acceptance testing stage

During this development stage the finished product is tested according to the test plans and procedures. In the event that the software does not satisfy a specified requirement then the SWE-IPT must decide to have the deficiency corrected, or to apply for a deviation or waiver for the product. A deviation represents a temporary acceptance of the software product with a known deficiency. The deficiency is to be rectified in an upcoming release or patch to the software product. The intent of a deviation is to permit the distribution or deployment of a software product with known requirement deficiencies. A waiver represents the stakeholders' agreement to permit the software product from not fulfilling a specified requirement, with no demands for the product deficiency to be correct in an upcoming release or patch.

2.2.7.1 Functional configuration audit

The function configuration audit (FCA) is a configuration management examination of the software product to verify, via testing, inspection, demonstration, or analysis results, that the product has met the requirements specified in the functional baseline documentation. The examination verifies that all authorized change proposals were incorporated into the product and documentation set prior to acceptance testing.

2.2.7.2 Physical configuration audit

The physical configuration audit (PCA) is a configuration management examination of the as-built (implemented) software product configuration against its technical documentation. The PCA includes a detailed examination of the engineering drawings, design documentation, and specifications to ensure that the documentation set is ready to support the post-development processes.

2.2.7.3 Deployment qualification review

The deployment qualification review is a technical-level review of the deployment process to ensure that the process and personnel are prepared for software product training. The results of this review should be presented at the deployment readiness review (DRR).

2.2.7.4 Training qualification review

The training qualification review is a technical-level review of the training process to ensure that the process and personnel are prepared for software product deployment. The results of this review should be presented at the DRR.

2.2.7.5 Sustainment qualification review

The sustainment qualification review is a technical-level review of the sustainment process to ensure that the process and personnel are prepared for customer and software product support. The results of this review should be presented at the DRR.

2.2.7.6 Deployment readiness review

The deployment readiness review is a project review that evaluates the status of the post-development processes and their documentation and readiness to release the software product to customers, consumers, and other stakeholders. The results of acceptance testing are reviewed to ensure that the product has satisfied its specified requirements. The results of the software product audits are reviewed to ensure that the product and associated documentation are ready to support post-development processes. Upon successful completion of the DRR the software product is transitioned from software development into operations reinforced by the operational state of the post-development processes.

2.3 Summary

The software development framework provides a structured approach to software development and project management. Stakeholder involvement throughout the development effort is achieved with their representation on the SWE-IPT. The IPPD philosophy accounts for the concurrent development of the PDSS processes. These PDSS processes must be established in a timely manner to support software product deployment and operations. The SBS embraces the IPPD philosophy and establishes the accountability for post-development processes within project plans, budgets, and schedules. The software development framework involves a series of project reviews and audits to provide the project management team and stakeholders an opportunity to maintain awareness of the status of the development effort. Project reviews determine the readiness of the technical effort to proceed to each subsequent development stage. Configuration audits are conducted to ensure that the implemented and tested software product configuration complies with the functional and physical baselines.

The software development framework provides a basis for discussing the need for the software engineering practices encouraged by this book. Because the software product takes different representations throughout the development process, software engineering principles, practices, and tools must be employed prudently. Because of this realization, much care has been given to how the software engineering tasks are explicitly stated to account for the status of the software product and the project within the development framework.

Software Architecture

CHAPTER OUTLINE

This chapter examines the software architecture that is the representation of an integrated software product and provides the foundation for software implementation. Because of the complex nature of a software product, there are several perspectives that must be comprehended to describe a software product. First, a software product is being developed to satisfy customer and stakeholder needs and expectations. Therefore, the software product requirements need to be agreed upon by all stakeholders and entered into the configuration management system as a requirements baseline. This baseline permits the tracking of change proposals against the baselined requirements.

The second element of the software architecture is the functional architecture that depicts the operational process, functional decomposition, performance, and specialty-engineering characteristics of the software product. The functional decomposition must address the behavior of the software product including aspects, such as data security, error and failure recovery, and safety-related actions. These behaviors have erroneously been referred to as nonfunctional requirements. These requirements should be considered specialty-engineering mandates that must be addressed within the functional architecture. Failure detection and response/recovery functions directly impact the software product's dependability coefficient. Product complexity, architectural integrity, and resilience directly affect the software product's maintainability coefficient and the ability to enhance, fortify, and extend functionality in future versions of the software product. However these nonfunctional requirements are specified, they must be incorporated into the functional architecture, and their behaviors, in a stimulus-response scenario, explicitly designed into the overarching representation of the functional architecture.

The final element of the software product architecture is the physical architecture that depicts the structural aspects of the software product and provides insight into how the product will be assembled and integrated to form one or more software configuration items. The physical architecture is derived from the functional architecture in a manner that involves a top-down conceptualization and a bottom-up manifestation. As the functional architecture is initially formulated the uppermost structural components of the physical architecture may be identified. The foundation of the physical architecture is derived from the functional units, which are grouped and synthesized to identify structural units. This exposes a gap in the structural configuration that is resolved with the establishment of a software integration strategy. This approach to configuring the physical architecture is explained in detail in Chapter 12.

Without the physical architecture, the software implementation effort cannot be properly defined, planned, and controlled. The software engineering integrated product team (SWE-IPT) is responsible for developing and controlling the software architecture and its integrated design and configuration documentation. The software architecture must characterize the design of the software product to be developed. This necessitates the crafting of different types of design diagrams, views, and documentation that depict the software architecture. The general categories of design documentations include:

- Descriptions of the functional architecture and its design representations, such as functional specifications, functional decomposition hierarchies, data flow diagrams, behavioral models, and data dictionaries.
- Descriptions of the physical architecture and its design representations, such as interface block diagrams, structural specifications, and configuration assembly and integration plans.
- Requirements baseline and its representations, such as software requirement specifications, software interface specifications, and database requirement specifications.
- Description of the computational environment.
- Post-development process specifications and design documentation.

There exist relationships and dependencies among all of these design descriptions that must be harmonized and synchronized to enable the project to consider potential software design opportunities, and respond to change requests and proposals by incorporating approved changes into the software architecture.

The elements of the software architecture, the computing environment, and the relationships and dependencies that exist among these elements are identified in Figure 3.1. These relationships are indicated by the arrows between any two elements of the software architecture. These relationships represent the dependencies a source element has with regard to the target element. These relationships and their dependencies are further examined in the following sections. Notice that the stakeholder needs, software implementation, and test and evaluation elements in the figure are grayed out to indicate that they are not elements of the software

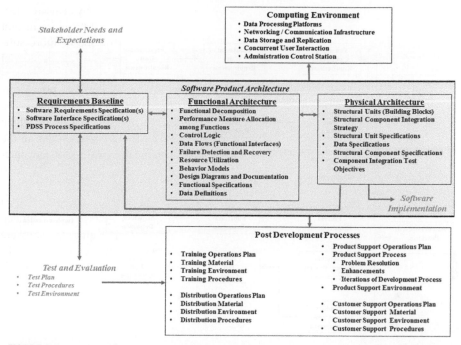

FIGURE 3.1

Software architecture elements.

architecture. They are included in the figure because of their interest in the establishment of the software architecture and their involvement with the software development effort.

The definition of the software architecture is the responsibility of the SWE-IPT. This multidisciplinary team involves representatives from all of the technical organizations involved in the software development effort. These representatives bring their technical knowledge and organizational interests to collaborate on the definition of the software architecture. The SWE-IPT is responsible for the generation and maintenance of diagrams, drawings, models, and documentation that comprise the product data package. The product data package provides the information necessary to enable the software implementation team to design, code, and test (fabricate) structural units, and to assemble, integrate, and test structural components into one or more complete software configuration items. The software data package is enhanced by the addition of the as-built documentation, generated during software implementation, which is necessary for software product sustainment. The software product configuration audits are performed against the data package prior to deployment readiness review (DRR) to ensure that the product data package accurately reflects the product implementation and incorporates all authorized change proposals.

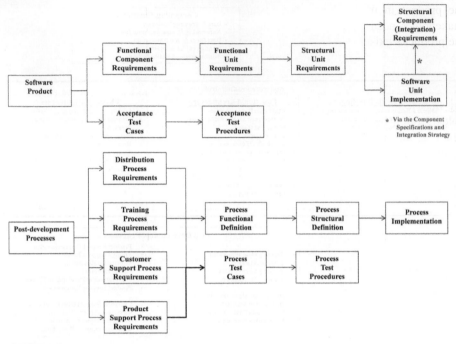

FIGURE 3.2

Chain of requirements traceability.

Because of these relationships and dependencies among the elements of the software architecture, the practice of requirements management and traceability must be extended to account for the broader converge necessary to support software development and product sustainment. The software requirements involve the software product, interfaces to external systems, the computational environment, and several post-development processes. There exists a chain of traceability from stakeholder needs to the software product requirements, functional and physical representations, and post-development processes that are essential to the implementation of the design solution. Figure 3.2 depicts this requirements traceability chain for the software product and post-development processes. The relationships and dependencies are identified and discussed in the following sections to emphasize the association among the architectural elements and how they coalesce into a software product configuration.

3.1 Stakeholder needs relationships and dependencies

Stakeholders have a vested interest in the development, operation, and sustainment of the software product. They derive some benefit or utility from the existence of the product in their professional occupation, personal affairs, or entertainment. Stakeholder needs establish the value, potential, motivation, and consequence of the product's existence and sustainment. Stakeholders' contribute their professional discrimination toward the definition of the product's composition, characteristics, and application within their profession, enterprise, and industry. When the product is finally deployed, stakeholders gain personnal benefits and satisfcation with having been closely assoicated with the product's development. Additionally, stakeholders often become advocates for the use of the product within their business ventures, industry, or social circles, and take great pride in their contribution to the development of a successful product. The prinicpal dependencies between stakeholder needs and software requirements are:

1. *Product operational characteristics (requirements baseline).* The stakeholders expect to utilize the product in their vocation, personal interests, or recreational interests. They will promote operational traits for the software product that can be exploited for their benefit, advantage, or entertainment value.

2. *Product performance characteristics (requirements baseline).* Stakeholders are interested in the effectiveness, responsiveness, and efficient execution of data manipulation, computation, and presentation.

3. *Product physical characteristics (requirements baseline).* Stakeholders are concerned with the style, sophistication, and aesthetic qualities of the software product due to their authoritative affiliation with it. The intellectual response to the attractive, creative, and innovative "look and feel" with graphical displays, user interfaces, and data presentation affect the acceptance by the user community at large.

4. *Product qualification requirements (requirements baseline).* Stakeholders must concur with the product qualification methods by which each requirement will be authenticated. The typical qualification methods include analysis, demonstration, inspection, and testing. Each method prescribes the manner by which test results will be analyzed to determine if the product conforms to specified requirements or exhibits the desired characteristics.

5. *Product interface requirements (requirements baseline).* Stakeholders are constrained by the existance of operational systems or other products that are utilized to support their business operations and professional assignments. Product interfaces provide the seamless data exchange among systems or products, and these product interfaces cannot be arbitrarily modified to facilitate the software product's design and implementation.

6. *Post-development processes (requirements baseline).* The requirements for post-development processes are contingent on the definition of the software product. The methods employed to package and distribute the product will be determined by industry norms and competitive approaches. The types of user training will depend on the complexitiy of the product, the business or operational missions it supports, and the number of external systems or products it interfaces with. The types and amount of customer and product support made available will

be determined by the magnitude of the customer base and the reliance of businesses or individuals on the product to achieve their professional transactions.

3.2 Software requirements baseline relationships and dependencies

The software requirements baseline consists of a number of specifications that are harmonized to articulate the expected functional, performance, physical, and quality characteristics to be exhibited by the software product, computing environment, and associated post-development processes. This set of requirements focuses on the activities that elaborate the software architecture and the definition of the acceptance test scenarios and procedures. The requirements are utilized during the functional and physical configuration audits as the standard against which software product implementation is assessed to determine its quality of workmanship. The requirements baseline involves the following relationships and dependencies with stakeholder needs or other elements of the software architecture:

1. *Development costs versus timeliness (Stakeholder Needs).* The software requirements will ultimately determine the cost of the development effort and will impact the product delivery milestones. Determining how to balance the software product requirements so that the development project remains stable and can proceed decisively toward conclusion is contingent on the accuracy and reasonableness of the requirements baseline to establish the conditions for the project to succeed.
2. *Software product requirement appropriateness (functional architecture).* The suitability, correctness, thoroughness, and precision of product requirements will impact the development effort. The breadth of the requirements will affect the product success in the marketplace. The software product requirements are interpreted and converted into the functional architecture. Vague or ambiguous requirements may obscure the optimal composition of the functional architecture in terms of orderly arrangement, complexity, and suitability. Requirements that are overstated will drive up development costs and threaten to increase product complexity.
3. *Scope of the test and evaluation effort (test and evaluation).* The requirements baseline establishes the scope of the test and evaluation effort for both the software product and the post-development software sustainment (PDSS) processes. Permitting the requirements to be excessive will significantly increase the number and complexity of test cases and scenarios. The testing effort may consume a significant amount of project resources in terms of budget, tools, equipment, and schedule.
4. *Scope of the post-development processes (post-development processes).* Increased product complexity impacts ease-of-use and training demands for users, as well as product and customer support costs.

3.3 **Computing environment relationships and dependencies**

The computing environment involves the collection of computer machinary, data storage devices, work stations, software applications, and networks that support the processing and exchange of electronic information demanded by the software solution. The computing environment involves the following relationships and dependencies with elements of the software architecture:

1. *Technology availability (requirements baseline).* The performance of the software solution is constrained by the computing environment and must be factored into software product requirements. The number of intructions that can be excuted, data transfer rates, graphics resolution, and rendering rates are typical computing equipment measures that affect the subsequent performance of the software solution.

2. *Resource utilization and conservation (software product architecture).* The availability of computer resources within the computing environment will constrain software product performance. Shared resource utilization models must be developed, especially for networked multi-user applications. A strategy for managing resources that establishes resource consumption, conservation, preservation, and recovery must be developed and incorporated into the software archtiecture.

3.4 **Test and evaluation relationships and dependencies**

The testing effort may consume a significant amount of project resources in terms of budget, tools, equipment, and schedule. The testing and evalution effort determines the suitability of the software product and post-development processes relative to the requirements baseline. The test and evaluation effort involves the following relationships and dependencies with the software architecture:

1. *Test coverage (software product architecture).* Software test coverage provides an important indicator of the software implementation progress. It is necessary to track test coverage against the three elements of the software architecture to ensure complete exposure of the software product to testing. During software implementation, the focus is on tracking software unit and component test coverage showing how much of the application you have exercised. During test planning, it is necessary to correlate test cases and scenarios with the requirements that they exercise.

2. *Test sufficiency (requirements baseline).* Testing the software product entails some deliberate scrutiny to identify a set of discriminating test cases and scenarios that will exercise the software product under simple, practical, and extreme conditions or circumstances. Boundary testing concentrates on the boundary

conditions of the software requirements. Boundary value analysis should be performed to ensure that the set of test cases are sufficient to demonstrate that software product requirements will be subjected to a sufficient set of tests.

3. *PDSS process test effort (post-development processes).* Each of the post-development processes will require a test and evaluation effort to ensure that the process is prepared to support the software product and its customers or users upon release. The post-development processes are closely associated with the software product architecture.

4. *Regression testing (requirements baseline).* During software implementation, existing code that has already undergone testing will need to be retested after changes have been accomplished, such as functional enhancements, patches, or configuration changes. Formal change proposals and technical change requests must account for the amount of regression testing that will be necessary to address the levels of structural component integration necessitated by proposed changes.

3.5 Functional architecture relationships and dependencies

The functional architecture describes what transactions the software product must carry out to satisfy the specified requirements. To determine this, the top-level functions must be decomposed to identify the sequence of subfunctions, control logic and decision branches, and inputs and outputs necessary to enable each function. Functions may require computing resources, such as data storage or data transmission bandwidth, to perform effectively. The functional architecture involves the following relationships and dependencies with the software architecture:

1. *Functional behavior verification (requirements baseline).* The functional decomposition of the software requirements results in the definition of functional behaviors that express the software response to identifiable stimulus. These behaviors depict functional flow timing, data flow, control flow, and resource utilization for each user interaction, software operation, and interface transaction. The accuracy and suitability of these behavioral models must be confirmed as a suitable interpretation of the software requirements.

2. *Performance allocation confirmation (requirements baseline).* The anticipated range of functional performance must be shown to satisfy the degree of performance specified by the software requirements. Functional performance budgets should be justifiable based on the computing environment vendors' published equipment characteristics.

3. *Functional specification integrity (requirements baseline).* The complete functional architecture must be shown to address all operational or system states and modes of operation, user inputs, interface message profiles, and fault detection, isolation, and recovery solutions.

4. *Functional assimilation (physical architecture).* Each of the functional units must be assigned to a structural unit where it may be combined, integrated, and blended with similar functions. The resulting structural unit requirements must be traceable to each functional unit specification.

3.6 Physical architecture relationships and dependencies

The physical architecture depicts the arrangement, interfaces, assembly, and integration configuration of the software product:

1. *Structural design verification (functional architecture).* The physical architecture must be verified to confirm that all of the functional requirements have been incorporated into the structural unit and component integration specifications.
2. *Structural design optimization (functional architecture).* The physical architecture design refinements and optimization must be shown to conform to the funtional specificiatons. Structural design refinements may be embraced to accommodate structural design discretion and resourcefulness and may require adjustment of the functional specifications.
3. *Structural performance validation (requirements baseline).* The estimated performance of the structural design must be determined using static mathematical or dynamic models. These performance estimates must be shown to satisfy the specified requirements.
4. *Measured product performance (software implementation).* The actual performance of the software implementation must be measured and verified against the predicted performance of the structural design.

3.7 Post-development process relationships and dependencies

The post-development processes involve their own specific development process that is not the subject of this material. However, their requirements are specified as an integral element of the software product development effort due to their close association with the software product. Therefore, the relationships identified here are intentionally general and broad:

1. *Process effectiveness verification (requirements baseline).* Each of the PDSS processes, in terms of procedures and trained, qualified staff, must be verified to ensure operational readiness and utility.
2. *Process completeness (software architecture).* The overall definition, design, and implementation of each post-development process must be verified to be consistent with the software architecture.

3.8 **Motivation for the software architecture**

Software development has a tarnished history of project and product failures and has earned a reputation as an undisciplined, naïve craft. While there have been many offenders, the numerous attempts to improve the state of practice have failed to make any significant advancement in software development efficiency, effectiveness, or product quality. The failure of past attempts can be attributed to the failure to devise a vigilant design paradigm that addresses the product requirements, functional and performance characteristics, and assembly and integration structural considerations. The software architecture, as addressed in this material, is intended to fulfill this software design liability.

The software architecture involves a number of elements or subarchitectures to be consistent with the integrated product and process development (IPPD) philosophy. The following list identifies the various subarchitectural elements found within the software architecture. Note that for each lowest-level subarchitecture there are three subelements: (1) requirements baseline, (2) functional architecture, and (3) physical architecture.

Software Architecture
- Product requirements baseline
- Product functional architecture
- Product physical architecture

Software Post-development Process Architecture
Product Distribution Process Architecture
- Distribution process requirements baseline
- Distribution process functional architecture
- Distribution process physical architecture

Product Training Process Architecture
- Training process requirements baseline
- Training process functional architecture
- Training process physical architecture

Product Sustainment Process Architecture
Customer Support Process Architecture
- Customer support process requirements baseline
- Customer support process functional architecture
- Customer support process physical architecture

Problem Resolution Process Architecture
- Problem resolution process requirements baseline
- Problem resolution process functional architecture
- Problem resolution process physical architecture

Product Enhancement Process Architecture
- Product enhancement process requirements baseline
- Product enhancement process functional architecture
- Product enhancement process physical architecture

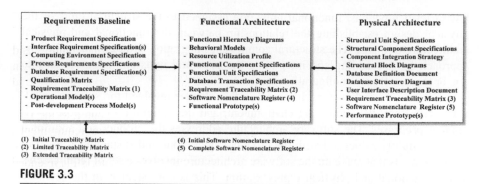

Requirements Baseline	**Functional Architecture**	**Physical Architecture**
- Product Requirement Specification - Interface Requirement Specification(s) - Computing Environment Specification - Process Requirements Specifications - Database Requirement Specification(s) - Qualification Matrix - Requirement Traceability Matrix (1) - Operational Model(s) - Post-development Process Model(s)	- Functional Hierarchy Diagrams - Behavioral Models - Resource Utilization Profile - Functional Component Specifications - Functional Unit Specifications - Database Transaction Specifications - Requirement Traceability Matrix (2) - Software Nomenclature Register (4) - Functional Prototype(s)	- Structural Unit Specifications - Structural Component Specifications - Component Integration Strategy - Structural Block Diagrams - Database Definition Document - Database Structure Diagram - User Interface Description Document - Requirement Traceability Matrix (3) - Software Nomenclature Register (5) - Performance Prototype(s)

(1) Initial Traceability Matrix
(2) Limited Traceability Matrix
(3) Extended Traceability Matrix

(4) Initial Software Nomenclature Register
(5) Complete Software Nomenclature Register

FIGURE 3.3

Typical software product architecture artifacts.

The software architecture discussed throughout this work is based on systems engineering practices and principles. The software architecture consists of an assortment of design artifacts typical of other engineering disciplines, such as diagrams, drawings, and static and dynamic models. The typical software architecture artifacts are shown in Figure 3.3. This architecture is used to control the product configuration and facilitate the inclusion of authorized changes within the product *design* framework. It accounts for the complex, nonmaterial nature of the software product, and its relationship to project management tools and techniques. The artifacts associated with the physical architecture forms the software technical data package that is provided to the software implementation team for software implementation design, coding, integration, and testing.

Every complex product development activity involves some form of product architecture derived from engineering principles. The following definition is provided for the term *product architecture*:[1]

> *Description of the way(s) in which functional elements of a product or system are assigned to its constituent components or subsystems, and of the way(s) in which they interact.*

This definition identifies the primary intent associated with the software product architecture—to describe the way in which functions are assigned to physical elements and how they interact. This implies that the product architecture involves two distinct design representations, one being functional and the second being physical. Product functions and performance objectives are derived from the product requirements. Functional decomposition breaks down a complicated problem space into smaller, less difficult tasks that can be less challenging to resolve. In its most basic form a functional decomposition is represented as a hierarchical decomposition with its performance characteristics budgeted among the constituent functions. The functional architecture description includes the functional inputs and resources needed by the function to generate outputs or provide a service. The

---

[1] See *http://www.businessdictionary.com/definition/product-architecture.html*.

lowest-level functions, functional units, are assigned to the structural units of the physical design establishing the relationship between the functional and physical architecture domains. The structural component integration strategy establishes the approach for assembling and integrating the structural units and components into one or more software configuration items.

The software architecture discussed in this chapter involved the software product architecture, the computing environment, and the definition of the post-development processes. The software architecture addresses the product and additional elements tightly associated with the product's operations and sustainment. Each of these elements that make up the software architecture involves a set of requirements and a functional and physical representation. This is consistent with the software breakdown structure (SBS) and IPPD philosophy addressed previously. The software product architecture involves the product requirements, product functional architecture, and product physical architecture. The elements of the software product architecture are examined in more detail in the following chapters of this book:

- Product requirements—Chapters 7–9
- Functional architecture—Chapters 10 and 11
- Physical architecture—Chapters 12 and 13

Understanding the Software Project Environment

4

CHAPTER OUTLINE

The effective and profitable execution of a software engineering project involves an understanding of the complex interactions and dependencies inherent in the project environment. This knowledge must be fortified with a set of supervisory tools that provide information concerning the current status of tasks and work products. This information contains obscure symptoms of potential situations that threaten the project's success or software product's quality and competitiveness in the marketplace. Software engineering exploits this information to permit its attentive practitioners to recognize disruptive trends and react in a positive manner to neutralize the root causes of problematic conditions.

There are three fundamental management tools that are used to guide a project toward successful completion. The first is the integrated master plan (IMP), which identifies the organizational roles and responsibilities, tasks to be performed, and expected outcomes. The second is the integrated master schedule (IMS), which provides a timeline of key events, milestones, reviews, and decision points. And finally, there is the project budget, which identifies the resources that are allocated to each organization to enable the execution of planned tasks. However, these project management instruments must be properly developed, monitored, and adjusted to reflect the ambiguity inherent in task estimation. Initial planning forecasts of anticipated productivity, performance, and results must account for project uncertainty. The level of confidence toward achieving project objectives involves understanding the assumptions that were involved in generating project plans and the probable outcomes if the assumptions prove flawed or inaccurate. The software engineering team can control the project's destiny by understanding the impact assumptions and decisions may have on project plans and anticipating the recovery strategy when progress is slowed or impeded by unforeseen circumstances.

Project plans, schedules, and budgets are simply restraining devices that are used to corral the project team toward product delivery in a timely and cost-effective manner. Initial plans are never accurate since there are too many unknowns concerning the software product to be developed. Additionally, it may not be possible to predict future or unexpected events. The number of stakeholders involved with the software development project makes it almost impossible to establish an accurate project plan. Therefore, the most important motive for employing software engineering practices is to fill in the gaps of understanding concerning the software product. This, in turn, helps refine the technical and project plans, schedules, and budgets so that the project can be successfully executed.

Software development projects are established with the aim of delivering a "new" software product to one or more customers. Therefore, until the software product definition is relatively complete, the project plans will always be imprecise. This implies that the project plans, schedules, and budgets are simply tools that direct the project team toward the definition, design, implementation, testing, documenting, and delivery of a software product. The dilemma faced by the project team is determining how to define the software product in such a manner that the project goals and objectives can be satisfied. Inherent in this situation is the fact that project plans, schedules, and budgets are simply a means to an end to the successful delivery of a software product on time (according to schedule) and without exceeding authorized funding thresholds (according to budget). As long as the project team can define and deliver an acceptable software product by the delivery date and does not expend more resources than authorized, the project should be deemed successful.

Within the project environment there exists a variety of decision points that represent opportunities to maintain the project scope so that goals and objectives can be attained. Software engineering practices and tools are structured to recognize when the definition of the software product presents an opportunity to revisit the project plan. At each opportunity, a decision must be made on which way to proceed among alternative approaches. Making proper architectural design decisions involves the following factors:

1. Understanding the product functions and characteristics that are important to stakeholders (requirements analysis).
2. Determining how each product characteristic will be provided (functional analysis and design synthesis).

3. Identifying which design approach best serves the current product stakeholders and the envisioned stakeholder community or customer base (trade-off analysis).
4. Eliminating unknown conditions that improve the likelihood of achieving project and product objectives (risk assessment).
5. Ensuring that every function or characteristic is necessary to the operation of the product and not in excess of what is needed (verification and validation).
6. Controlling product complexity to simplify software operational and support costs (integrated product and process development, IPPD).
7. Refining technical and project plans, schedules, and budgets to reflect the selected course of action (control).

Fundamentally, the software product architecture determines the project effort necessary to successfully implement, test, deliver, and support the product throughout its life cycle. If the project definition is allowed to drive the software product definition, then the product may be less beneficial and noteworthy in a competitive environment. The project scope must be aligned to provide the resources (personnel, facilities, equipment, tools, budget, schedule, etc.) necessary to define, design, implement, test, and deliver the software product to its customers. The software product must be developed to accommodate the needs and expectations of all stakeholders, including users, support staff, training staff, investors, and enterprise management. When the product definition and project scope are unbalanced, then the software engineering, technical, and project management teams must collaborate to stabilize the situation.

The software engineering effort represents the total technical effort within the project scope. As such, the software engineering leadership is responsible for defining the software product architecture in a manner that is consistent with the project scope. When it is perceived that the product value to its customers (consumers, operators, investors, etc.) can be enhanced with the application of additional project resources, then change proposals are generated to establish the merit of the enhancement. This occurs whenever the enhancement cannot be accommodated within the established project cost and schedule objectives. Figure 4.1 depicts the role of software engineering within a project environment.

The complexity of a software development effort can be appreciated by examining the multitude of products that must be addressed throughout the development project. Figure 4.2 provides a list of significant work products that must be generated, coordinated, and controlled by six organizations within the software development project. Table 4.1 identifies the work load assigned to each of the software development project organizations. The software engineering organization is directly responsible for one-quarter of the total work plan. However, software engineering is the lead for the total technical effort involving the work products of the other technical organizations—everything except the project management products. This accounts for 77.5% of the work effort. In addition, as the lead technical representative, the software engineering organization provides representatives to contribute to the generation, coordination, and control of the project management work products.

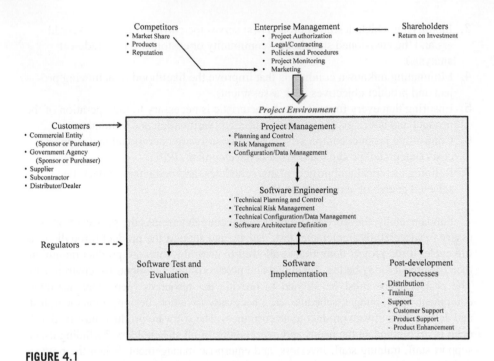

FIGURE 4.1

Role of software engineering within a project environment.

Software development projects with little or no software engineering practices have very little chance of success. Conducting software development without an effective software engineering approach is analogous to building a house without the architectural and engineering drawings. It would not be wise to permit the construction of a house to begin without the architectural drawings being finalized. Then why would it be acceptable to begin coding without the software product's architecture being available? Software engineering practices provide the following advantages to the software development project:

- Maintain the balance between the total technical effort and project objectives.
- Establish the software product architecture.
- Control the complexity of the software product.
- Coordinate change proposals and requests with all stakeholders.
- Coordinate organizational work plans to maintain alignment of technical plans with project objectives.

The remainder of this chapter identifies and discusses the software engineering practices and tools that contribute to achieving software product and project alignment.

Project Management

Project Planning
1. Project Plan
2. Integrated Management Plan
3. Integrated Management Schedule

Resource Control
4. Work Breakdown Structure
5. Work Packages
6. Budget and Cost Allocations

Data Management
7. Specification Tree
8. Specifications
9. Drawings and Diagrams
10. Plans and Procedures
11. User Manuals

Configuration Management
12. Configuration Management Plan
13. Change Control Board
14. Configuration Identification
15. Configuration Status Accounting
16. Change Management

Risk Management
17. Risk Management Plan
18. Risk Repository
19. Risk Status Reporting
20. Risk Abatement Strategy

Software Engineering

Software Analysis and Control
1. Software Engineering Plan
2. Technical Change Control Board
3. Trade-off Study Reports
4. Technical Risk Assessments
5. Computing Environment Requirement Specification
6. PDSS Requirement Specifications
7. Product Dictionary

Requirements Baseline
8. Software Requirement Specifications
9. Software Interface Specifications
10. Requirements Traceability Matrix
11. Operational Model

Functional Architecture
12. Functional Component Specifications
13. Behavioral Models
14. Functional Unit Specifications
15. Functional Hierarchies

Physical Architecture
16. Structural Unit Specifications
17. Structural Component Integration Specifications
18. Software Integration Strategy
19. Structural Block Diagrams
20. Structural Integration Hierarchies

Software Implementation
1. Software Implementation Plan
2. Software Unit Development Folders
3. Software Unit Source Code
4. Software Unit Testing Procedures
5. Software Unit Testing Results
6. Software Component Integration Procedures
7. Software Component Testing Procedures
8. Software Component Testing Results
9. Change Requests
10. Data Dictionary

Software Test and Evaluation
1. Software Test Environment
2. Software Test Plan
3. Acceptance Test Cases
4. Acceptance Test Procedures
5. Acceptance Test Results
6. Regression Test Data Files
7. Software Quality Evaluation Procedures
8. Software Quality Evaluation Reports
9. Change Requests

Computing Environment Definition
1. Computing Environment Definition Plan
2. Computing Environment Design
3. Network Implementation Plan
4. External Applications
5. Operating Systems and Middleware
6. Computing Environment Testing Plan
7. Computing Environment Testing Procedures
8. Computing Environment Testing Results
9. Change Requests

Post-development Processes

Software Distribution Process
1. Distribution Process Definition Plan
2. Distribution Process Design
3. Distribution Process Tools
4. Distribution Process Procedures
5. Distribution Process Testing Plan
6. Distribution Process Testing Procedures
7. Distribution Process Testing Results

Software Training Process
8. Training Process Definition Plan
9. Training Process Design
10. Training Course Material
11. Training Environment
12. Training Tools
13. Training Process Testing Procedures
14. Training Process Testing Results

Software Sustainment Process
15. Customer Support Environment
16. Customer Support Tools
17. Customer Support Procedures
18. Customer Support Records
19. Problem Reports
20. Problem Resolution Report
21. Software Patches/Fixes
22. Software Enhancement Development

FIGURE 4.2

Software development work products.

Table 4.1 Software Development Project Organizational Work Load

Organization	No. of Work Products	% of Work Plan
Project management	20	22%
Software engineering	21	23%
Software implementation	10	11%
Software test and evaluation	9	10%
Computing environment definition	9	10%
Post-development software sustainment	22	24%
Total	91	

4.1 Integrated product teams

Integrated product teams (IPTs) are the organizational construct used to manage the complexity of the software development effort and ensure proper stakeholder participation in the decision-making process. IPTs are the basis of organizing development personnel and stakeholder representatives to enable IPPD. Implementation of IPTs represents a transition from a functional stovepipe organizational arrangement to a product and process focus. Teamwork drives the functional disciplines into a mutually supportive relationship that helps remove barriers to software development success. The teams can be formed at all levels of the organization and are empowered to make critical life-cycle decisions for the development of a software product or sustainment process. Figure 4.3 identifies several recommended software IPTs. Additional IPTs should be formed to oversee the development of individual product elements or sustainment processes, depending on the critical nature of the article.

The software engineering IPT is chaired by the chief software engineer and involves representatives from the technical organizations and stakeholder groups. The team is responsible for establishing and controlling the software product and process architectures in a manner that ensures the symmetry and harmony of the interests of all representatives. Issues that cannot be resolved by this team should be raised to the project control IPT for deliberation. It acts as the technical change control board (CCB) for change requests that can be accommodated within the current scope of the development project. Change requests that cannot be accomplished within available technical resource levels should be elevated to the project control IPT for consideration.

The project control IPT is responsible for monitoring project progress toward the achievement of project objectives, as well as stakeholder satisfaction with the software product. The team acts as a filter for change proposals that require the application of additional resources to execute. Change proposals that cannot be accommodated within available project resource levels should be elevated to the project CCB.

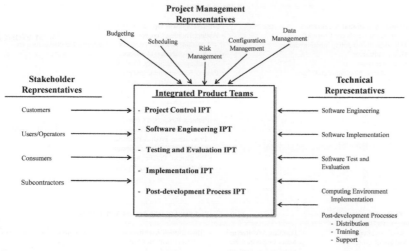

FIGURE 4.3

Recommended software development IPTs.

4.2 Software architecture

The software architecture identifies the operational and business needs and characteristics associated with the software product. Software engineering establishes a software architecture to address the functional and physical configuration of the software product and influences the post-development processes. Thus, the software architecture involves the software product architecture and the architectures for each of the post-development processes. Figure 4.4 shows the software architecture and its relationships to the software product and post-development process architectures.

Each architecture involves three distinct but integrated perspectives: requirements baseline, functional architecture, and physical architecture. The *requirements baseline* represents the set of requirement specifications that address the software product or post-development process area. The *functional architecture* represents the functional and performance decomposition of the requirements into functional components and units. One or more behavioral models can be developed to depict the functional flows, data flows, timing, and execution logic in terms of loops and business rules (e.g., If ... Then ... Else ..., Select ... Case constructs). Each functional element is characterized by a specification that provides the details concerning its performance, behaviors, and handling of error conditions. The *physical architecture* represents the structural design of the software product or post-development process area. It is derived from the lowest-level functional units and addresses the component integration strategy that guides the assembly, integration, and testing of the software product or post-development process area.

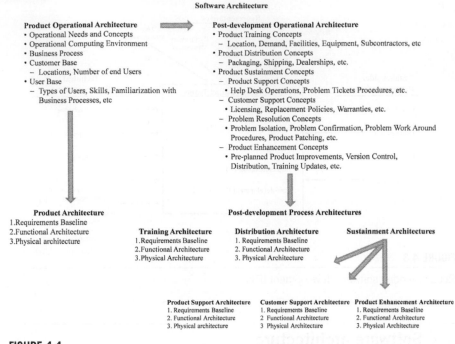

Software Architecture

Product Operational Architecture
- Operational Needs and Concepts
- Operational Computing Environment
- Business Process
- Customer Base
  - Locations, Number of end Users
- User Base
  - Types of Users, Skills, Familiarization with
    Business Processes, etc

Post-development Operational Architecture
- Product Training Concepts
  - Location, Demand, Facilities, Equipment, Subcontractors, etc
- Product Distribution Concepts
  - Packaging, Shipping, Dealerships, etc.
- Product Sustainment Concepts
  - Product Support Concepts
    - Help Desk Operations, Problem Tickets Procedures, etc.
  - Customer Support Concepts
    - Licensing, Replacement Policies, Warranties, etc.
  - Problem Resolution Concepts
    - Problem Isolation, Problem Confirmation, Problem Work Around
      Procedures, Product Patching, etc.
  - Product Enhancement Concepts
    - Pre-planned Product Improvements, Version Control,
      Distribution, Training Updates, etc.

Product Architecture
1. Requirements Baseline
2. Functional Architecture
3. Physical architecture

Training Architecture
1. Requirements Baseline
2. Functional Architecture
3. Physical Architecture

Distribution Architecture
1. Requirements Baseline
2. Functional Architecture
3. Physical Architecture

Sustainment Architectures

Post-development Process Architectures

Product Support Architecture
1. Requirements Baseline
2. Functional Architecture
3. Physical architecture

Customer Support Architecture
1. Requirements Baseline
2 Functional Architecture
3 Physical Architecture

Product Enhancement Architecture
1. Requirements Baseline
2. Functional Architecture
3. Physical Architecture

FIGURE 4.4

Elements of the software architecture.

1. *Software product operational architecture.* The product operational architecture profiles the business and market essentials concerning the new software product that is being considered for development. It should provide the information concerning the operational computing environment, the business process it supports, the customer base by industry, and the number of potential corporate entities and end users that would utilize the product. The types of end users and associated skill levels should be categorized to provide a basis for establishing the software product training and help systems. The issues of product licensing, warranties, and return policies must be addressed.

2. *Post-development operational architecture.* The post-development operational architecture should establish the anticipated approach to providing software product distribution, installation, training, and support capabilities. The use of existing facilities, subcontractors, and software dealerships versus enterprise direct sales, training, and support staffs should be considered.

3. *Software product architecture.* The software product architecture identifies product requirements and functional and physical characteristics to be implemented and tested. Chapter 3 provides a detailed description of the software product architecture.

4. *Post-development process architectures.* Each of the post-development processes should be defined to address how the software product will be distributed and sustained, and end-user training provided.

- *Training process architecture.* The training process architecture should identify the training program in terms of training courses, materials, facilities, and automated aids that must be provided to assist the end user gaining an understanding and proficiency in the software product operation. The use of third-party training organizations, training of customer training staff, or enterprise training capabilities should be considered.
- *Distribution process architecture.* The distribution process architecture should identify the various approaches by which the software product will be shipped, installed, and transitioned into operational status. Software media content (executable files, installation, and users' manuals) should be identified and the means of distributing the media should be addressed. The use of boxed media versus electronic media delivery should be evaluated to determine the best avenue for transmitting the software product and manuals to customers.
- *Sustainment process architecture.* The sustainment process architecture should identify the types of product and customer support that must be provided. The problem resolution process and procedures should be defined, and the facilities, tools, and staffing requirements for product sustainment should be specified. The approach to developing and distributing problem remedial patches and preplanned product enhancements should be described and characterized.

4.3 Complexity control mechanisms

A major focus of the software engineering effort is the relationship between product and project complexity. A number of software engineering practices are utilized to manage this relationship and monitor progress toward achieving project objectives. Each of these complexity control mechanisms will be discussed as they apply to the software product. However, they are just as applicable to the definition of the computing environment and the post-development processes.

4.3.1 Work breakdown structure

The work breakdown structure (WBS) decomposes work activities into manageable tasks that are expressed as work packages. Each work package identifies the sequence of tasks that must be accomplished to complete an intermediate work product or outcome. Work packages identify the inputs from other sources, labor, meetings, travel expenses, and material resources needed to complete the task. Work scheduling identifies the anticipated start dates, conditions necessary to begin a task, the time interval when the task will be performed, and the anticipated completion date and deadline that identifies when a delay in task completion begins to affect other tasks.

The most common technique for defining a WBS is to use the product breakdown structure to identify the effort necessary to define, design, implement, and test the various parts of the product, and perform assembly, integration, and testing of components. This permits each of the project organizations to identify the work associated with each element of the software product, identify the staff work assignments, and ensure that staff skills and expertise are properly applied across all work products. Each work package should be assigned a work authorization or cost accounting control number used to track cost accrual over time.

The work package definition establishes the dependencies among task execution that provide the information necessary to construct a work plan, schedule, and budget. The work plan should identify the activities and tasks that must be accomplished to generate work products, the organizational roles and contribution to each task, and the level of effort and resources necessary to perform the identified work. Risks to task execution should be identified and incorporated into the work plan and schedule to identify potential problematic situations that must be monitored, and the anticipated response to adverse occurrences.

The WBS has long been a project management tool used to define, organize, and track progress toward achieving project objectives. It captures the work to be performed necessary to deliver the software product and establish the post-development processes. It illustrates the numerous interactions among the software development organizations required to coordinate and collaborate on development activities. However, a new software development product cannot be defined in terms of its product breakdown structure during the early stages of development. Therefore, the work packages and cost allocations must be continually revisited and elaborated to reflect the software architecture as it evolves.

The WBS provides an excellent gage of the project and product complexity relationships. The number of dependencies among tasks provides a basis for establishing a critical path for achieving project objectives. The slack time (time between planned completion and deadline) indicates how compressed the work plan has been constructed. The smaller the slack time between elements on the critical path indicates the relative stress and significance the tasks on the critical path are to be accomplished according to the plan. Slack time should be built into the schedule's critical path to account for unforeseen events that may cause tasks to be delayed.

4.3.2 Product breakdown structure

The product breakdown structure (PBS) represents the decomposition of the software product into software configuration items, multiple levels of structural components, and structural units. The PBS is essential since it provides the basis for software component integration and testing, as well as the refinement of work packages and budget allocations. However, the initial PBS can only address the top level of known configuration items and software components. The initial PBS becomes increasingly accurate as a result of developing the software product architecture.

The complete definition of the PBS is extracted from the software product physical architecture and reflects the work effort to design, code, and test software units and the integration of these units into software components and configuration items. Therefore, the initial PBS that supports early project and technical planning is based on abstract software components that represent large wedges of anticipated work. These initial planning approximations are known as ballpark estimates and provide a placeholder within the work plan that must be enhanced in precision as more knowledge of the software product architecture is made available. Figure 4.5 depicts a conceptual evolution of the PBS as the software product physical architecture is refined and characterized. This occurs when software requirements are analyzed, design alternatives are investigated, and a design approach is chosen. The figure only shows a partial decomposition for one configuration item. The definition of the PBS is expanded throughout the early software definition activity, but should be finalized by critical design review (CDR). By this milestone, the software product physical architecture should be complete with a full set of identified structural units and software integration strategy.

4.3.3 Specification tree

The specification tree is a schematic diagram that identifies the requirement specifications and their relationships for the software product and post-development processes under development. Each element of a product or process breakdown structure should have a specification that stipulates the performance or essential characteristics that a stakeholder requires and that must be delivered. Specifications are written usually in a manner that enables the developer and stakeholders to measure the suitability of the software product's intended operational or business purpose. Specifications represent an output, product, or result of a work package identified by the WBS. The specification tree supports cost estimation, budgeting, and configuration control activities within a development project.

4.3.4 Documentation tree

The documentation tree is a schematic diagram that identifies the design drawings, diagrams, documents, and technical manuals associated with a software product or post-development processes under development. Each element of a product or process breakdown structure should have one or more documentation items that record its design characteristics. Documentation represents an output, product, or result of a work package identified by the WBS. The documentation tree supports cost estimation, budgeting, and configuration control activities within a development project.

4.3.5 Software product baselines

The *requirements baseline* identifies the required software functional, performance, and interface characteristics that must be present for the product development to be

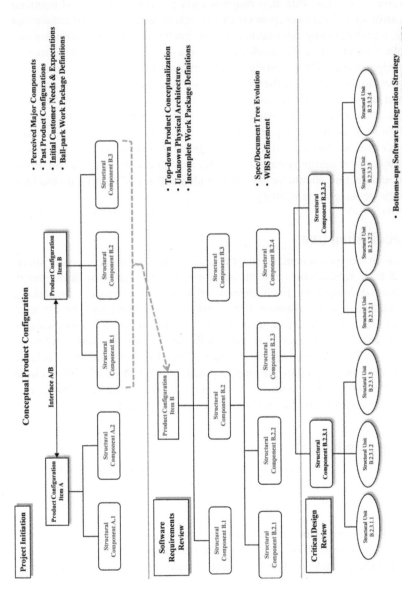

FIGURE 4.5

Evolution of the PBS.

completed. It addresses the verification fundamental to demonstrating the achievement of those specified requirements. The requirements baseline is comprised of the software and computing environment requirement and interface specifications that will be used by the software test staff to confirm the product's completeness during acceptance testing. The traditional software requirements baseline has been referred to as the functional baseline by the configuration management discipline. However, this baseline only addresses the software product functionality and ignores the functionality provided by the elements of the computing environment. Because a software product cannot be executed without the properly configured computing environment, the term *requirements baseline* has been introduced. In essence, the requirements baseline is comprised of the functional baselines of the software configuration items (if there are multiple software configuration items) and the computing environment.

The *allocated baseline* defines the configuration items making up a software product and identifies how software functional and performance requirements are allocated across lower-level configuration items.[1] It includes all functional, performance, and interface characteristics that are allocated from top-level software configuration items to functional components and units that comprise the functional architecture.

The *product baseline* describes all of the necessary functional and physical characteristics of a software configuration item and the tests necessary to demonstrate the compliance of the configuration items with its specified requirements. The product baseline includes "code-to" specifications for software structural units and components that comprise the physical architecture.

4.3.6 Requirements traceability guidelines

It is vital to have a complete understanding of the relationships among the software product and post-development processes and the project management and control mechanisms. It is not sufficient to have software requirements traceability among requirements specifications and test artifacts. To be responsive to design decisions, configuration alterations, requirements change proposals, and evolving stakeholder needs, many of the software development documentation artifacts (specifications, diagrams, plans, schedules, budgets, work packages, etc.) must be associated and tracked via one or more traceability tools. Figure 4.6 identifies the types of software design, documentation, planning, and project control artifacts that should be included in requirements traceability guidelines.

---

[1] The term *configuration item* is typically used to identify an integrated, deliverable software product. A software product may be one or more software configuration items. Every element of the software architecture (functional and structural components and units) represents configuration elements that are addressed by the allocated and product baseline.

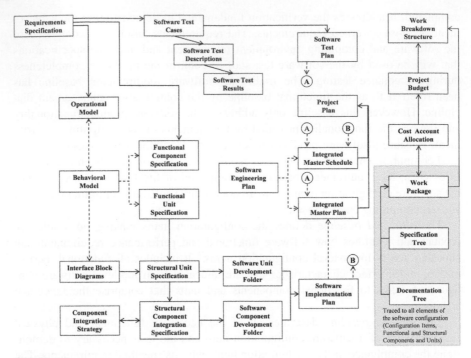

FIGURE 4.6

Recommended requirements traceability coverage.

There is a minimum set of traceability relationships that must be managed to support software verification and validation evaluations and configuration audits. These are shown as a solid line in Figure 4.6.

4.3.7 Trade-off analysis

Trade-off analysis is an exploratory tool by which stakeholder needs, software requirements, or architectural design alternatives are assessed to determine a preferred course of action. A software trade-off analysis should be conducted whenever there are competing solutions under consideration rather than making assumptions or design decisions with less-than-ideal information. It is important to understand how each decision affects the software product architecture in terms of complexity, effort required to implement the solution, and impact on post-development processes and life-cycle costs. Each potential alternative must be evaluated from several perspectives, including performance, innovativeness, cost to implement, usability, customer appreciation, competitive posture, and post-development sustainment ramifications. In addition, alternatives should be assessed to understand

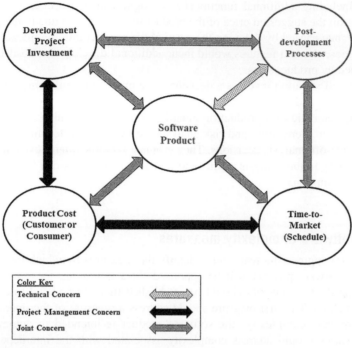

FIGURE 4.7

Fundamental trade-offs during software development.

the potential risks to achieving project objectives if the alternative were chosen. Understanding the risks with each alternative enables many risks to be avoided.

There are eight fundamental trade-offs that must be considered before making any decision to sanction a software requirement or design approach (Figure 4.7). The trade-offs occur among the primary competing factors that affect software development and product success. These trade-offs properly consider development project expense as an investment in the product being developed. Time-to-market addresses the importance of distributing the product sooner to capture market share and establish a customer base. Product performance recognizes that each increment of functionality or performance aggravates the work effort, which increases product cost and development expense.

It is important to understand the relationship among these product development and project characteristics. Development program expense represents the cost to develop the software product, while development speed addresses the schedule consideration with product introduction to a market or delivery to a customer. Product cost intimates the customer or consumer value for the software product given product performance, characteristics, and competitive factors. Product performance addresses the functional and performance characteristics provided by the software product. Including additional functionality or significant performance advantages should permit the suggested price of the product to be increased due to the potential loss of revenue caused by delaying the entry of the product into the marketplace. In addition, those product features would incur additional development costs that must be recouped by product sales.

A trade-off situation involves a decision to be made with full comprehension of both the upside and downside of a particular choice. It implies forfeiting one feature or characteristic of a product or situation in return for gaining another feature or characteristic. Sensitivity and risk analysis are two notable techniques that support the trade-off analysis decisions. They evaluate possible alternatives in terms of the uncertainty in the analysis results and how these variations can be attributed to different assumptions.

4.3.8 Software complexity measures

The software engineering team must identify the measures by which the complexity of the software product will be appraised. At a minimum, these measures of software product complexity should be established that can be used to aid design decision making. The first measure should address a measure of the operational or business process complexity[2] the software product is intended to automate. The other measures should address complexity associated with the interdependencies among elements within the software product architecture.

The process complexity can be obtained by constructing a static or dynamic model of the software product operations within the operational or business environment. The software product complexity necessitates three interrelated measures that address the evolution of the product architecture:

1. The number of stakeholder requirements and the perceived *computational intricacy* that can be applied against the software requirements specifications.
2. The *functional collaboration dependency* that addresses the number of user, database, external, and internal interactions or data exchanges identified within the functional architecture.
3. The *structural density* of the product architecture that addresses the number of component integration actions needed to assemble the software product.

These three measures provide a gage for each element of the software product architecture. Tables 4.2, 4.3, and 4.4 provide a description for the computational intricacy, functional collaboration dependency, and structural density software complexity measures.

---

[2]G. M. Muketha, A.A.A. Ghani, M. H. Selamat, and R. Atan (2008). A Survey of Business Process Complexity Metrics, available at *http://scialert.net/fulltext/?doi=itj.2010.1336.1344&org=11*.

Table 4.2 Computational Intricacy Complexity Measure Descriptions

	Name	Description
Measure	Computational intricacy	The overall challenge imposed by the software product requirements concerning the technical implementation in terms of algorithmic efficiency, performance, resource utilization, and other estblished measures of performance.
Parameters	Unprecedented (U)	The number of requirements that characterize a data processing challenge for which no prior solution is known.
	Complicated (C)	The number of requirements that characterize a data processing challenge for which the solution is understood, but the implementation of which may not be satisfactorily realized.
	Demanding (D)	The number of requirements that characterize a data processing challenge for which the solution may be inadequately supported by computer and software technology.
	Moderate (M)	The number of requirements that characterize a data processing challenge for which a solution is known and the implementation is relatively undemanding.

		Example
Method of calculation		Each requirement is categorized based on the perceived level of difficulty to be satisfied effectively and efficiently given the availability of software technology, programming language constraints, and the level of experience and skills inherent with the software implementation team. Each requirement is evaluated by subject matter experts to assign an intricacy rating (10 for extensive; 7 for excessive; 4 for significant and 1 for moderate) and the overall collaboration complexity rating is computed by summing the rating for each category. The intricacy rating is then divided by the total number of requirements to derive the computational intricacy measure of complexity.
Formula	$(10 \times (U) + 7 \times (C) + 4 \times (D) + (M))/$ Total no. of requirements	For this example problem, assume that the software requirement involves the following parametrics involving architectural and implementation challenges:
		U = 1 requirement implies an unprecedented challenge to deriving an acceptable solution.
		C = 4 requirements imply a complicated challenge to deriving an acceptable solution.
		D = 7 requirements imply a demanding challenge to deriving an acceptable solution.
		M = 38 requirements imply a moderate challenge to deriving an acceptable solution.
		$(10 \times 1) + (7 \times 4) + (4 \times 7) + (38) = 104$
		Total no. of requirements $= 1 + 4 + 7 + 38 = 50$ $104/50 = 2.08$
		This example of computational intricacy identifies a *moderately* complex software solution
Complexity levels		Extremely complex: >5
		Very complex: between 4 and 4.999
		Highly complex: between 3 and 3.999
		Moderately complex: between 2 and 2.999
		Routine complexity: between 1 and 1.999

Table 4.3 Functional Collaboration Dependency Complexity Measure Descriptions

	Name	Description
Measure	Functional collaboration	The overall challenge imposed by the arrangement of functional elements in term of dependencies and interfaces.
Parameters	Extensive (EX)	The number of functional dependencies or interfaces among a functional element (functional component or unit) exceeds 6.
	Excessive (E)	The number of functional dependencies or interfaces among a functional element (functional component or unit) is for 4 or more.
	Significant (S)	The number of functional dependencies or interfaces among a functional element (functional component or unit) is 2 or more.
	Moderate (M)	The number of functional dependencies or interfaces among a functional element (functional component or unit) is less than 2.

	Example
Method of calculation	Each functional element evaluated by subject matter experts and categorized based on the number of functional elements that impose a dependency or interface requirement on the function. The number in each category is multiplied by its complexity rating (10 for extensive; 7 for excessive; 4 for significant; 1 for moderate) and the overall collaboration complexity rating is computed by summing the total rating for each category. The collaboration complexity rating is then divided by the total number of functional elements to arrive at a functional collaboration measure of complexity.
Formula	$(10 \times (EX) + 7 \times (E) + 4 \times (S) + (M))/$ Total no. of functional elements
	For this example problem, assume that the software structural configuration involves the following parametrics involving structural component integration:
	EX = 1 functional element involves more than 6 functional dependencies or interfaces.
	E = 4 functional elements which involve more than 4 functional dependencies or interfaces.
	S = 7 functional elements which involve 2 or more functional dependencies or interfaces.
	M = 38 functional elements which involve less than 2 functional dependencies or interfaces.
	$(10 \times 1) + (7 \times 4) + (4 \times 7) + (38) = 104$
	Total no. of functional elements $= 1 + 4 + 7 + 38 = 50$ $104 / 50 = 2.08$
	This example of functional collaboration identifies a *moderately* complex functional solution.
Complexity levels	Extremely complex: > 5
	Very complex: between 4 and 4.999
	Highly complex: between 3 and 3.999
	Moderately complex: between 2 and 2.999
	Routine complexity: between 1 and 1.999

Table 4.4 Structural Density Complexity Measure Descriptions

	Name	Description
Measure	Structural density	The overall challenge imposed by the structural arrangement of a software configuration item in terms of the software integration effort.
Parameters	Extensive (EX)	The number of structural components that involve the integration of 10 or more structural elements.
	Excessive (E)	The number of structural components that involve the integration of 7, 8, or 9 structural elements.
	Significant (S)	The number of structural components that involve the integration of 4, 5, or 6 structural elements
	Moderate (M)	The number of structural components that involve the integration of 3 or fewer structural elements.
		Example
Method of calculation		Each structural component evaluated by subject matter experts and categorized based on the number of structural elements (subcomponents or units) that are involved in its integration. The number in each category is multiplied by its complexity rating (10 for extensive; 7 for excessive; 4 for significant; 1 for moderate) and the integration complexity rating is computed by summing the rating for each category. The integration complexity rating is then divided by the total number of structural components to arrive at a structural density measure of complexity.
Formula	$(10 \times (EX) + 7 \times (E) + 4 \times (S) + (M)) /$ Total no. of structural components	For this example problem, assume that the software structural configuration involves the following parametrics involving structural component integration: EX = 1 structural component which involves the integration of 10 or more structural elements. E = 4 structural components which involve the integration of 7, 8 or 9 structural elements. S = 7 structural components which involve the integration of 4, 5 or 6 structural elements. M = 38 structural components which involve the integration of 3 or fewer structural elements. $(10 \times 1) + (7 \times 4) + (4 \times 7) + (38) = 104$ Total no. of structural components = $1 + 4 + 7 + 38 = 50$ $104 / 50 = 2.08$ This example of structural density identifies a *moderately* complex software configuration.
Complexity levels		Extremely complex: > 5 Very complex: between 4 and 4.999 Highly complex: between 3 and 3.999 Moderately complex: between 2 and 2.999 Routine complexity: between 1 and 1.999

```
Software Product                          1.2 Physical Configuration
1. Configuration Item X                        1.2.1 Structural ComponentX.1
1.1 Functional Configuration                       1.2.1.1 Structural ComponentX.1.1
    1.1.1 Functional ComponentX.1                      1.2.1.1.1 Structural UnitX.1.1.1
        1.1.1.1 Functional ComponentX.1.1              1.2.1.1.2 Structural UnitX.1.1.2
        1.1.1.2 Functional ComponentX.1.2          1.2.1.2 Structural ComponentX.1.2
        1.1.1.3 Functional ComponentX.1.3              1.2.1.2.1 Structural UnitX.1.2.1
            1.1.1.3.1 Functional UnitX.1.3.1           1.2.1.2.2 Structural UnitX.1.2.2
            1.1.1.3.2 Functional UnitX.1.3.2           1.2.1.2.3 Structural UnitX.1.2.3
    1.1.2 FunctionX.2                          1.2.3 Structural Interfaces
        1.1.2.1 SubfunctionX.2.1               1.2.4 External Interfaces
        1.1.2.2 SubfunctionX.2.2           2.   Configuration Item Y
    1.1.3 Functional Interfaces                     ⋮
          ⋮                               3.   Glossary of Names
```

FIGURE 4.8

Suggested structure for the nomenclature registry.

4.4 Software nomenclature registry

The registry identifies the architectural elements of the software product architecture, and provides meaningful information about each element and their relationships to other elements within the architecture. The registry provides the configuration identification information pertaining to each entry in the registry. A glossary should identify the unique names for functional and structural components and units to ensure that there are no duplicate names used within the definition of the product architecture. The glossary of names should be arranged alphabetically and associated with the architectural element to which it pertains using the product unique identifier. Figure 4.8 depicts a suggested structure for the nomenclature registry.

4.5 Software integration strategy

The software integration strategy is developed while preparing the software product physical architecture. It identifies how structural units will be combined into a set of structural components. Structural units are derived from the functional architecture by grouping common functional units and assimilating the unit specifications to eliminate conflicts, duplication, and inconsistencies. Structural components are then synthesized by grouping structural units and assimilating their specifications to establish structural component specifications. Structural component specifications should not reiterate structural unit requirements, but should address those unique behavioral characteristics and interfaces that result from the integration. This understanding of an integrated software component's behavioral characteristics results from the synthesis of lower-level structural elements into an integrated structural component. This integration strategy may involve the integration of nondevelopmental items, such as commercially available or reusable software components.

The software integration strategy forms the basis for the software implementation team's work plan to perform component integration and testing. Therefore, the identification of structural components must result in an assembly structure for the software configuration items and product. Each software component must be comprised of sufficient functionality and test stubs to be independently tested and evaluated.

4.6 Project and technical planning

The execution of the software development project is guided by a set of project and technical plans. However, it is the planning exercise and decisions that are central to the success of the project. The plans themselves only document the approach or course of action designed to achieve immediate or short-term objectives. Initial plans established for the software development project will need to be revised as the software requirements and architecture are ascertained and characterized. It is not possible to establish a comprehensive plan addressing the entire software development effort during the early stages of development. Therefore, it is necessary for project and technical plans to be revised prior to each review or milestone to reflect the understanding obtained during the preceding phase of development. Figure 4.9 shows the evolution of the software architecture throughout the first three development phases and how this leads to improving project and technical plans.

At the start of the software development effort project plans should simply establish the major milestones to be achieved and the technical activities, documentation, and models that will be generated to define the software requirement. Prior to the software requirements review, project and technical plans should be extended to address the technical activities that will be conducted to delineate the product functional and physical architectures. These technical plans are summarized in the IMP and arranged as a time-based IMS. The IMS is a networked, multilayered schedule showing the significant tasks required to establish the software product architecture. These project and technical plans should be the fundamental elements reviewed at the software requirements review (SRR). Successful completion of the SRR would authorize the work articulated by these planning devices. Throughout the software development effort, these plans should be revised to align the technical work with the effort remaining to complete the project objectives.

4.6.1 Technical organization plans

The software engineering plan is the central technical management document that guides the software development effort. It focuses on the integrated technical work necessary to define and control the software architecture. It should identify the organizational roles and responsibilities, integrated product team purpose and composition, and phase-specific results and success criteria.

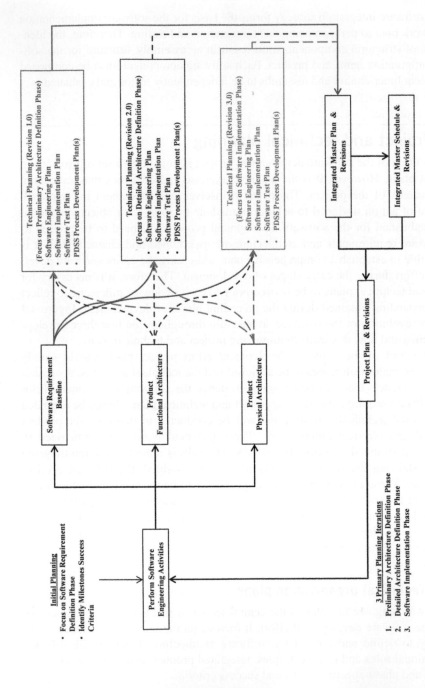

FIGURE 4.9

Technical and project planning.

Each technical organization should prepare its individual work plan, which identifies how work assignments will be accomplished. The lead technician responsible for each task and the interaction with other technical organizations that contribute to task execution must be identified. The software implementation plan identifies how structural units will be designed, coded, and tested, and the component integration strategy will be executed. The software test plan addresses how product acceptance testing will be conducted, including the dry-run testing to ensure that the software product is ready for formal acceptance testing. Software product deficiencies uncovered during dry-run testing should be resolved and retested prior to conducting the testing readiness review. The post-development process development plans should address the approach to designing, implementing, and testing each of the post-development sustainment processes based on the software product architecture.

4.6.2 Project plans

The IMP and IMS represent the project plans that address the technical work to be performed. The IMP provides an integrated, hierarchical view of important technical efforts (activities, high-level tasks, reviews, and milestones). The IMP is not a date-driven plan but is characterized by technical results that must be achieved. Each effort must be defined by explicit results and the associated criteria that will be utilized to confirm attainment of the desired results. The IMS is derived from the IMP and provides additional levels of detail for tasks that are necessary to accomplish technical results. The IMS aligns anticipated start dates, durations, and relationships of tasks to other tasks to provide a network of integrated tasks. The IMS provides a calendar-based view of the task details necessary for the execution, monitoring, and control of project progress. The IMS must be directly traceable to the IMP and must be linked to the WBS.

Software Integrated Product and Process Development

5

CHAPTER OUTLINE

Integrated product and process development (IPPD) is a central theme of software engineering that affects the software product architecture and sustainment processes. The object of IPPD is to control the product definition in a manner that reduces complexity and life-cycle support costs. IPPD addresses two prevalent concerns within the system development community: first, concurrent engineering, which is to ensure that the entire product''s life cycle is taken into consideration during the design process; and second, that all product disciplines, including all implementation, assembly, test and evaluation, maintenance, and support, should be involved in the early design phases. This chapter will discuss how IPPD should be adapted for software engineering efforts. Successful implementation of IPPD can result in:

- Reduced time-to-market.
- Reduced product development costs.
- Reduced development risk.
- Improved product quality.
- Reduced sustainment costs.

Traditional IPPD addressed the tight relationships between product design engineering and production capabilities. Products that involve hardware elements must address the manufacturing and assembly line capabilities to produce quantities of units with consistent dimensions, properties, or characteristics. Engineering tolerances must be specified to allow reasonable leeway for imperfections and inherent variability in production quality without significantly affecting functioning of assembled components. Therefore, the engineering design specifications for hardware parts must incorporate production process capabilities. Furthermore, the manufacturing process must incorporate adequate process control devices to ensure a significant yield of acceptable parts and reduce manufacturing waste and rework. This demands that design engineers of products that must be manufactured must be cognizant of the capabilities of the production tooling and manufacturing process.

A software product is a complex "system" that is made up of many collaborating parts. It is not sufficient to simply decompose software requirements and allocate them to software components and units. Software IPPD must resolve design challenges and complexity by establishing the product architecture. The development of the functional architecture addresses software control flow, data exchanges, performance, resource utilization, and detection and response to failure conditions. The physical architecture addresses the manner in which software structural units and components collaborate and are integrated to comprise the final software product. The software architecture represents the design of the software product with sufficient information to permit structural units and component behaviors to be specified.

Software IPPD differs from traditional software development due to the nature of the software product of which the implementation design is dependent on the capabilities and programming constructs inherent in the compilation language. The software functional and physical architectures must be developed with an understanding of implementation and testing challenges. This requires the involvement of software implementation and testing subject matter experts in software engineering activities. In addition, the post-development software sustainment processes must be addressed so that they can be established and tested in a timely manner to support software product distribution. Therefore, the software engineering integrated product team (SWE-IPT) must involve representatives from all software technical organizations. This permits the software product architecture to be developed with an appreciation for software implementation and sustainment issues. This approach reduces life-cycle costs, minimizes risk to achieving project schedules, and restricts the potential for requirements creep.

Additionally, software engineering IPPD ensure that sufficient time is invested in establishing the product architecture where early design decisions can have the most significant impact on project and process success. During the architecture definition phases, design alternatives should be evaluated via modeling and prototyping to determine the best approach to proceed with. Prototyping should not be left until software implementation because it defers important design decisions to later phases of development. Software implementation should be simplified to the design of software units against the specification established by the physical architecture. This approach is more consistent with hardware development where detailed models and equipment prototypes are developed during detailed design to confirm design suitability.

Table 5.1 Comparison of Hardware and Software Development Phases		
Hardware Development Phases	**Traditional Software Development Phases**	**Software Engineering Development Phases**
HWCI preliminary design—evaluates the system requirements allocated to hardware configuration items and prepares a specification of requirements.	*CSCI preliminary design*—evaluates the system requirements allocated to software configuration items and prepares the software component specifications (allocation of software requirements).	*Software architecture preliminary design*—evaluates the software requirements and generates the software product's functional architecture. Generates behavioral models to assess product performance. Results in the identification and specification of functional components and units.
HWCI detailed design—develops models and prototypes to assess design concepts and generates manufacturing engineering drawings and diagrams.	*CSCI detailed design*—evaluates the software component requirements and prepares the software unit specifications (allocation of software requirements).	*Software architecture detailed design*—evaluates the software functional units and establishes the software product's physical architecture. Generates models and prototypes to support design trade-off analysis. Results in the identification and specification of structural units and integrated components. Establishes the software integration strategy.
HWCI fabrication—the production organization utilizes the engineering drawings and produces a working prototype for testing.	*CSCI code, testing, and integration*—designs, codes, and tests software units against unit specifications. Performs software component integrations and testing.	*Software implementation*—designs, codes, and tests software units. Performs software integration and testing according to the software integration strategy. Performs product testing to ensure the software product is ready for acceptance testing.
HWCI testing—formally test the hardware items against their requirements specifications.	*CSCI testing*—formally tests the software configuration items against their requirement specifications.	Acceptance testing—formally tests the software product against its requirement specifications.
HWCI = Hardware Configuration Item; CSCI = Computer Software Configuration Item.		

Table 5.1 aligns the traditional software development, software engineering, and hardware development phases to highlight the differences between these approaches. Notice that software implementation and the designing, coding, integration, and testing of the software product is aligned with the hardware fabrication phase. This alignment suggests that the software implementation effort is analogous to hardware manufacturing. Therefore, the predominance of the software product

design effort, including modeling and prototyping, should be accomplished prior to initiating software implementation.

5.1 Application of IPPD to software

Integrated product and process development is based on fundamental guidelines and assumptions that have served the systems engineering community since the early 1990's. The guiding principles of IPPD have been embraced by most agencies within the federal government and commercial corporations that develop large, complex products. The fundamental principles of IPPD were first established by the secretary of defense, who mandated the use of IPPD in all systems acquisition programs.[1]

IPPD is defined as a management process that integrates all activities from product concept through production/field support, using multifunctional teams to simultaneously optimize the product and its manufacturing and sustainment processes to meet cost and performance objectives. Its key tenets are as follows:

1. *Customer focus:* The primary objective of IPPD is to satisfy the customer's needs better, faster, and at less cost. The customer's needs should determine the nature of the product and its associated processes.
2. *Concurrent development of products and processes:* Processes should be developed concurrently with the products that they support. It is critical that the processes used to manage, develop, manufacture, verify, test, deploy, operate, support, train people, and eventually dispose of the product be considered during product development. Product and process design and performance should be kept in balance.
3. *Early and continuous life-cycle planning:* Planning for a product and its processes should begin early in the science and technology phase (especially advanced development) and extend throughout a product's life cycle. Early life-cycle planning, which includes customers, functions, and suppliers, lays a solid foundation for the various phases of a product and its processes. Key program events should be defined so that resources can be applied and the impact of resource constraints can be better understood and managed.
4. *Maximize flexibility for optimization and use of contractor unique approaches:* Requests for proposals (RFPs) and contracts should provide maximum flexibility for optimization and use of contractor unique processes and commercial specifications, standards, and practices. They should also accommodate changes in requirements and incentivize contractors to challenge requirements and offer alternative solutions that provide cost-effective solutions.
5. *Encourage robust design and improved process capability:* Encourage use of advanced design and manufacturing techniques that promote achieving quality through design and products with little sensitivity to variations in the manufacturing process (robust design), and focus on process capability and continuous process improvement.

---

[1] DoD Guide to Integrated Product and Process Development, Version 1.0, Feb. 5, 1996.

6. *Event-driven scheduling:* A scheduling framework should be established that relates program events to their associated accomplishments and accomplishment criteria. An event is considered complete only when the accomplishments associated with the event have been completed as measured by the accomplishment criteria. This event-driven scheduling reduces risk by ensuring that product and process maturity are incrementally demonstrated prior to beginning follow-on activities.

7. *Multidisciplinary teamwork:* Multidisciplinary teamwork is essential to the integrated and concurrent development of a product and its processes. The right people at the right place at the right time are required to make timely decisions. Team decisions should be based on the combined input of the entire team (e.g., engineering, manufacturing, testing, logistics, financial management, and contracting personnel) to include customers and suppliers. Each team member needs to understand his or her role and support the roles of the other members, as well as understand the constraints under which other team members operate. Communication within teams and among teams should be open with team success emphasized and rewarded.

8. *Empowerment:* Decisions should be driven to the lowest possible level commensurate with risk. Resources should be allocated at levels consistent with authority, responsibility, and the ability of the people. The team should be given the authority, responsibility, and resources to manage their product and its risk commensurate with the team's capabilities. The team should accept responsibility and be held accountable for the results of their effort.

9. *Seamless management tools:* A framework should be established that relates products and processes at all levels to demonstrate dependency and interrelationships. A single management system should be established that relates requirements, planning, resource allocation, execution, and program tracking over the product's life cycle. This integrated approach helps ensure teams have all available information thereby enhancing team decision making at all levels. Capabilities should be proved to share technical and business information throughout the product life cycle through the use of acquisition and support databases and software tools for accessing, exchanging, and viewing information.

10. *Proactive identification and management of risk:* Critical cost, schedule, and technical parameters related to system characteristics should be identified from risk analyses and user requirements. Technical and business performance measurement plans, with appropriate metrics, should be developed and compared to best-in-class industry benchmarks to provide continuing verification of the degree of anticipated and actual achievement of technical and business parameters.

While many of these principles integrate project management and technical competencies, the adaption of IPPD to software development must emphasize the technical challenges associated with software engineering. The software engineering practices discussed in this book are passed on an IPPD approach. Therefore, the following sections will address how IPPD tenants have been applied to the engineering of software products.

5.1.1 Customer focus

This tenant of IPPD identifies four central themes for establishing a quality software product:

1. Customer needs should determine the nature of the software product and processes.
2. Products should satisfy customer needs better (improved quality).
3. Products should satisfy customer needs faster (time-to-market).
4. Products should satisfy customer needs at lower cost (reduced product and life-cycle costs).

These themes are admirable goals that are not easy to achieve. If methodologies or approaches to software development were sufficient to fulfill these mandates, then there would be no need for further research or rhetoric about improving software development. However, according to the CHAOS[2] reports for a period of 15 years, the success rate for software development projects hovers around 28%, an average of 37% of the projects were considered challenged,[3] and the remaining 35% were impaired.[4] Therefore, one can surmise that the current methodologies, tools, and techniques for software development are not adequate to fulfill this tenet of IPPD. Throughout this material, these customer focus themes have been incorporated as the nucleus of the software engineering philosophy.

Throughout the software engineering process the emphasis of verification and validation is to ensure that the software product architecture definition will satisfy stakeholder needs and expectations. The term *stakeholder* is used to represent all customers of the technical effort, including project management, customers, end users, suppliers, and product sustainment organizations. The concept of achieving a balance among product requirements, product architecture, sustainment processes, and project objectives is supported by the conduct of trade-off analysis and risk assessments.

5.1.2 Concurrent development of products and processes

The total scope of a software development project must address the development of the software product, as well as the processes by which the product will

---

[2]CHAOS, The Standish Group Report, 1995.
[3]The project is completed and operational but overbudget, over the time estimate, and offers fewer features and functions than originally specified.
[4]The project is cancelled at some point during the development cycle.

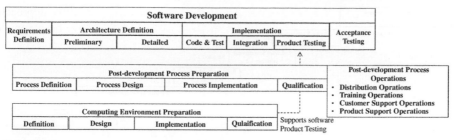

FIGURE 5.1

Concurrent development of products and processes.

be implemented (software equivalent of manufacturing), tested, and supported. In addition, a software product requires the establishment of a computing environment within which it operates. The computing environment involves a number of computing devices, workstations, storage devices, networking equipment, the target operating systems, middleware, and associated applications (e.g., database management system, DBMS).

Within the software development project there are a number of processes that are affected by the definition of the software product architecture. The three primary processes involved in the product development are software implementation, computing environment implementation, and software testing. The three primary processes involved with product sustainment are product distribution, product training, and product support. Product support can be further decomposed into several processes, such as customer support or help desk operations, problem resolution, and product enhancements. However a software development project identifies these processes, they must be defined, designed, implemented, and tested concurrently with the development of the software product. Figure 5.1 aligns these process development efforts with the software development framework that addresses the software product development phases.

Each of these software processes involves facilities, equipment, staffing, procedures, and associated resources to be available to support execution of assigned tasks. These process areas must be defined, designed, implemented, and tested in a timely manner to support the software product development schedule. The definition of these processes is influenced by the definition of the software product and cannot be implemented independently. Therefore, the mandate imposed by an IPPD philosophy is that these processes must be defined simultaneously with the software product. Software product design approaches may have significant impacts on one or more of these processes and life-cycle costs. Therefore, representatives from these process areas must be involved in the software engineering activities that define the software product architecture. This collaborative arrangement will be discussed further in the "Multidisciplinary Teamwork" section later in the chapter.

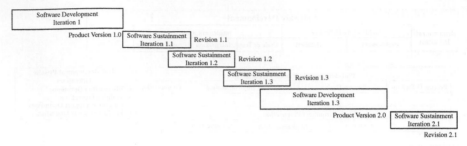

FIGURE 5.2

Iterative and/or incremental software life-cycle planning.

5.1.3 Early and continuous life-cycle planning

The IPPD philosophy expands the definition of development to address the product life cycle. This involves more than the development of the product—establishing the infrastructure for post-development software sustainment. This involves considering how the product may be evolved over time through a number of iterative development efforts, as well as how the advancement of computing technology may affect the product design and computing environment composition. The variable element of the product life cycle must be identified early to ensure that the software product architecture is established to facilitate the product's evolution. Planning the product development and life-cycle sustainment activities must begin early in the product conceptual definition. The planning activities must be revised to continually incorporate the most current knowledge and understanding of the effort needed to complete the initial product development and initiate the post-development efforts.

This captures the premise behind iterative and incremental software development approaches. They recognize that a software product will evolve throughout its life cycle. Therefore, it is prudent to plan the software product's evolution around several iterations of software development to provide increments of product functionality and performance. Under the IPPD philosophy, the initial development of the software product represents a large development effort due to the need to establish the product architecture. During software sustainment, the product is modified, enhanced, or extended by additional iterations of the development activities. Whenever the software product must undergo significant architectural redefinition, a new software development project should be established. For each major iteration of software development, the associated life-cycle processes may need to be redeveloped to accommodate the changes in the product's architecture. Figure 5.2 shows the sequence and alignment of software development projects and post-development software sustainment iterations.

5.1.4 **Maximize flexibility for optimization and use of contractor unique approaches**

This tenant of IPPD focuses primarily on agreements between customers, developers, suppliers, and subcontractors. Innovative techniques to software development can be both beneficial and detrimental to project success. While new or unproven approaches may appear advantageous, they should be selectively instituted under trial conditions to ensure they produce the desired results.

The second statement within this tenant addresses a concept of challenging requirements and offering alternative solutions that prove cost effective. This is a valuable idea that provides several benefits whenever it is applied. Challenging the validity of requirements improves the precision by which software requirements are captured and expressed. Stakeholder representatives typically view the software product from their own perspective. Thus, they will support the requirements that embellish the characteristics of the software product they are concerned with. Stakeholders must be challenged to identify what the software product must do and not overemphasize the importance of features or characteristics that are nice, sophisticated, or impressive.

Software requirements must be solicited and gathered from many sources. The complete set of requirements must be clarified and prioritized to establish the precedence of product functions, features, and other characteristics. Each individual requirement imposes a cost on the development effort, therefore challenging the validity of the assists in weeding out the unnecessary or secondary stakeholder needs and expectations. The objective must be to reduce the set of requirements to the minimal necessary to result in a viable product that supports customer and stakeholder needs, are clearly specified so that there is no confusion concerning what is intended by the requirements statement, and fit within the project scope of resources and scheduled milestones.

In some instances, stakeholders do share the financial burden associated with their defense of particular requirements. If a company is funding a software development effort, its representatives may feel responsible for getting the most prolific product for their money. They may misrepresent the importance of features and may argue the merit of unnecessary requirements with the software development team. Such representatives do not understand that they may cause the development effort to be doomed from the start by overburdening the development effort with excessive requirements. It is always necessary to challenge the validity of software requirements and to prioritize them before determining the minimal set that fits within the development project's constrained resources.

Once the software development effort has begun, any proposed changes to the requirements baseline must be challenged immediately. The addition of new or modifications to existing requirements may necessitate significant rework to incorporate the change into the product architectural design. The cost associated with a requirement change must account for the effort to incorporate the design modification throughout the affected product documentation. In addition, the organizational plans, technical plans, work packages, schedules, and related planning documents must be updated to address each change. If a proposed change can be delayed and incorporated in a future version of the software product, then it may be best to accept the change but to postpone its incorporation into the software product.

5.1.5 Encourage robust design and improved process capability

This tenant addresses improving the software design (software engineering), implementation, testing, and post-development process cohesion. The intent is to establish software design techniques that facilitate software implementation (design, coding, integration) and testing. This tenant is satisfied by establishment of the software architecture as the foundation for software implementation. The transition from software product architectural design to software implementation is enhanced by developing software product specifications for every structural unit and component. The software integration strategy is developed during the detailed architecture definition activity and provides a roadmap for software integration and testing. Therefore, the material contained herein is intended to fulfill this tenant by improving the software product design and development processes.

5.1.6 Event-driven scheduling

Whenever this material addresses scheduling, it refers to the integrated master plan and schedule (IMP/IMS). The IMP is an event-driven schedule that identifies the accomplishments that must be achieved and the criteria that must be satisfied for work to be considered complete. The IMS is a date-driven schedule that aligns organizational and technical plans with the project milestones. This is addressed in Chapter 4 and is further discussed throughout the remainder of this book as needed.

5.1.7 Multidisciplinary teamwork

Conducting the software engineering practices expressed in this book requires the use of IPTs. The primary integrated product team is the SWE-IPT, which is responsible for developing the software architecture. Additionally, four additional IPTs are identified that address software implementation, software test and evaluation, post-development software sustainment processes, and project control. Each IPT should involve members whom advocate for stakeholder needs, as well as representatives from each of the technical organizations. Additional IPTs may be established by the project or SWE-IPT as deemed advantageous to achieving project objectives.

5.1.8 Empowerment

The software development planning and scheduling activities involve all technical organizations that prepare detailed plans for accomplishing the tasks assigned to them via work packages. These plans are integrated by the SWE-IPT to form an integrated technical plan and schedule (ITP/ITS). The ITP and ITS are combined with the work plans of other project management and support organizations to form the IMP and IMS. The work breakdown structure, IMP, and IMS provide the basis for task execution, and each technical organization must be held accountable for achieving results.

Technically, the software product architecture establishes the structural unit and component specifications for software implementation. These specifications permit the software implementation team members to design, code, and test software units with complete design decision authority. The software integration strategy establishes the approach for software component integration and testing and the software implementation team should be authorized to establish the procedures for software integration and testing.

5.1.9 Seamless management tools

This book provides the basis for establishing integrated software engineering tools that provide planning, product architecture definition, progress tracking, status reporting, configuration control, extended requirements traceability, and risk management capabilities. An integrated tool environment could provide a multidisciplinary, collaborative tool framework and data repository.

5.1.10 Proactive identification and management of risk

Risk identification and management is addressed as an important element of software analysis, which is fully explained in chapter 14, Software Analysis Practice. A risk is anything that could potentially be encountered that would negatively affect the achievement of project objectives. Since planning and design entail some form of decision making, it is best to identify the risks inherent with each alternative. This will enable the SWE-IPT to make architectural design decisions with more knowledge of the inherent risks being assumed. Risk abatement plans are encouraged to address risk-tracking procedures and the criteria that would initiate each contingency course of action.

5.2 Software engineering and development

The current situation confronting software development projects is assessed in chapter 6, Impediments to Software Design. The success of every software development project is dependent on establishment of a product architecture as the foundation upon which the software product can be implemented (programmatically designed, coded, integrated and tested), tested and supported throughout its lifecycle. The remainder of this book will address the software engineering and development tasks. The software engineering tasks are addressed throughout Section 2. Each chapter in that section focuses on a major element of the software engineering

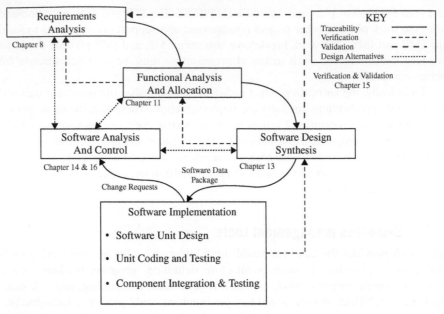

FIGURE 5.3

Software engineering practices.

Table 5.2 Alignment of Chapters to Software Engineering Practices	
Element of Software Engineering	**Chapter Number and Title**
Requirements analysis	7—Understanding Software Requirements
	8—Software Requirements Analysis Tasks
	9—Software Requirements Management
Functional analysis and allocation and application design synthesis	10—Formulating the Functional Architecture
	11—Functional Analysis and Allocation Practice
	12—Configuring the Physical Architecture
	13—Software Design Synthesis Practice
Software analysis, control, verification and validation	14—Software Analysis Practice
	15—Software Verification and Validation Practice
	16—Software Control Practice

process identified in Figure 5.3. Table 5.2 identifies the chapters that address each element of the software engineering process. Each chapter within Section 3 identifies the organizational tasks that must be performed during a phase of software development, including software engineering, computing environment definition, software implementation, software test and evaluation, and post-development software sustainment.

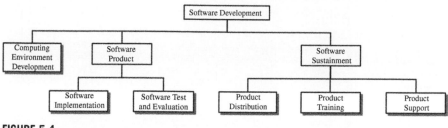

FIGURE 5.4

Software IPPD organizational framework.

The software development project must be organized around the IPPD philosophy and tenants. To accomplish this, the scope of the software development effort must recognize and address the dependency of the software product on the computing environment, and the lack of a "manufacturing" phase of the software life cycle. Software products involve a form of distribution where the electronic distributable files are either replicated, packaged, and shipped to distributors or retailers, or the files are provided via web services for download. Therefore, the software IPPD organizational framework for work to be performed must reflect the structure identified in Figure 5.4. The boxes that are shaded represent separate project elements that should be managed utilizing an IPT. Each of these IPTs should be responsible for the definition, implementation, and qualification of the software product or process they govern.

Impediments to Software Design

This chapter investigates the challenges associated with the development of a software product. This investigation concentrates on identifying the inherent features of software that obstruct the design of software products and the informal practices applied to influence a software design. The characteristics of software as a "raw material" are discussed, which contributes to the challenges of fashioning a software product. This exploration investigates the history of programming as it has evolved since Charles Babbage designed the first programmable computer, called the Analytical Engine, in 1837. The history of software development is examined to expose the challenges that threaten every software development project. The value of software engineering is substantiated to demonstrate how it provides a progressive, disciplined, and beneficial approach to software development.

In 1995, the Standish Group published the first CHAOS report from 1994, which assessed the success rates associated with software development throughout the industry. This report depicted the state of software development as being woefully deficient. The Standish Group's research showed that a staggering 31% of commissioned software projects fail or are cancelled before they are completed, and 53% of projects experienced cost overruns of 189% of their original estimates. U.S. companies and government agencies spent $81 billion for cancelled software projects and an additional $59 billion to complete projects that exceeded their budgets. Software development had become a liability to the United States and worldwide economic growth at that time.

The CHAOS study has been conducted every two years since 1994. The 2008 report published in 2009 indicated an increase in software development success rates to 32% while only 44% of projects were challenged (late, over budget, and/or with less than the required features and functions). Still, the failure rate (cancelled

Table 6.1 CHAOS Reports Summary

	1994	1996	1998	2000	2002	2004	2006	2008
Successful	16%	27%	26%	28%	34%	29%	35%	32%
Challenged	53%	33%	46%	49%	51%	53%	46%	44%
Failed	31%	40%	28%	23%	15%	18%	19%	24%

prior to completion or delivered and never utilized)[1] for software development projects averaged 20% over the 15-year reporting period. This indicates that current software development practices are incapable of reliably delivering software products on time or within budget. Table 6.1 provides a summary of the CHAOS report results for the 15 years the data has been collected.

What has caused this chaotic situation is the premise that software, as a material, lacks physical characteristics and, therefore, the application of traditional engineering practices cannot be applied to the development of software products. Software practitioners were left with no technical supposition on which to establish a software engineering discipline. Trailblazers in the software industry have devised a myriad of software development methodologies that have delivered little recognizable improvement with software development success. There is only one other profession in which a 30% success rate is considered respectable, and no one expects a baseball player to consistently hit above a 0.350 average.

Software has become a critical element of many consumer products. This is a major concern since software is integrated into systems the public, government agencies, and public and private institutions must depend on every day. The issues of software liability and consumer protection are refocusing attention on the inadequacies of current software development methods, techniques, and fads. The software industry must establish formal software engineering practices upon which software development can evolve into a dependable profession and significantly improve software development project success rates and product dependability. Figure 6.1 illustrates a conceptual progression of software development trends from initial laboratory experimentation to consumerism. The evolution of software programming languages and design techniques are associated with each stage of evolution to demonstrate how these technologies have supported the procession of software development as a legitimate profession.

The progression shown in Figure 6.1 represents a typical evolutionary path for most new technologies. Consumer laws and protection agencies exist to ensure that products that introduce new technologies will not cause serious injury, damage, or destruction of property. The introduction of software into critical systems and the consumer marketplace will be an incentive for the inevitable transition of the software craft to a professional stature. Current software development tools,

---

[1] See *http://www.projectsmart.co.uk/the-curious-case-of-the-chaos-report-2009.html*.

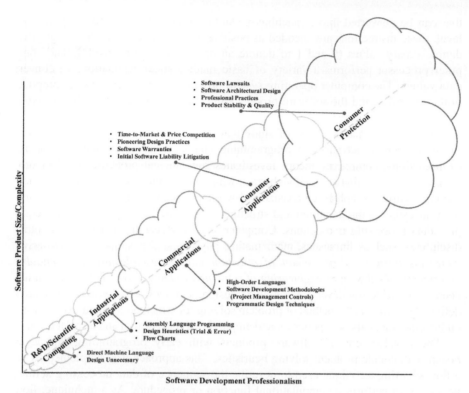

Software Product Size/Complexity

- Software Lawsuits
- Software Architectural Design
- Professional Practices
- Product Stability & Quality

Consumer Protection

- Time-to-Market & Price Competition
- Pioneering Design Practices
- Software Warranties
- Initial Software Liability Litigation

Consumer Applications

Commercial Applications

- High-Order Languages
- Software Development Methodologies
  (Project Management Controls)
- Programmatic Design Techniques

Industrial Applications

- Assembly Language Programming
- Design Heuristics (Trial & Error)
- Flow Charts

R&D/Scientific Computing

- Direct Machine Language
- Design Unnecessary

Software Development Professionalism

FIGURE 6.1

Evolution and proliferation of software development technologies.

techniques, and practices must be reinforced by practical engineering practices, policies, and procedures.

There has been considerable research performed to apply some precepts to the development of software products. The following sections will review the conditions confounding the software industry by examining the evolution of software development technologies, development, and management practices.

6.1 Software as a raw material

Engineering is the application of science, mathematics, and technologies to design human-made structures, machines, and other manufactured products. This involves the conversion of raw materials or parts that are fabricated, assembled, and integrated to form larger, more complex products. Software as a "raw material" does not exhibit any scientific properties that guide the design of a software product. Software is fundamentally a set of routines composed of instructions in a language that can be converted into a machine-readable format. At the computer processor level, these instructions are encoded as positive and negative electrical charges that denote binary values (0 and 1 to denote an on/off state, respectively). The computer processor performs a variety of basic mathematical calculations to convert data values. The computer operating system provides the management of computational execution and the software product's interaction with computer input/output devices and data storage equipment.

Computer science is a field of study that provides a research and development thrust to promote advances in programming languages and computational theory. Computational complexity theory investigates fundamental properties of data processing algorithms that are highly abstract, while other branches of computer science, such as computer graphics, emphasize real-world applications. The study of programming investigates the definition and structure of software languages to address complex data processing transactions. Computer science research often intersects other disciplines, such as linguistics, mathematics, physics, statistics, and logic. *However, there has been a paltry amount of attention paid to establishing a dependable approach to the design or engineering of software products.* Most of the research has been relegated to low-level programmatic design heuristics. The *Encarta Dictionary* defines *heuristics* as "a method of problem solving for which no formula exists, based on informal methods or experience, and employing a form of trial and error iteration."

The development of software products with early programming languages began with simple problem solving heuristics. This approach was supplemented by a flow-charting technique used to describe the sequence of data processing actions necessary to perform a computational function or procedure. As a technique, flow charts were useful to identify control mechanisms (decision blocks and control flow), input/output procedures, data processing steps (e.g., $X=X+1$), calls to subroutines (typically detailed in a separate flow chart), and data processing concurrency. The use of flow charts lost favor in the early 1980s due to the undesirable use of *goto(s)* to describe arbitrary jumps in control flow. This resulted in "spaghetti" code, which made understanding data processing flow difficult and impacted the software maintenance challenge. However, the use of *goto(s)* was purely a result of unstructured programming or improper programmatic design techniques.

Software is a very broad term used to identify a variety of computer programs that operate computers and devices embedded with computer technologies. The term *hardware* is used to describe the physical elements of a system or computer-based system, while *software* refers to various types of programs or applications used to operate a computer-based system. Software code is a set of instructions that can be converted into a format that a computer can perform. Code is broken into procedures, routines, functions, modules, objects, or other constructs to form parts or elements of a larger program. This partitioning of data processing transactions originated due to the challenge with the ever-increasing size and complexity of computer programs.

Within the software domain, there are references to a variety of terms that must be clarified to distinguish some basic properties of software. Table 6.2 provides a general explanation of these software product–related terms.

Table 6.2 Key Software Terms and Definitions

Term	Definition
Code	Instructions expressed in the syntax of a programming language that can be compiled and executed regardless of the correctness of the code or the validity of the data processing results.
Module	An early structured programming term to refer to a self-contained routine or procedure that represents a part or element of a larger program. Modules represent a separation of concerns and improve software maintainability by enforcing boundaries referred to as interfaces. Modules are executed within a larger program through the invoking of the module's interface. A module interface expresses the data items that are provided to and returned by a module when invoked.
Modularity	The compartmentalization and interrelation of the parts of a software program. Module programming can be performed even where the programming language lacks explicit syntactic features to support named modules.
Object	In object-oriented programming, a class is a module that encapsulates the data attributes and set of procedures used to set and retrieve their values. An object is an instance of a class that has a unique identity (specific values that distinguish it from other objects of that class), a state that describes the data values stored within an object, and behaviors that specify the interfaces by which the object can be accessed.
Program	A combination of modules or objects that perform an array of business or operational data processing tasks. The executable form of a program is in binary form, which a computer can execute. The human-readable form is expressed in source code in a software language that the programmer can edit. A program in source code form must be compiled, assembled, and linked with other essential referenced library routines to produce an executable file.
Application	A specialized program designed to perform business or operational tasks. Application is a term used to distinguish general-purpose programs, such as word processors, spreadsheets, video players, etc., from system software and middleware. Applications manage and integrate a computer's capabilities, but do not directly support the user in performing a business or operational task.
System software and middleware	Middleware is software that provides computing services to software applications beyond those available from the operating system, or provides connections between software applications so that they can exchange data.
Product	Any software program or application that is being developed for the express purpose of commercial distribution, customer delivery, or to facilitate enterprise processes. A generic term used to address the focus of a software development effort on the product and its post-development processes.

Software should be viewed as a set of data processing transactions that facilitate a business or operational process. Data processing transactions describe the stimulus-response nature of software execution. Almost all software modules are initiated by some stimulus, perform some computational action or function to produce some result, and transfer data processing control to another transaction. A large software program involves a number of possible transactions that are accomplished by the execution of a series of modules or routines. The sequence of module execution is dependent on the outcome of the computational action, and some form of decision or control logic determines how the transaction should proceed.

Because of its lack of physical characteristics, software represents a form of artificial language used to:

- Perform mathematical computations or process symbols into meaningful data.
- Construct logical arguments that guide the flow of data processing transactions.
- Preserve data in digital format for future access.
- Interact with elements of the computing environment.
- Interact with elements of the business or operational system.

Therefore, software is a combination of linguistics, semantics (the study of meaning), mathematical notation, logic, knowledge representation, and systems engineering (problem solving in the presence of complexity).

As software products have grown in size and complexity, the application of systems engineering practices to software development became more apropos due to its emphasis on analyzing design challenges and reducing design complexity. However, there has been no authoritative dictate to motivate or encourage the software industry to adopt systems engineering precepts. Software pundits emerged proposing numerous methodologies targeted at providing better software development stratagems. However, most of these software methodologies were driven by rapidly advancing computer technologies or program language–driven refinements, such as object-oriented programming. As a result, most software practitioners lack the fundamental skills necessary to cope with the convoluted dilemma associated with the design of a software product.

6.2 Evolution of software technologies

The software field of study is still in its early stages of refinement. It involves a number of research topics that are struggling to keep pace with the advances in computer technology. In addition, the application areas for software technology are spreading rapidly into almost every facet of society, including transportation (aircraft, ships, automobile, trucks, trains, and traffic management systems), communications, entertainment, business information processing, health care, construction, manufacturing, utilities, wholesale/retail, financial services (banking and investment), education, personal computing, etc. However, the advancement of programming and, most importantly, techniques for designing software products has been overwhelmed and derailed by a growing demand for software.

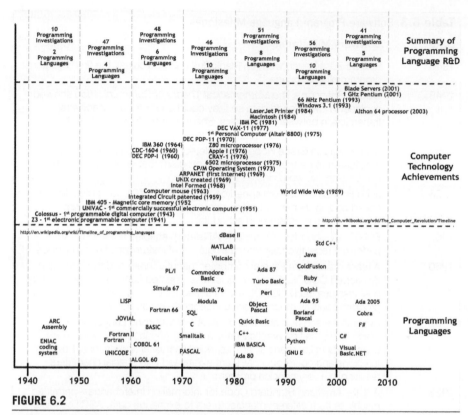

FIGURE 6.2

Timeline of selected computer and programming technologies.

The advances of software as a technology can be better appreciated by viewing a timeline of software-related technologies. Figure 6.2 provides a 70-year overview of the evolution of selected advances in computer technology and programming languages.[2] This figure highlights the prominent programming languages that enable the development of software products. The highlights associated with software programming between 1945 and 1985 are presented in Table 6.3.[3] Programming began as a specialized craft practiced by laboratory technicians working toward advancing computing systems. These scientists originally worked in machine code (binary 1's and 0's) to program very simplistic computations on very large computers with vacuum tubes. Machine code is a set of instructions executed directly by a computer's central processing unit (CPU).

---

[2] See *http://en.wikipedia.org/wiki/Timeline_of_computing* and *http://en.wikipedia.org/wiki/Timeline_of_programming_languages*.
[3] See *http://www.computerhistory.org/timeline/?category=sl*.

Table 6.3 Software Program Language Milestones

Date	Software Milestones
1945	Konrad Zuse began work on Plankalkul (Plan Calculus), the first algorithmic programming language.
1948	Claude Shannon's *The Mathematical Theory of Communication* showed engineers how to code data so they could check for accuracy after transmission between computers. Shannon identified the bit as the fundamental unit of data and, coincidentally, the basic unit of computation.
1952	Mathematician Grace Hopper completed the A-0 Compiler, what is considered to be the first compiler, a program that allows a computer to use English-like words instead of numbers.
1953	John Backus completed speed coding for IBM's 701 computer. Although speed coding demanded more memory and compute time, it trimmed weeks off of a programming schedule.
1957	FORTRAN (short for FORmula TRANslator), enabled a computer to perform a repetitive task from a single set of instructions by using loops.
1960	A team drawn from several computer manufacturers and the Pentagon developed COBOL, Common Business Oriented Language. Designed for business use, early COBOL efforts aimed for easy readability of computer programs and as much machine independence as possible.
1962	Kenneth Iverson published his book, *A Programming Language* (APL), which led to the first practical programming language. APL was widely used in scientific, financial, and especially actuarial applications. Powerful functions and operators in APL are expressed with special characters, resulting in a very concise program.
1963	ASCII—American Standard Code for Information Interchange—permitted machines from different manufacturers to exchange data. ASCII consists of 128 unique strings of 1's and 0's. Each sequence represents a letter of the English alphabet, an Arabic numeral, and an assortment of punctuation marks and symbols or a function such as a carriage return.
1964	Thomas Kurtz and John Kemeny created BASIC, an easy-to-learn programming language, for their students at Dartmouth College.
1965	Object-oriented languages got an early boost with Simula, written by Kristen Nygaard and Ole-John Dale. Simula grouped data and instructions into blocks called objects, each representing one facet of a system intended for simulation.
1969	AT&T Bell Laboratories programmers Kenneth Thompson and Dennis Ritchie developed the UNIX operating system on a spare DEC minicomputer. UNIX combined many of the time-sharing and file management features offered by Multics, from which it took its name. (Multics, a project of the mid-1960s, represented the first effort at creating a multi-user, multitasking operating system.) The UNIX operating system quickly secured a wide following, particularly among engineers and scientists.
1976	Gary Kildall developed CP/M, an operating system for personal computers. Widely adopted, CP/M made it possible for one version of a program to run on a variety of computers built around 8-bit microprocessors.

(Continued)

Table **6.3** Software Program Language Milestones (*Continued*)	
Date	**Software Milestones**
1979	Harvard MBA candidate Daniel Bricklin and programmer Robert Frankston developed VisiCalc, the program that made a business machine of the personal computer, for the Apple II. VisiCalc (for Visible Calculator) automated the recalculation of spreadsheets. A huge success, more than 100,000 copies sold in one year.
1981	MS-DOS, or Microsoft Disk Operating System, the basic software for the newly released IBM PC, came out.
1985	The C++ programming language emerged as the dominant object-oriented language in the computer industry when Bjarne Stroustrup published *The C++ Programming Language*. Stroustrup, at AT&T Bell Laboratories, said his motivator stemmed from a desire to write event-driven simulations that needed a language faster than Simula.

Following the introduction of C++, most of the contributions to the programming field involved extensions of existing languages to accommodate object-oriented programming or web-based application development. The early part of the 1990s began the introduction of integrated development environments (IDEs), such as Microsoft's Visual Studio. An IDE provides an integrated set of tools for software development, such as source code editor, graphical user interface (GUI) constructors, software component libraries, debuggers, and build automation tools. The evolution of software programming languages seems to have run its course as the emphasis had shifted to improving programmer productivity.

During the 30-year period from 1960 to 1990, the rapidly changing landscape of programming languages consumed the attention of students, instructors, and practitioners as they struggled to maintain their proficiency and marketable skill set. New programming languages cropped up and old languages were evolved to incorporate features that could take advantage of the dramatic increases in computing power. Changes in computing platforms, languages, storage technology, computer graphics, and multimedia technologies have challenged the software industry's ability to produce products of which the dependability and longevity satisfies the needs of customers, consumers, enterprise management, or investors.

6.2.1 Software development methods and standards

The development of software products has evolved through a series of forms that have been dictated by programming languages, computer technologies, and software methodologies. Early software programs were small, noncomplex assemblages of routines, subroutines, functions, or modules. Flow-charting techniques were initially used to provide a design foundation from which software code could be generated, converted to machine-executable format (compiled and assembled), and verified to perform correctly. As the size and complexity of software programs

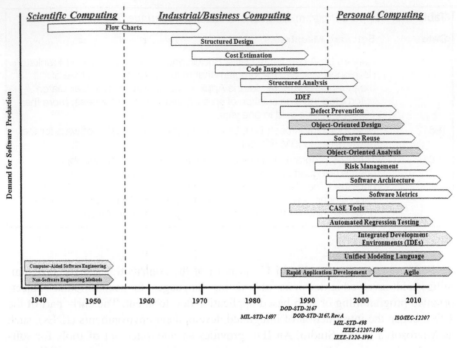

FIGURE 6.3

The progression of software development methods and standards.

became larger and more industry specific, they became known as software applications. However, the flow-charting techniques could not scale accordingly to express these larger design dilemmas.

A series of progressive software methodologies or design techniques were promoted since the 1960s that attempted to improve the software development success rates. Figure 6.3 provides a timeline that identifies the emergence of various software development methodologies, techniques, and standards.[4] This figure identifies 12 topics that are of concern to software engineering or the design of a software product, 5 topics that are not related to software engineering, 3 topics associated with programming automation, and 7 standards that address software development best practices. Each of these categories of topics are briefly addressed in Table 6.4.

Despite all of these efforts by the software industry to regiment the development of software products, the state of the practice is still chaotic. It is essential for software development approaches to be bolstered by rigorous design techniques that can contend with the difficulties associated with developing products out of a material known as software. Developing any product requires disciplined adherence

[4]Data extracted and refined from David F. Rico, "Short History of Software Methods."

Table 6.4 Categorized Software Development Topics

Topic Area	Specific Items	Discussion
Software engineering related	Flow charts Structured design Cost estimation Code inspection Structured analysis Defect prevention Software reuse Risk management Software architecture Software metrics	These topics represent areas that apply to software engineering, but do not constitute a standalone technique for developing a software product architecture. Several are not unique to software engineering and are typical project management practices.
Not related to software engineering	Object-oriented design Object-oriented analysis Agile Unified modeling language Rapid Application Development (RAD)	Three of these topics are associated with the implementation of object-oriented programming languages. RAD and Agile are nonstructured team management approaches focused on rapid prototyping and short-term planning.
Automated tools	CASE tools Automated regression testing Integrated development environments	Automated tools that support software implementation, especially code generation and testing.
Software development standards	MIL-STD-1679 (Navy) DOD-STD-2167 DOD-STD-2167, Rev A MIL-STD-498 IEEE-12207-1996 IEEE-1220 (Systems Engineering) ISO-IEC-12207	Industry and Department of Defense standards that address software development activities and tasks. Emphasis is on software project management, documentation, and configuration control. *Note:* IEEE-1220 represents the most definitive standard on systems engineering principles and practices.

to a set of scientific principles and practices established to enable the raw materials to be fabricated into human-made parts and components; assembly and integration of these parts into larger, more complex components; and testing of parts, components, and the final product. Within the manufacturing industry this process is known as fabrication, assembly, integration, and testing (FAIT). In addition, there is an investigative element of all product development efforts that strives to understand the fundamental needs for a new product. This exploratory and analytical element of product design establishes the specifications for the product, components, parts, and FAIT strategy. This investigative element is responsible for the specification, analysis, and synthesis (SAS) of the product, components, and parts from which the product is to be produced.

Software engineering practices provide a framework for accomplishing the SAS and developing the FAIT strategy, which results in a complete, noncomplex software product architecture. The software requirements analysis practice transforms stakeholders' needs and expectations into the software product, structural component, and unit specifications. The functional analysis provides the systematic techniques for understanding what data processing transactions the software product must perform to accomplish the product requirements as they are decomposed into software functions. The software design synthesis practice establishes the structural configuration of the software product and the FAIT strategy. The result is a completely specified software product architecture documented as the software technical data package (TDP). This software TDP includes the specifications, diagrams, drawings, and software integration strategy that facilitate software implementation (programmatic design, coding, integration, and testing).

The software industry has not been able or willing to step up to the demands of transitioning from a chaotic craft to a disciplined engineering profession. The unwillingness of software professionals to adopt a more disciplined set of practices for developing software products is a result of their unawareness and inexperience with other engineering disciplines. Ignorance is bliss goes the old saying! This implies that it is often preferred not to know something due to the unpleasant or foreboding consequences of knowing and accepting the truth. This is not to blame or insult software professionals; ignorance is simply a lack of awareness, knowledge, or education that prohibits their pursuing a better approach to designing software products. Because software personnel do not have awareness that there is a better way to perform their vocation, they continue to flail about clutching onto newly proposed stratagems in hopes of hiding their lack of competency. Most software professionals have been trained to program, which is predominantly a low-level design tactic. There has been no software methodology that offers a comprehensive approach to design a complete software product.

Software prototyping logically emerged as a way to rapidly develop software products with little or no effort to design the complete product. This approach has been renamed and repackaged in various clandestine attempts to divert attention away from the obvious lack of a formal design approach and permit software mavens to perform what they know how to do, which is program. This concept of software prototyping originated as a software development methodology entitled Rapid Application Development (RAD). The RAD philosophy suggests that a software product can be developed with "minimal planning and the incremental building of a prototyping. The 'planning' of software developed using RAD is interleaved with writing the software itself. The lack of extensive preplanning generally allows software to be written much faster, and makes it easier to change requirements."[5] This has led to the establishment of the Agile Manifesto, which attempts to formalize prototyping as a genuine software development methodology.

Fundamentally, the software development occupation will only be elevated to professional status when a set of principles and practices that guide its teaching, conduct, and management has been established. Software development

---

[5] See *http://en.wikipedia.org/wiki/Rapid_application_development*.

methodologies cannot be permitted to continually morph into new fads that avoid the reason for the chaotic state of the software development industry. Software development suffers for lack of attention to *designing* a product. Most methodologies properly accept that requirements are important and code generation is easy. However, there has been no significant contribution to instituting a rigorous and meticulous method of a establishing design for a complete software product. Programmatic design practices are at the coding level of the design hierarchy, and, therefore, completely insufficient for the establishment of a software product architecture.

The term *architecture* is used within this manuscript to distinguish it from what most engineering disciplines refer to as design. Software products represent a composite of various subroutines that contribute to data processing transactions. There are no established design guidelines upon which to structurally arrange or organize these software routines. This is a fundamental challenge to the generation of new software products and is a consequence of software's lack of physical properties. Systems engineering principles and practices provide the most relevant discipline upon which to base software engineering competencies. Systems engineering provides a rigorous approach to establishing the architecture for a complex product. Therefore, software engineering practices that are derived from systems engineering must be promoted as the founding guidelines for a software engineering profession.

6.2.2 Agile manifesto

The proponents of the Agile Manifesto must have been confounded by the situation they found themselves in regarding their profession. No software development methodology, technique, or practice enabled them to achieve success. Therefore, the Agile proponents formulated a manifesto to establish a guild surrounding a set of principles for software development based on rapid prototyping, incremental product delivery, and *absolutely no product design*. They needed to convince executives that there was a manner in which software products could be delivered that provided "value" to their customers. To accomplish this they devised a diversionary tactic that, if accepted, would enable them to do what they have been trained to do—program. The Agile Manifesto is presented in Figure 6.4 to provide a basis for discussing its merits and shallow misrepresentations.

The manifesto begins with a proclamation that the advocates of Agile Software Development were "uncovering better ways of developing software by doing it." On the surface, this statement implies that by the mere act of developing software the design methods and techniques were spontaneously improving. However, the 40-plus-year history of software development techniques has not resulted in such perceptiveness. The software development industry's record of success has been below 30%, and since the adoption of Agile techniques, has not improved noticeably. Therefore, there is a lack of substantiation for this claim of recognized improvement in the art of software development.

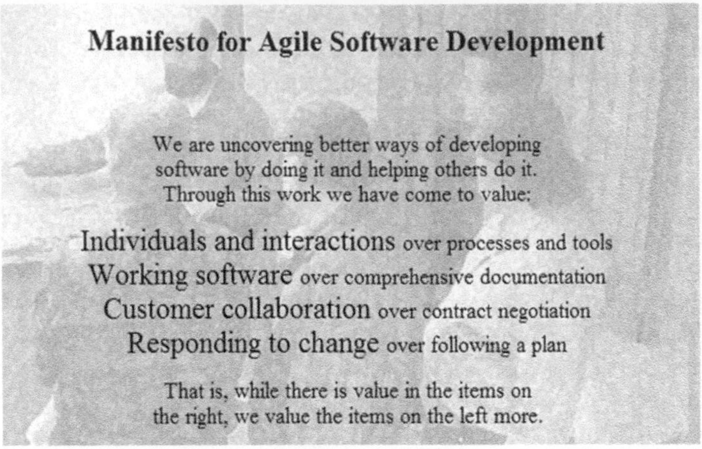

Manifesto for Agile Software Development

We are uncovering better ways of developing
software by doing it and helping others do it.
Through this work we have come to value:

Individuals and interactions over processes and tools
Working software over comprehensive documentation
Customer collaboration over contract negotiation
Responding to change over following a plan

That is, while there is value in the items on
the right, we value the items on the left more.

FIGURE 6.4

Agile Manifesto.[6]

The Agile Manifesto identifies the convictions that the advocates value. These beliefs were revealed by their experiences in past software development efforts and are interpreted as follows:

1. *Individuals and interactions over processes and tools.* Software personnel and the manner in which they work together are more important to the success of a software development effort than processes or tools. There is no underlying basis for this claim as most professional occupations have concluded that processes and tools are vital to success, cost control, and quality results.
2. *Working software over comprehensive documentation.* This statement implies that Agile is based on a rapid prototyping methodology that produces working prototypes. The prototypes are evolved and enhanced to provide the final, deliverable software product. The belittling of software documentation infers that documenting the software design does not contribute to the development of the software product. If the software design is not documented, then how is it comprehended by the team of programmers? This suggests that software development is best served by the development of software prototypes, which are not designed or documented.
3. *Customer collaboration over contract negotiation.* Within the ISO standard on software development processes there is a process for establishing an agreement that guides the software development effort. The agreement may be a formal contract between business entities or internal to an entity between management and the software development project. However, contracts or agreements are

---

[6] See *http://agilemanifesto.org/principles.html*.

used to hold the software development team accountable. The Agile proponents do not want to be held accountable. (Wouldn't every employee enjoy being compensated with no accountability? Agile is every derelict's dream employment arrangement!)

4. *Responding to change over following a plan.* Change is inevitable, but there must be a plan upon which progress can be measured. By suggesting that a software product can be produced without a plan is hypocritical. Every product development project must have a plan against which progress can be measured and the development team held accountable. Oh, that's right! With Agile, software development organizations are not held accountable. So what benefit is a plan? The definition of design is to create a detailed plan of something. Besides, as the customers keep changing their desires, the software development team can enjoy a prolonged engagement and continued employment because they cannot be held accountable for schedule delays. (When will the product be finished? Who cares!)

The authors and proponents of the Agile Manifesto certainly did not intend for Agile's guiding principles to be interpreted so blatantly and conspicuously. They obviously have given up trying to follow standard project management and software development techniques due to the high rate of disappointing results while encumbered by these practices. They were unaware of any approach that would result in the achievement of software development plans, objectives, or agreements. They determined that their best chance for success was to do what they had been trained to do—program. This resulted in a manifesto for a technical discipline that abolishes plans, schedules, design and documentation, agreements, or culpability when the project fails.

> When a dance couple trains unrelentingly to win the world championship in the Waltz competition, they are dedicated to their profession. When their opportunity finally presents itself and the music begins … and it's a tango … the couple dances the waltz. After all, the waltz is what they have been trained to execute and any other response would lead to disappointment, so why not dance the dance they know how to perform?

The previous assessment of Agile must be taken in context. Agile is a programming methodology and works well as a form of software implementation. However, Agile cannot succeed unless it is fortified by software engineering and a predefined software architecture. The proponents of Agile are just unaware of software engineering as described in this manuscript and therefore are attempting to "do the best that they can." As I reviewed my initial treatise on the Agile Manifesto I became aware that what they are proposing has value when it is relegated to the software implementation stage of software development. The usefulness of Agile or any other software methodology is greatly enhanced when coupled with a preceding software engineering effort. The next section discusses how an architecture-driven approach to software development, which combines software engineering and an agile methodology, would greatly enhance the probability of success of a software development project.

6.3 Architecture-driven software development

The current state of software development is greatly impaired because there has not been guidance on how to develop a software product architecture. Every attempt to generate a software product based on programmatic design techniques or methodologies has failed. Even those efforts that were deemed successful have resulted in software products that suffer from a poorly conceived architectural structure. This results in a costly software sustainment effort and reduces the longevity of the software product life cycle.

Software engineering provides the technical nucleus and governance that enable software implementation to be well planned and executed. Programmers who have not been educated in software engineering struggle with understanding stakeholder requirements, maintaining a tactical plan of action, and balancing perceived customer value with project resources. If a software development project is driven only by delivery objectives, then there is little chance of ensuring that the software product will ever be delivered. Therefore, why not simply accept the inevitable need to incrementally deliver incomplete products that hopefully will placate customers and management. It may be comforting to believe that customers are receiving value with an unending stream of incremental deliveries. However, customers faced with a continual need to be retrained on an ever-changing product configuration will eventually abandon their hope of ever receiving a complete, stable product. While product improvements are desirable, frequent and radical changes will only make the product architecture unstable and more suspect to eventual collapse, disorder, and turmoil.

The need for a software product architecture is paramount for establishing an initial software product release that can be evolved over time with future enhancements and new features. Software engineering is compelled to resolve stakeholder confusion, comprehend the problem space, and establish a structural design solution that provides a stable and enduring product foundation. Any software development effort that attempts to develop a product without an architectural framework has, as history demonstrates, a 30% chance of success.

The architecture-driven software development model described in this manuscript is represented in Figure 6.5. In the center of the Venn diagram are the software engineering practices that are paramount to successful software product development. Aligned on top of this model is the project management framework, which is generalized to address project objectives, budgets, plans, and schedules. The remaining six interleaving circles represent the typical software development stages, including requirements definition, architectural definition, software implementation, and acceptance testing. The preliminary and detailed design stages have been redefined to establish a software product architecture based on software engineering practices. The software technical data package provides the specifications and supporting design information needed for the product to be *implemented*.

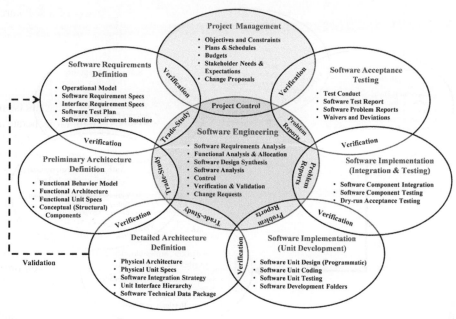

FIGURE 6.5

Architecture-driven development model.

This model provides a holistic approach to software development that is predicated upon employing software engineering as the nucleus for planning and executing the software development effort. It involves representatives from a variety of software disciplines to ensure that the software product requirements are complete and consistent, the technical plans can be accomplished with the established resource budgets, and the software product architecture provides a structurally dependable framework for software enhancements and evolution throughout the product life cycle.

The failure of previous software methodologies is due to a lack of understanding how to design and foster a software product architecture. While software development standards and management practices have been well devised, software methodologies have leveraged the strengths of programming languages to facilitate proper programmatic design techniques. What has been lacking is the knowledge and skills necessary to establish a software product architecture. Figure 6.6 depicts an Agile-driven model of software development. This model leaves out the software engineering centerpiece and the definition stages focused on establishing a software product architecture. Without this software engineering foundation, Agile simply sidesteps the all-important "design" dilemma and proceeds from requirements directly into software implementation. (Note: Based on the Agile Manifesto, it is difficult to determine the need for the project management element so it has been included in the Agile-driven model.)

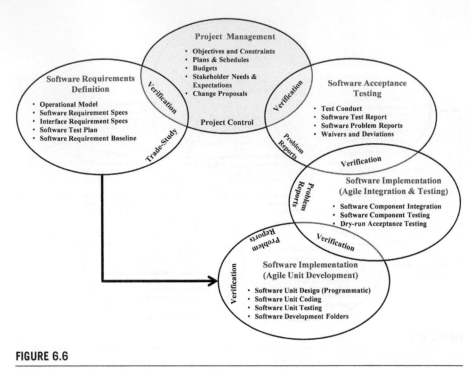

FIGURE 6.6

Agile-driven software development model.

The Agile-driven software development model is a result of years of frustration on the part of software professionals who could not understand why software development was so difficult and failure-prone. Therefore, the proponents of Agile have established a guild of software professionals whom have come to believe that the incremental delivery of an evolving product is delivering value to the customer. To "sell" this methodology they insulated themselves from the most problematic elements associated with software development:

- Deriving a complete set of requirements before the coding begins.
- Focusing on incremental delivery versus a comprehensive project plan.
- Ignoring the need to design and document the software product.

Less time wasted on unnecessary overhead tasks and more time spent fixing the product so it works.

Conversely, these problematic elements associated with software development happen to be the competencies of software engineering. Software engineering provides the basis for coalescing stakeholder needs and expectations into a complete and consistent set of software requirements. Changes to the established software requirements baseline are interrogated against the software architecture, project plans, and resource allocation to ensure that a proposed change can be accommodated. Changes that are necessary can be incorporated into the technical plans

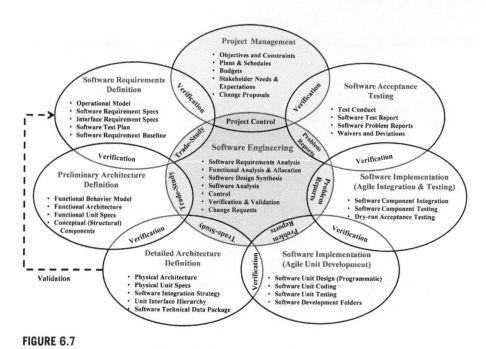

FIGURE 6.7

Software development combining software engineering and Agile.

and schedule if there are sufficient resources to ensure project success. Otherwise, changes should be scheduled for a future revision.

Establishment of a software architecture permits the software implementation effort to be properly scoped, planned, and accomplished efficiently. Each structural unit identified by the physical architecture is adequately specified to permit programmatic-level design, coding, and testing. The software integration strategy is established during detailed architecture definition to permit software integration and testing to proceed according to an established work plan. The software work breakdown structure identifies the work packages and resources allocated to each software implementation activity. The result should be an uncomplicated, systematic software implementation and testing of a complete software product deliverable.

This assessment of the Agile methodology acknowledges that software implementation is difficult to plan and accomplish in an organized manner if there is no software architecture. Software engineering establishes the structural foundation upon which the software implementation plan can be predicated. What must be appreciated is that any software methodology or approach that ignores the value of a software architecture is doomed to fail. Figure 6.7 depicts the software development Venn diagram including both software engineering and the Agile methodology. This model can be altered to accommodate any software implementation methodology. Simply insert the preferred software implementation methodology wherever the term Agile appears!

Software Engineering Practices

This section introduces the six software engineering practices that are utilized to develop the software architecture. These practices provide the underlying foundation for all engineering disciplines and are uniquely customized for each discipline. These software engineering practices have been adapted from the system engineering discipline because they deal with controlling product complexity. Each of the practices is expressed in a set of tasks that contribute to exploring a problem/solution space in a quest for a viable, affordable architectural resolution.

These practices are not independent and must be applied iteratively and recursively, as needed, to devise a material solution or further constrain the problem space to enable a feasible solution to be realized. The practices apply iteratively to permit a problem/solution space to be explored in a layered approach. In addition, the practices must be applied iteratively to reconsider implications of architectural decisions on previously defined elements of the architecture. This iterative application of software engineering practices permits a problem/solution space to be refined in a top-down, structured approach.

These practices are applied recursively to permit a deep dive into the problem/solution space and bring to the surface technical challenges that affect upper-level architectural solutions. The practices may be invoked on successive layers as the problem is explored and again on the return to higher levels of the architecture. Each iteration or recursive application of a practice is focused on the current level of the architectural problem/solution space being considered.

Each of the software engineering practices provide the fundamental constructs associated with all professional engineering disciplines. These constructs are defined in the following table.

Software Engineering Practice	Engineering Constructs
Requirements analysis	The evaluation of stakeholder needs and operational conditions that affect the architectural solution. Provides an analytical means of specifying requirements that are unambiguous to stakeholders, developers, and project management personnel.
Functional analysis and allocation	The investigation into behaviors that bound the functional and performance characteristics associated with the product, operational environment, and sustainment processes. Identifies failure conditions that the product must be prepared to encounter, as well as the availability of resources to support effective operations.
Design synthesis	Identifies "material" solutions that contribute to satisfying specified requirements. Derives design drawings and models to confirm the effectiveness of a design solution to fulfilling the requirements. Establishes the structural configuration of the product and generates the "build to" drawings and specifications against which the physical element (part, component, etc.) will be fabricated.
Software analysis	Provides the supervision of design alternative comparisons to assess the merits and disadvantages of potential solutions to determine the most balanced approach with which to proceed. This involves assessing the risk associated with each proposed architectural alternative to understand the potential ramifications of adopting an architectural solution.
Verification and validation	Ensures that the three perspectives describing the architectural solution are consistent with the evolving architectural definition. The three perspectives include the product requirements and functional and physical architectures.
Control	Ensures that architectural design decisions and authorized changes are consistently assimilated throughout the product configuration documentation and project plans. Provides stability for the artifacts of the engineering activities to ensure that they are properly stowed within a controlled library for record-keeping purposes.

The systems engineering practices provide the mechanisms for investigating architectural design problems and establishing an effective, efficient architectural solution. These practices are applied at every level of design, or product decomposition, to ensure that the problem space is fully comprehended and that the solution addresses all potential operational situations that could arise.

These software engineering practices have been adapted to support the engineering of software products. They have been defined in terms of the various software engineering tasks that should be performed to fulfill the intent of each practice. These tasks have been composed using a set of software-specific functional and structural elements that permit readers to understand where in the product decomposition the task applies.

Within the functional architecture there is a distinction made between functional components and units. Functional components represent complex data processing actions that should be further examined to reveal the subcomponents or units that are necessary to support the functional component. Naturally, there are several (more than two or three) levels of functional components necessary to describe even moderately complex software behaviors. Functional units represent noncomplex functions that do not require further decomposition.

Within the physical architecture there are three distinct tiers in which emergent structural elements are discussed. At the topmost tier the conceptual components are identified to represent placeholders for large software product design segments. The bottommost tier involves the fundamental structural units that are derived from functional units as the basic building blocks for the physical architecture. One level above structural units are the fundamental structural components that form logical or operational groupings of units that contribute to achieving a common data processing function. The design chasm between the fundamental and the conceptual structural elements is populated with integrating components of which the purpose is to facilitate the software integration and test strategy.

Requirements must be specified for every element of the software architecture. Therefore, the requirements analysis practice must be rationally applied for each functional and structural element of the architecture. The requirements analysis practice, as a whole, should be applied to assist the exploration of each level of functional decomposition to ensure that the problem/solution space is comprehended.

The software analysis practice should be employed whenever there are multiple possible tactics by which requirements may be specified, complex data processing functions can be decomposed, or structural elements can be arranged or integrated.

Software verification and validation should be performed periodically to ensure that the evolving software architecture is coherently delineated. This involves verifying that the three architectural perspectives are aligned and consistently stipulated. Validation involves ensuring that the complete structural configuration has been properly engineered to satisfy the software specifications.

Software control provides a variety of tasks that capture completed architectural artifacts and maintain control over the evolving architectural documentation. This includes the processing of change requests and proposals and the updates to technical plans, schedules, and work packages.

Several additional chapters are included to provide detailed commentary concerning the development of the three architectural perspectives. Chapters 7, 9, 10, and 12 are for informational purposes and should not be considered definitive or conclusive portrayals of the practice to which they pertain. These chapters are provided to assist readers in gaining an appreciation for each software engineering practice and its application.

Developing the software product architecture

The software engineering practices provide a set of tasks for translating stakeholder needs into a complete, consistent, and effective software product architecture. A fundamental flaw emerges when the practices are applied as sequential steps in the establishment of the architecture. These practices should not be interpreted to imply that the architecture is formulated by first establishing the requirements baseline, then the functional architecture, and lastly the physical architecture. This sequence implies a waterfall approach that inhibits proper exploration of the problem/solution space. The primary practices of software requirements analysis, functional analysis and allocation, software design synthesis, and software analysis provide the basis for deriving an integrated architectural solution in a manner that is aligned with stakeholder needs and expectations, as well as project resource constraints, technology readiness, and staff proficiency.

There are several conceptual approaches to evolving the software product architecture that must be considered when planning the software engineering effort. This involves how the software engineering practices will be applied to result in the architecture. Most software methodologies fail to provide for the iterative nature of the design process. Therefore, early architectural design decisions are assumed to be final and are never revisited, even when they impose risks to achieving project objectives. Popular software development methodologies (e.g., iterative, incremental, and agile) have been embraced due to the inability of the software development team to grasp a complete architectural solution. Regardless of the methodology chosen, every software development project will derive enormous benefits from the proper application of software engineering and establishing a durable architectural foundation for a software product.

Software architectural approaches

Every architecture can be viewed as a series of progressively detailed descriptions of the software product. The layers of the architecture provide a means of compartmentalizing aspects of the overall problem/solution space. This concept has been described as peeling the onion, in which a layer of the architecture is considered before diving below the surface to the next layer of detail. This provides a reasonable approach for describing the resulting architecture to stakeholders by introducing them to the architectural solution incrementally. For example, a book is composed of chapters; chapters are comprised of sections; sections are comprised of paragraphs; paragraphs are comprised of sentences; and sentences are constructed from words. The book is meant to tell a story with each chapter providing a basis for the follow-on chapter in which the story progresses toward its conclusion. Reading ahead to see how the story ends causes readers to miss many of the valuable aspects of the tale that are intended to make the story more complete, satisfying, and enduring.

Developing a software architecture establishes a structural foundation for the software product. Every element of the architecture fulfills a purpose and its reason for existing defensible; otherwise, it should not be included in the solution. The purpose for each element of the structural configuration or physical architecture must be traceable to an element of the functional architecture, a specified software requirement, and a stakeholder need. However, this does not mandate that the architectural solution be devised in a layered approach. Additionally, if the software architecture is permitted to evolve incrementally or iteratively, the stability and durability of the software architecture may erode over time as new features or enhancements are incorporated. Therefore, the initial software architecture must be derived in a manner that accommodates the software requirements intended for the first release of the software product while establishing the foundation for product evolution and future extensions.

It may be prudent to adopt an architectural development strategy that is driven by critical-path or risk-reduction analysis. Critical-path analysis recognizes that the software product must be designed to enable one or more essential or crucial data processing operations. This approach establishes the data processing scenarios, behaviors, and structural elements necessary to enable the most important data processing objectives. The secondary or less important data processing objectives are then integrated into the architectural configuration in a manner that is most efficient, effective, and pragmatic. Risk-reduction analysis focuses the establishment of an architectural configuration around the data processing operations that resolve the most challenging aspects of the solution. This provides an initial emphasis on tackling the most difficult and precarious design endeavors to establish a feasible technical solution. The remainder of the functional and structural elements can then be integrated into the architectural configuration in a manner that is efficient, effective, and pragmatic. Both of these approaches explore a limited architectural solution in depth to establish an underlying architectural framework for the entire software product.

Iterative software engineering application

The software engineering practices provide a strategic manner of problem solving analogous to systems thinking.[1] Each software engineering practice provides

---

[1] *Systems thinking* has been defined as an approach to problem solving, by viewing problems as part of an overall system, rather than reacting to specific parts, outcomes, or events, and potentially contributing to further development of unintended consequences. Systems thinking is not one thing but a set of *habits or practices* within a framework that are based on the belief that the component parts of a system can best be understood in the context of relationships with each other and with other systems, rather than in isolation. See *http://en.wikipedia.org/wiki/Systems_thinking*.

a distinct, unavoidable, and compelling perspective of the problem being solved and available solutions. Therefore, these practices should not be employed in isolation to one another as a set of sequential tasks. Viewed in operation, each practice can lead to two or more of the related practices. A practice can be interrupted to facilitate an excursion into another practice, as needed, to clarify some aspect of the problem being explored or solution being investigated. Each iteration returns to the interrupted practice with additional information upon which further analysis or synthesis can be performed. Assumptions can be tested and confirmed while faulty speculation marginalized. This iteration provides clarity for the software engineering team about the problem space that results in a more effective and efficient architectural solution. It provides a level of comprehension that facilitates creativity, ingenuity, and resourcefulness. This results in a solution that is operationally suitable, resource efficient, unfaltering, and structurally enduring.

Most software development methodologies struggle with the concept of iteration. They emphasize the need to follow a structured approach in which the requirements are established before the design solution is derived. This encourages a typical *requirements, design, code, and test* strategy. However, it must be recognized that the requirements for a software product must be achievable. The preferred manner in which to ensure requirements feasibility is to venture into the realm of design, even prototyping, to ensure that each specified requirement can be satisfied. As the overall software development situation is appraised, there is an intriguing dynamic of opposing forces that mandates an iterative approach to any engineering problem. Interactions by the technical team with stakeholders warrants an evolutionary disclosure of the broadening understanding of the software operational boundaries, product characteristics, and performance challenges, and the underlying structural components upon which the solution will be founded. This is referred to as the top-down or structural analysis approach to software development. The instinctive reaction of most programmers is to "prototype" a solution and socialize it among the stakeholders. This is referred to as the rapid application development or agile approach to software development. Neither approach has emerged with an irrefutable record of success, and the software development industry remains stymied by its futile attempts to establish a credible approach upon which to forge an engineering discipline.

The software engineering practices that are prescribed in this section establish an iterative paradigm that accommodates the dynamic forces encountered during software development efforts. These underlying forces involve the need to:

1. Establish a feasible set of software requirements.
2. Establish a solid structural foundation for software implementation.
3. Incrementally expose the emerging solution with stakeholders to ensure continual consensus.
4. Ensure that the resulting product can be delivered according to project or contractual provisions.

As the software engineering team endeavors to associate the solution with its driving requirements, there arises a disconcerting dilemma that must be appreciated to devise a unified product solution. The manner by which an engineering solution must be fostered involves a concurrent refinement of a solution in both a top-down and bottom-up manner. The top-down architectural conception provides a continual unraveling of the problem space as expressed by stakeholder needs and software requirements. The bottom-up fulfillment clarifies the needed building material from which a product can be assembled. Bridging these two coalescing perspectives involves a dualistic impetus to translate data processing threads of behavior and provide a strategy for software component integration.

This dualistic imperative leads to a software design chasm that will be further examined in Chapter 12. The software product architecture matures in a top-down, conceptual manner while striving to be definitive in the identification and specification of structural elements in a bottom-up manner. The smallest structural parts or units represent the building-block material from which the software product will be implemented. Each structural unit must be precisely specified so that the software implementation team may perform programmatic design, coding, and testing of each software unit against the structural unit's specification. The design chasm naturally forms as the gulf of space between the upper layers of conceptual components and the lower layers of structural elements. The design chasm can be bridged by further top-down functional decomposition, by determining a bottom-up software integration strategy, or by working in both directions.

Therefore, the software engineering practices are not individual steps in a process by which the software product architecture is generated. They are elements of a single, inclusive problem investigation and design discovery paradigm configured to address the myriad of potential software architectural pitfalls. Because of the vast array of potential architectural anomalies and inconsistencies, it is impossible to establish an unequivocal description of each software engineering practice. Therefore, it should be recognized that the software engineering practices presented in this section are defined with an emphasis on presenting a 90% complete and satisfactory set of software engineering practices.

Understanding Software Requirements

CHAPTER OUTLINE

Software development projects are confronted with the challenge of satisfying multiple stakeholders, each of whom assert a biased perspective affecting the design of the software product. Each stakeholder represents an important aspect or role associated with the software product, such as product performance, testing, appreciation for software implementation, product support, and user training. Each class of stakeholder views their concerns and expectations associated with the software product as significant features or characteristics that must be incorporated into the software requirements.

Each stakeholder champions different and often competing objectives, opinions, and expectations that must be addressed by the software engineering integrated product team (SWE-IPT) during the definition of software requirements. This diverse set of interests creates design challenges that necessitate the conduct of trade-off studies to resolve. Table 7.1 identifies the objectives and motivations of each class of stakeholder. The primary objectives of the SWE-IPT are to:

1. Solicit stakeholder needs and expectations.
2. Specify the software requirements for the product and post-development processes.
3. Generate the integrated technical plans for accomplishing the software development effort.
4. Translate stakeholder requirements into a complete, specified architectural description.
5. Ensure that the software technical data package is sufficiently detailed to facilitate an efficient and effective software implementation.
6. Monitor the progress of development efforts and the establishment of post-development processes.
7. Assess the impact of proposed changes to the software product to ensure that the change can be accommodated within available project resources.

The majority of these objectives involve software requirements. Software requirements must address the complete scope of the development effort, including the computing environment, software product and its interfaces, and post-development processes. Technical plans are derived from the software requirements, and the progress of the project team toward achieving project objectives is measured against the technical plans. Change proposals directly involve new or modifications to the requirement baseline that can be suggested by any stakeholder. Change requests affect the software product design that is expressed by the product architecture. This architecture is derived from the software requirements and is specified by the software data package. Solicitation of stakeholder needs and expectations is necessary to understand the software product's purpose, functions, features, and performance characteristics that determine the project scope and software requirements.

The objective of most interest, and thereby warrants further elaboration, concerns the software technical data package. The technical data package is the collection of technical drawings, diagrams, and specifications that is provided to the software implementation team to guide the programmatic design, coding, integration, and testing of the software product. Software implementation represents the construction or manufacturing activity in the housing or system development industries. The building architect generates a set of engineering plans and drawings that provides the details necessary for the construction team to build a house, building, bridge, or other structure. This includes a bill of material that identifies the types and quantities of building materials necessary to execute the architectural plans. In manufacturing, the engineering drawings or schematics are provided to the production team that fabricates, assembles, integrates, and tests products to ensure compliance with the schematics. The software technical data package includes the architectural specifications, drawings, and diagrams necessary for the software product to be implemented. This includes a software bill of material that identifies and specifies every structural unit to be designed, coded, and tested during

Table 7.1 Stakeholder Objectives and Motivations

Stakeholder	Objectives	Motivations
Customer	• Effective and efficient software application • Procurement cost • Delivery schedule • Operational costs	• Extensiveness of the application functionality • Execution performance and responsiveness • Computer environment resource utilization
End user	• Ease of use • Product learning curve • Responsive product support	• Intuitive user interaction • Appealing, innovative user interface • Effective training and user documentation • Customer support • Problem resolution and rectification
Enterprise management	• Customer satisfaction • Industry reputation and market growth • Project return-on-investment	• Project progress and status • Risks to successful project completion • Project cost accumulation and escalation
Project management	• Achievement of project objectives • Predictable work estimates • Project scope preservation	• Project planning • Cost and schedule reserves
Software implementation	• Ease of implementation • Product acceptability • Product quality	• Product complexity • Changing product requirements • Specification completeness and accuracy
Software test and evaluation	• Product acceptance • Product quality	• Unambiguous specifications • Test environment, tools, and procedures • Computing environment and multi-user load tolerance
Post-development processes	• Distribution process readiness • Training program and aids readiness • Support process readiness	• Product packaging and distribution • Reseller agreements • Executable file replication • Training material • Problem reporting and resolution • Customer support • Software product enhancements and extensions • Product registration

implementation. In addition, it provides the software integration strategy, which depicts how the structural units and components should be assembled, integrated, and tested until an integrated software product configuration is realized.

Stakeholder needs and expectations must be accumulated, deconflicted, harmonized, and prioritized. The resulting set of needs must be pruned to balance the work forecasted necessary to satisfy the needs with the scope of resources available to the software development project. Once the software requirements are agreed upon, the set of software specifications should be baselined and placed under configuration control.

The software requirements provide the basis for refining and elaborating the technical work plans. The SWE-IPT utilizes software engineering principles and practices to conceive the technical plans for the software development project. Technical planning begins with the identification of tasks, task dependencies, and interrelationships to identify workflows and the requisite results of each task and workflow. The roles of each of the technical organizations must be identified and the resource requirements determined. These task definitions and resource requirements are coalesced into work packages and aligned within the project timeline. Task-based work packages are combined into larger elements of work (activities) and organized into the technical work breakdown structure (WBS). The WBS is completed by adding the project management and other nontechnical work packages to represent the total work to be performed and the respective budget and schedule information. The WBS provides the details necessary to prepare technical and project plans, such as the software engineering plan, integrated master plan (IMP), integrated master schedule (IMS), and project plan.

Establishing software requirements specifications and technical and project plans requires a rigorous, disciplined approach that involves trade-off analysis (technical), cost-benefit analysis (management), and risk assessments to ensure that the requirement specifications are complete and can be achieved by the resulting plans, schedules, and resource budgets. The identification and determination of the scope of each task must reflect the effort to define, design, and implement the software functionality and features specified by the software requirements. Figure 7.1 depicts how the software requirements are established and reflected in technical and project plans. The following sections describe each step of this workflow that translates stakeholder needs into requirement specifications and realistic technical and project plans.

7.1 Step 1: Soliciting stakeholder needs and expectations

The stakeholder needs and expectations are collected, analyzed, and deconflicted to generate the software requirements specifications. The various stakeholders will express their needs utilizing operational or business process terms or expressions relating to their particular field or expertise. Each of the stakeholders provides a different perspective as it relates to the desired software product. It is necessary to collect, analyze, and prioritize the stakeholder needs to develop the software

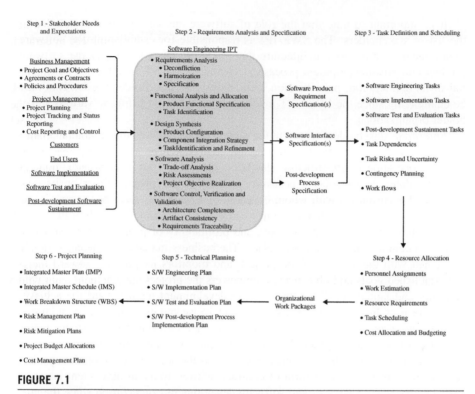

Step 1 - Stakeholder Needs
and Expectations

Business Management
• Project Goal and Objectives
• Agreements or Contracts
• Policies and Procedures

Project Management
• Project Planning
• Project Tracking and Status
  Reporting
• Cost Reporting and Control

Customers

End Users

Software Implementation

Software Test and Evaluation

**Post-development Software
Sustainment**

Step 2 - Requirements Analysis and Specification

Software Engineering IPT

• Requirements Analysis
  • Deconfliction
  • Harmoization
  • Specification
• Functional Analysis and Allocation
  • Product Functional Specification
  • Task Identification
• Design Synthesis
  • Product Configuration
  • Component Integration Strategy
  • TaskIdentification and Refinement
• Software Analysis
  • Trade-off Analysis
  • Risk Assessments
  • Project Objective Realization
• Software Control, Verification and
  Validation
  • Architecture Completeness
  • Artifact Consistency
  • Requirements Traceability

Software Product
Requirment
Specification(s)

Software Interface
Specification(s)

Post-development
Process
Specification

Step 3 - Task Definition and Scheduling

• Software Engineering Tasks
• Software Implementation Tasks
• Software Test and Evaluation Tasks
• Post-development Sustainment Tasks
• Task Dependencies
• Task Risks and Uncertainty
• Contingency Planning
• Work flows

Step 6 - Project Planning

• Integrated Master Plan (IMP)
• Integrated Master Schedule (IMS)
• Work Breakdown Structure (WBS)
• Risk Management Plan
• Risk Mitigation Plans
• Project Budget Allocations
• Cost Management Plan

Step 5 - Technical Planning

• S/W Engineering Plan
• S/W Implementation Plan
• S/W Test and Evaluation Plan
• S/W Post-development Process
  Implementation Plan

Organizational
Work Packages

Step 4 - Resource Allocation

• Personnel Assignments
• Work Estimation
• Resource Requirements
• Task Scheduling
• Cost Allocation and Budgeting

FIGURE 7.1

Establishment of software specifications and project plans.

Table 7.2 Priority of Stakeholder Needs	
Priority	**Stakeholder Needs**
Essential	• Enterprise management • Customer
Very important	• Project management • End user
Important	• Software implementation • Software test and evaluation

Significant	• Post-development processes
	  • Distribution
	  • Training
	  • Product sustainment

requirement specifications. The prioritization of stakeholder needs should be driven by the relative importance of each stakeholder class and the significance of each need as they relate to product acceptance. In general, Table 7.2 provides a relative prioritization scale for the stakeholders involved in a typical software development effort.

It is important to note that the role of software engineering is not included in the list of stakeholders. The SWE-IPT is responsible for establishing the software requirements and product architecture that guide the development of the software product and post-development processes. Therefore, the SWE-IPT must be impartial in its deliberation, prioritization, and analysis of stakeholder needs. This may be challenging since the SWE-IPT involves representatives from the various stakeholder organizations.

Enterprise stakeholders represent the organizational entities that enable and oversee the software development project for the enterprise. The enterprise provides the business operational infrastructure (facilities, equipment, etc.), personnel, policies and procedures, and resources necessary to conduct the project either on its own behalf or for customers with whom contracts or agreements have been established. The business management team is concerned with the continued growth of the enterprise, its reputation within its industry, and profitability of projects or the software product within a competitive marketplace. The business management team is mostly concerned with the success of the project, and monitors its progress toward meeting established goals and objectives. It empowers the project management team with authority and latitude to direct the software development team toward the achievement of project directives that best serve the enterprise and its customers or end users.

Customers represent business entities that enter into contractual arrangements with the software development business. In some situations, the customer may be an organization within the same business entity as the software development project organization. In that case, a form of contract referred to as an agreement is established between the customer and software development organization since the customer's organization is dependent on the software product for improving business process efficiency, reducing operating costs, or increasing profitability. The customer's needs and expectations must be understood prior to establishment of the terms and conditions of the contract or agreement under which the software product will be developed, documented, and delivered. The contract or agreement should establish the cost, schedule, and operational and performance characteristics the software product must exhibit upon delivery.

Project management represents the project oversight team empowered to plan, monitor, and direct the engineering and development of the software product and associated post-development processes. The project management team acts as the primary interface with business management, customers, and software engineering and development organizations. Its focus is on the achievement of project goals and objectives, project status reporting, customer interactions toward the fulfillment of the contract or agreements, and the delivery and acceptance of the software product by customers, end users, and other stakeholders. The project management team involves the project planning and control, configuration management and change control, cost tracking and accounting, risk management teams, and the interface with contracting and legal organizations.

End users represent customer employees or individuals who will operate the software product. End users are concerned with the user interface, application interactions, data storage and retrieval, data analysis, and report generation. Ease of use, errorless data processing, and intuitive interactions are the primary concerns of end users. Real-time systems, which control larger systems involving hardware components, are concerned with systems operations, failure modes, and graceful degradation of system performance, warning mechanisms, and corrective actions when system operations encounter adverse conditions.

Software implementation is the organization responsible for translating structural unit specifications of the physical architecture into software unit designs, coding and testing these code segments, and conducting software component integration and testing. It provides representatives to the SWE-IPT to offer insight into the software implementation issues and concerns inherent with the evolving architecture.

Software test and evaluation represents the organization responsible for establishing the software product and post-development process test plans and procedures. It provides representatives to the SWE-IPT to offer insight into the test issues and concerns inherent with the evolving architecture. It also ensures that software requirements are properly stated to provide a complete, consistent, and affordable testing strategy; conducts software dry-run and acceptance testing; and performs software quality assurance inspections to ensure adherence to software development plans, procedures, and guidelines.

Post-development sustainment represents the organizations responsible for defining, designing, implementing, and qualifying post-development processes. Qualification of these processes is a test and evaluation exercise that ensures that the processes are sufficient to facilitate anticipated post-development activities in an effective and efficient manner. These organizations provide representatives to the SWE-IPT to contribute insight into post-development issues and concerns inherent with the evolving software product architecture. This organization involves staff members proficient in software distribution, software training, and software support subject matter.

The various stakeholders have different, often competing interests, needs, and expectations that must be addressed by the software engineering effort. This diverse set of interests creates design challenges that might necessitate the conduct of trade-off analysis to be resolved. Stakeholder needs and expectations must be translated into a set of requirements for the software product and post-development processes. These requirements are documented as one or more specifications against which the software architecture and testing program will be developed. The requirements specifications should not be baselined (placed under configuration control) until the requirements are nonvolatile and determined to be achievable within project cost and schedule objectives.

7.2 Step 2: Requirement analysis and specification

The translation of stakeholder needs into a feasible, effective, and efficient software solution involves exploration of the problem space expressed by customers and evaluation and analysis of potential designs approaches. Only when the design solution is sufficiently mature and technical risks eliminated or minimized should the requirements be specified. This requires the application of software engineering practices to derive a design solution that balances the various stakeholder needs against cost and schedule constraints. The general approach to deriving a software solution involves the following three areas of interest:

1. The translation of stakeholder needs and expectations into a software architecture.
2. The specification of a balanced, achievable set of software requirements.
3. The incorporation of the solutions into work packages and technical and project plans and schedules.

Stakeholder needs and expectations must be evaluated, harmonized, and deconflicted to ensure that stakeholder expectations are properly established before the project enters into more detailed engineering activities. Abstract solution boundaries are generated in the form of ideas, considerations, and constraints that restrict the problem to be solved by design alternatives. Having the problem bounded permits the elaboration of product concepts that address the most important stakeholder needs and technical challenges. Initial product concepts should address how the product will operate within a larger business or operational context. The top-level or predominant functionality and performance challenges should be examined to gain an appreciation for the extent of the effort necessary to realize a product solution. An initial physical solution should be prepared that identifies the key structural components of the software product and attempts to reduce the product complexity.

The initial product concepts should be assessed against operational scenarios, project objectives, technical feasibility, and product sustainment concepts. Certain technical solutions may result in very eloquent and user-satisfying products. However, the technical challenges confronting software implementation and testing efforts may increase product training or support costs. The product technical solutions should be as noncomplex as possible to reduce implementation, testing, and sustainment costs. At this juncture, the product concepts should be assessed in terms of its total life-cycle costs resulting from the post-development process definitions. These processes are conceptualized and initial process definitions generated to support this assessment. Eventually, the initial software architecture should be specified in terms of the product and process requirements, and the initial functional and physical architectures. The complete software architecture is represented by the combination of the product and post-development process architectures.

The challenges involved with this initial exploration of the stakeholder needs are:

1. Balancing and deconflicting stakeholder needs.
2. Maintaining the scope of the project to ensure that project cost and schedule objectives can be achieved, including the following:
   - The cost associated with implementing the complete set of software requirements.

- The cost associated with testing the software product based on the assorted set of operational threads, control mechanisms, and interfaces with external systems and applications.
- The cost associated with defining and establishing the post-development processes.
- The software development timeline and task dependencies necessary to accomplish each stage of software development.

3. Ensuring the availability of experienced software personnel with the technical skills required to design, code, and test the software product.

7.2.1 Balancing and deconflicting stakeholder needs

Resolving conflicting stakeholder needs so that the software requirements can be specified, and understanding how each need affects the software architecture, project costs and schedule objectives, product complexity, and post-development processes. The costs and risks associated with each need must be estimated to provide a basis for proceeding with generating an achievable set of software requirements. The stakeholder needs must be prioritized based on the cooperative agreement of potential costs and risks to project objectives and product viability. This set of prioritized needs, with estimated cost, schedule, and risk information, provides a basis for resolving conflicts among stakeholders needs, and gaining stakeholder acceptance of recommended compromises that form the basis for establishing software specifications.

Further analysis of prioritized stakeholder needs may involve functional analysis and allocation and design synthesis to gain a better understanding of the ramifications on the software product, post-development processes, and project cost and schedule objectives. Trade-off analysis and risk assessments should be performed to distinguish among the design alternatives and permit design decisions to be made with more accurate information. This further analysis will provide the supporting data and rationale that can be used to assist stakeholders to appreciate the impact of their vague or excessive requests.

7.2.2 Maintaining the scope of the project

The scope of the software development effort must be maintained within the established project cost and schedule boundaries. It must be recognized that several influences will affect project scope and planning, such as:

- Ambiguity of stakeholder needs or software requirements that result in misinterpretations affecting the scope of the technical effort. Ambiguity occurs when the personnel assume they understand stakeholder needs and do not scrutinize each need or requirement with the intent of eliminating statements that may have more than one possible meaning or interpretation. Software professionals need the assistance of subject matter experts who are familiar with the business or operational environment within which the software product is expected to function. This expertise will alleviate the ambiguity associated with interpreting stakeholder needs.

- Changing stakeholder needs and expectations as the software development effort progresses. This represents an evolution associated with the understanding and clarity of stakeholder needs as it affects the software product. Continual changes in product requirements will impair the ability of the project team to stabilize the software specifications and progress with software implementation.
- Underestimating the scope of effort involved with the incorporation of new or modification of old software functionality and features. Each change must be comprehensively examined to address the impact of incorporating the change into the product architecture, associated documentation, and technical plans.

Every change to project scope will have a varying level of impact on the planned software development effort. An objective of software engineering is to prepare the product architecture in a manner that can be implemented and tested within project cost and schedule parameters. Changes late in the project timetable, after preliminary design review (PDR) or critical design review (CDR), will require revisions to the software specifications, software architecture, and test plans and procedures. Changes to project scope must account for the total project effort needed to revise the specifications, architecture design documentation, and technical plans. Otherwise, the project will be challenged to exceed the anticipated work reflected in the work packages. The act of incorporating changes in scope also impacts the project by derailing technical progress to address the effort necessary to adjust the software architecture, reprogram and reallocate resources, and update project and technical plans to reflect the incorporation of the change.

7.2.2.1 Cost associated with implementing the complete set of software requirements

Every software requirement involves a cost and schedule burden that impacts the planned software development effort. The desired functionality and level of performance must be understood to properly establish the work effort necessary to satisfy a requirement. The WBS must provide a basis for tracing software requirements to project and technical plans. The later a change in scope is considered, the greater the impact of that change. This is due to the need to reevaluate architectural impacts, redesign, code, and test existing software units, reintegrate and test software components, and accommodate the changes within technical plans and documentation. This should be recognized as a form of rework necessary to refine an already generated work product to conform to a new set of conditions.

As a rule of thumb, software requirements should reflect the software product's role in business or operational processes. The requirements should be minimal in number, but sufficiently articulated to ensure that the testing strategy adequately demonstrates the effectiveness and efficiency of the product performance when subject to various levels of operational stress. Operational concepts must be translated into technical terminology to guide the establishment of a complete, efficient, and noncomplex product architecture. Chapter 8 will provide further guidance on how an operational model can be utilized to assist in establishing a solid requirements baseline.

Testing is performed against software requirements specifications and is intended to demonstrate that the product conforms to the requirements as they are specified. If the specifications do not accurately capture stakeholder needs and expectations, then the delivered software product may not provide a value proposition for all stakeholders. To ensure that the software product will satisfy stakeholders, the test strategy, plans, and procedures should ensure conformance with the operational concepts through a variety of scenarios and stressful multi-user operational conditions.

7.2.2.2 Cost associated with testing the software product

Identifying the magnitude of the software test and evaluation effort must be accommodated within the confines of project scope and resources. Testing occurs throughout the software implementation stage and must emphasize the achievement of specified performance measures. Functional requirements identify *what* the software must do, while performance measures address *how well* a function must be accomplished. Some requirements may be specified that cannot be demonstrated without special test facilities or equipment. Others may be cost prohibitive to qualify prior to delivery. If a requirement precludes the establishment of a clear or cost-effective test approach, then the requirement should be highlighted within the test plan to elevate this situation.

An example of this would be an Internet-based game that permits thousands of real-time users to interact within a digital world. It may be challenging and cost prohibitive to conduct performance testing with the anticipated number of users. Therefore, the approach to assessing the performance of the software product under extreme conditions must be able to extrapolate and forecast performance measures utilizing advanced load testing tools and techniques.

7.2.2.3 Cost associated with defining and establishing the post-development processes

The integrated product and process development (IPPD) philosophy emphasizes the need to concurrently accomplish the efforts associated with establishing the post-development processes. The software product should not be deployed unless the post-development processes have been defined, designed, implemented, and tested. These processes provide the infrastructure necessary to distribute the software product, train users, and provide customer and software support. The software development project should encompass the resources and management oversight necessary for the formulation of these essential software post-development processes.

7.2.2.4 Software development timeline and task dependencies

The accuracy of project and technical plans, budgets, and schedules involves management processes that are responsive to changes in project scope and product architectural design. Initial plans will never account for the true scope of the development effort because the understanding of the stakeholder requirements may be limited. The purpose of software engineering is to investigate stakeholder needs and expectations so that a technical solution may be formed. As the software product architecture is developed, more insight into the technical work effort is made available and plans and schedules increase in accuracy. Rather than being driven by initial planning assumptions, project and technical plans must be continually revised and updated to reflect the improved information resulting from the software engineering effort. Design decisions made during the software engineering effort will require the project team to continually reevaluate plans, work packages, and risks to reallocate budgets and realign task schedules and dependencies.

7.2.3 The availability of experienced software personnel

The availability of talented, experienced, and trained software professionals is crucial to executing technical plans. Task durations and costs will vary depending on the level of expertise embodied by the technical staff. Representatives from the software implementation, test and evaluation, and post-development process organizations must be adequately trained to perform the tasks identified in technical plans. Additionally, these personnel must be educated concerning the evolving architectural design as it affects their technical duties. Work packages must be established and revised to account for the availability of software professionals, their combined skill set, and their familiarity with the nature of the software product, development methodologies, procedures, and use of automated tools.

The technical and project plans must be revised to accurately reflect the evolving software requirements and product architecture. As stakeholder needs and expectations are translated into software requirements and interface and post-development process specifications, these documents and supporting analysis provide a basis for refining the scope and effort necessary to perform each development task. Project plans and management controls must be aligned to reflect the current, most accurate state of the development project. As the software engineering effort progresses, the analysis that leads to design decisions provides a more realistic estimate of the scope of each task, resource requirements, skill sets, and level of effort necessary to perform each task.

7.3 Step 3: Task definition and scheduling

Each requirement must be evaluated by the SWE-IPT to establish organizational roles, responsibilities, and task definitions. The software engineering practices should be applied to gain a complete understanding of requirements' functional and performance characteristics needed to be satisfied by the software product. The software implementation and test organizations must utilize this understanding to reframe the scope of their tasks. Organizational tasks should be evaluated to identify potential risks and uncertainty associated with task performance. Contingency plans should be identified for each risk abatement approach and the conditions that would warrant their activation must be identified. The dependencies among tasks must be aligned to establish the criteria for task initiation and provide a view of the overall workflow and schedules.

7.4 Step 4: Resource identification, estimation, and allocation

The resources required to execute each task must be identified in terms of manpower, facilities, equipment, office supplies, and computer automated software engineering (CASE) tools. Resources may include any item that contributes to project costs including travel expenses, reproduction, and software-related skills training. The costs associated with resources should be allocated among technical organizations participating in executing the task. Lower-level tasks should be combined to establish higher-level task cost estimates. This exercise leads to the identification of budget estimates for organizational and integrated technical work packages. Work packages can be combined to summarize the cost of performing each element of the WBS.

Initial work package cost estimates must be reconciled against available project resources. Task scope and resource requirements may need to be revised to provide a complete set of work packages consistent with project budget constraints. Work packages that involve an identified risk should incorporate a contingency reserve budget based on the magnitude of the risk, its probability of occurring, and the resources needed to execute the contingency plan of action.

7.5 Step 5: Establish organizational work packages

The WBS is a central project management tool that is tightly coupled with project plans, budgets, and schedules. Each technical organization should maintain its own version of the WBS that identifies the organizational task descriptions, resources, and results. Technical organizations must convert their contribution to tasks execution into an organizational set of work packages. These organizational work packages form the basis for organizational and technical planning.

7.6 Step 6: Technical planning

Each technical organization utilizes its WBS to generate or revise organizational plans and schedules. These plans should identify the organizational role and responsibilities associated with each work package. Task descriptions, dependencies, duration (start and stop dates), resource requirements, expected results, risks, and contingency plans should be addressed. The SWE-IPT is responsible for ensuring that organizational plans are consistent with established project objectives, budgets, and milestones. An integrated technical plan (ITP) and schedule (ITS) must be established by combining organizational plans, eliminating duplication of effort, and preparing integrated work package definitions.

The software engineering plan (SWEP) must be prepared or revised to capture the detailed tasks for the impending stage of software development. The SWEP addresses the focus of the SWE-IPT by identifying the approach to developing the desired results for the stage of development it is addressing. It should identify any known risks that will be monitored and the contingency plans of action that will be initiated to redirect planned activities toward an alternate design solution. Plans to conduct trade studies for identified design challenges should be conveyed, the competing alternatives described, and the selection criteria established.

The primary software engineering activities involve requirements analysis, functional analysis, and application design synthesis. They are supported by software analysis, control, verification, and validation activities. Software analysis involves the conduct of risk assessments and trade-off studies, and is applied whenever deemed necessary. The control, verification, and validation activities will be different during each stage of software development as the focus of the effort progresses from stakeholder needs and expectations to the software architecture, implementation, and acceptance testing. The SWEP, ITP, ITS, and organizational plans must be updated to reflect the evolution of the software development effort as it progresses through each stage.

7.7 Step 7: Project planning

The project management team, with support from the lead software engineer, should utilize the technical plans to establish or revise the project plans and schedules. Work packages for project management activities, such as project control, cost tracking, configuration, and data management, should be integrated with technical work package descriptions. These integrated project work packages are utilized to establish an IMP and IMS, project-level WBS, and budgets.

This general flow for establishing project plans is intended to ensure that technical and project plans accurately reflect stakeholder needs, specified software requirements, and focus on the achievement of project objectives. This approach is facilitated by a stakeholder requirements analysis activity that explores the problem area and assesses software design solutions and alternatives. Once a software solution is recognized, the project, technical, and organizational plans must be revised to provide an accurate and consistent representation of the work to be performed. This planning sequence emphasizes the importance of conducting adequate software engineering analysis to generate the software requirement specifications that guide technical and project planning efforts. This is intended to ensure that the software development effort is driven by the stakeholder needs and software requirements rather than erroneous and inaccurate project plans developed at the onset of the project.

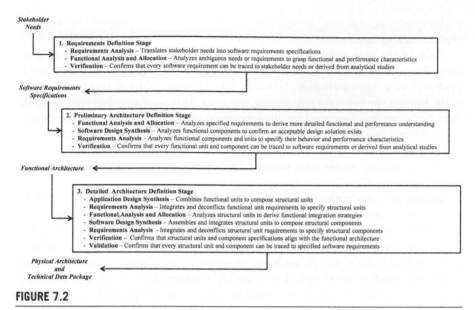

Stakeholder Needs

1. Requirements Definition Stage
- **Requirements Analysis** – Translates stakeholder needs into software requirements specifications
- **Functional Analysis and Allocation** – Analyzes ambiguous needs or requirements to grasp functional and performance characteristics
- **Verification** – Confirms that every software requirement can be traced to stakeholder needs or derived from analytical studies

Software Requirements Specifications

2. Preliminary Architecture Definition Stage
- **Functional Analysis and Allocation** – Analyzes specified requirements to derive more detailed functional and performance understanding
- **Software Design Synthesis** – Analyzes functional components to confirm an acceptable design solution exists
- **Requirements Analysis** – Analyzes functional components and units to specify their behavior and performance characteristics
- **Verification** – Confirms that every functional unit and component can be traced to software requirements or derived from analytical studies

Functional Architecture

3. Detailed Architecture Definition Stage
- **Application Design Synthesis** – Combines functional units to compose structural units
- **Requirements Analysis** – Integrates and deconflicts functional unit requirements to specify structural units
- **Functional Analysis and Allocation** – Analyzes structural units to derive functional integration strategies
- **Software Design Synthesis** – Assembles and integrates structural units to compose structural components
- **Requirements Analysis** - Integrates and deconflicts structural unit requirements to specify structural components
- **Verification** – Confirms that structural units and component specifications align with the functional architecture
- **Validation** – Confirms that every structural unit and component can be traced to specified software requirements

Physical Architecture and Technical Data Package

FIGURE 7.2

Conceptual application of software engineering practices.

7.8 Exploring stakeholder needs

Establishing detailed technical plans can only be achieved when stakeholder needs and expectations have been properly translated into an achievable set of software requirements. Eliciting, harmonizing, and prioritizing stakeholder requirements are important steps in aligning work plans with project objectives. However, before the software requirements can be specified, some amount of design conceptualization and exploration must be performed to ensure that the product can be developed and delivered within the project resource constraints. The software requirements baseline represents a binding agreement (sometimes contractual) between the technical, project management, and stakeholder representatives concerning the product characteristics and operational effectiveness. To ensure that the project team can successfully deliver the software product and achieve project cost and schedule objectives, some amount of effort must be expended to amplify the architectural concept. Early and continual examination of the software architecture, especially the areas that are technically challenging or risky, provides the assurances necessary to have confidence that the technical and project plans can be satisfied.

Establishing the software product architecture involves performing several iterations of the software engineering practices. In concept, each of the first three stages of software development involve performing most of these practices at least once to produce the requirements specifications and functional and physical architectures. Figure 7.2 shows how the software engineering practices are applied to generate the desired results for each stage of development. However, within each stage these practices may be repeated, as necessary, to revise, refine, or elaborate the software product architecture.

Each of the first three stages of software development is intended to progress the software architectural definition toward a state of specificity that is sufficient to guide software implementation. Unfortunately, the titles of these stages are *similar* to the titles of the software engineering practices. This similarity has caused confusion. Software development practitioners mistakenly assumed that only the identified software engineering practice was to be performed during these early stages of development. However, it is essential for software engineering practices to be applied, as needed, within each stage of development to eliminate risks or to establish a design solution.

Historically, the preliminary design stage resulted in an allocation of requirements throughout a functional hierarchy. Functional components and units were inappropriately considered elements of the preliminary design configuration. The distinction between a functional and physical architecture was not comprehended since software, as a design medium, resembled functional notations. Software languages involve statements that resemble mathematical or logical functions. Early programming languages involved procedures, functions, and subroutines as their basic structural elements. Therefore, it was easy for software practitioners to assume that the architectural definition was complete when the functional decomposition was fully established. However, it must be understood that every product has a physical configuration. The functional analysis and allocation practice enables software requirements to be translated into the essential data processing actions the software product must be able to perform. However, this does not conclude the definition of the software architecture. The physical configuration must be synthesized to provide a coherent, noncomplex solution.

Each of the software engineering practices *must* be utilized whenever its sphere of influence is implicated by the delineation of the problem/solution space. This iteration of software engineering practices must always revisit the requirements analysis activity to revise or refine the software product requirements. For example (see Figure 7.2), during the detailed architecture definition stage of development, the requirements analysis practice occurs twice. The first occurrence addresses the specification of structural units and the second occurrence addresses the specification of structural components.

During software requirements definition, there may be stakeholder needs that necessitate modeling or prototyping efforts to ensure that stakeholder needs are understood, to investigate design challenges, and to minimize risks to the development effort. These analytical tools should be used to ensure that the software requirements are unambiguously specified. This undertaking must be considered an excursion into the realm of design for the purpose of clarifying stakeholder needs. The term *excursion* is used to emphasize that it represents a departure from the normal or planned application of software engineering practices. The development of models or prototypes should be achieved by rapid application of software engineering techniques to establish models or prototypes for the purpose of clarifying software requirements. Models must still exhibit some functionality and performance characteristics that enhance the accuracy of requirements specification. Prototypes will involve a software implementation effort to develop a mock-up of the prototype design. These models and prototypes must be viewed as tools that facilitate an enhanced comprehension of the stakeholder needs.

Software Requirements Analysis Practice

Software requirement analysis is the software engineering practice that, at the top level of the software architecture, translates stakeholder needs and expectations into a viable set of software requirements. As the software product architecture is systematically revealed, these tasks should be selectively applied to specify the requirements for each element of the architecture. This set of tasks applies to the software product (application and computing environment), as well as post-development software sustainment processes. Software requirements analysis involves a set of analyses and assessments to examine stakeholder needs and software requirements to comprehend the implications of each requirement on the scope of the development effort.

The complexity associated with the design solution must be understood before the requirements are baselined and placed under configuration control. In addition, requirements analysis must assess the feasibility of satisfying the complete set of software requirements within program cost and schedule constraints. This can only be achieved by exploring the solution space for each requirement and correlating the sensitivity of project variables to various levels of performance. This may necessitate conducting exploratory architectural investigations (functional analysis and application design synthesis) and trade-off analyses to achieve a balanced set of requirements that can be successfully implemented within program cost and schedule objectives.

This chapter discusses the primary tasks that are involved with software requirements analysis given the environment the application is constrained to operate within. This involves exploration of the operational and sustainment processes to determine the functional and performance characteristics needed to satisfy the stakeholder of the software product. The execution of these software requirements analysis tasks results in the generation of specifications for the software product (computing environment, software application, the application interfaces) and the software sustainment processes. These specifications must be informally controlled until the product design is determined to be sufficiently defined and agreed upon by stakeholders to be placed under configuration control. The baseline software requirements and interface specifications form the basis for the software test and evaluation effort. Figure 8.1 depicts the tasks that contribute to software requirements analysis.

These tasks have been classified to emphasize the area of investigation each task addresses. These categories include project, operational, product, and post-development process analyses, and project assessment. The analytical tasks are intended to examine the software product to understand it in the context of its project, operational, and sustainment environments. Project assessment tasks are performed on preliminary requirements to understand the feasibility of achieving project objectives if the requirements are to be endorsed, baselined, and placed under project configuration control.

8.1 Project analysis tasks

The project analysis tasks involve gathering the information concerning the product to be developed to establish the criteria for product and project success. The specification of software requirements must be accomplished in a manner that keeps the project scope capable of being successfully executed.

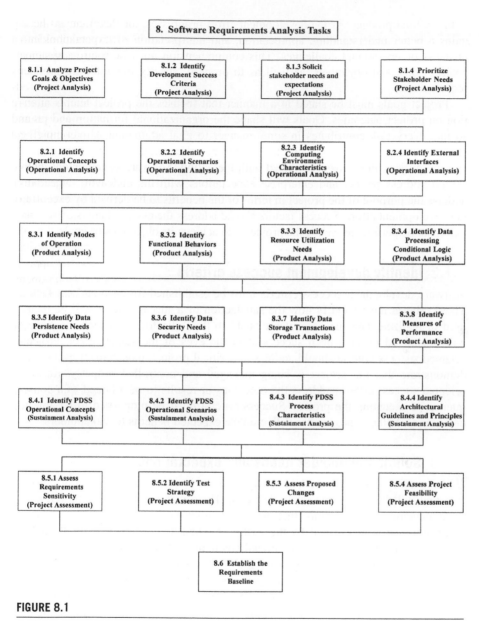

FIGURE 8.1

Software requirements analysis tasks.

8.1.1 **Analyze project goals and objectives**

Every software development project is established with a set of goals and objectives that guide the project team's efforts. Initial project goals and objectives are purposefully abstract and grandiose in nature given the lack of clarity associated with the final product. As the development effort progresses, the development team gains a better understanding, appreciation, and interpretation of the stakeholder's business or operational challenges. This comprehension must be used to enhance project goals and objectives, as well as to properly specify the software product requirements.

Project goals must be stated in a manner that focuses the project team's attention on project outcomes. Goals will shape the organizational formation and plans so that every task contributes in some manner to goal attainment. Goals must be measurable and address an accomplishment to be achieved, the results of the action, and the project milestones associated with the action. Software development goals should address project and enterprise expectations with the endeavor. Objectives address the purpose of the project in terms of the benefits to be derived by executing the development effort. Success factors should address the essential areas of activity that must be performed well if the project is to achieve its objectives or goals.

8.1.2 Identify development success criteria

Software development success criteria must be established for each success factor. These criteria must identify how the satisfaction of a success factor will be measured or realized. The success criteria establish the indicators by which the project will be judged to have been successful in the eyes of the stakeholders. Project-oriented success criteria should address the critical project management events that demonstrate that the project is being managed and controlled properly. Results-oriented success criteria address the outcomes or results to be attained as a consequence of executing the project. Success criteria must be monitored to be able to determine whether a project has delivered the expected benefits to stakeholders.

8.1.3 Solicit stakeholder needs and expectations

Understanding customer needs and expectations is central to developing a solution that will be acceptable when delivered. History is wrought with flawed software development programs that were delivered late, exceeded program cost constraints, or were rejected by the customer when the system was finally delivered. Requirements creep—the continual changing and addition of requirements—is a major dilemma confronting programs. Software development managers fail to restrain the customer from attempting to continually change or add requirements throughout development. It must be recognized that each requirement implies an expense to the development effort, including driving up test costs and impacting the delivery schedule.

Fundamentally, customers do not have requirements, they have needs and expectations. When faced with the cost associated with a new requirement, customers will often change their stated needs or drop the requirement altogether. The greatest challenge a software development manager will face is establishing a requirements baseline and not allowing it to change. As the software engineering process is executed, derived requirements will emerge that affect the ability of the development effort to deliver the solution on time and within budget. Allowing requirements to be changed or added to the effort will only make this situation worse. If a requirement is to be changed, then it should be modified in a manner that simplifies the development work effort by reducing or eliminating risks to the program.

Customer needs and expectations must be captured as the source of the requirements that will be specified for the computational environment and software application. Every effort should be made to minimize the number of customer needs and expectations by capturing them in terms of how the solution is expected to operate or support the customer's business processes. Customer expectations should not imply a design constraint on the solution, but should address the way in which data will be accessed and processed.

Software development projects are typically established within an enterprise organization. The enterprise represents a business entity, government, or social organization that operates for stated business purposes. All enterprises have policies and fiscal responsibilities. Development programs that do not perform as expected impact the enterprises' financial stability. When a program is established, the enterprise establishes cost and schedule objectives that constrain what can be achieved and delivered by the software development program. In addition, policies may dictate the conduct of technical reviews, quality programs, use of technologies, etc., all of which affect the development effort and the final solution.

Enterprise and program constraints must be captured since they will form the basis for governing the software development effort. Constraints affect the solution space and burden the development effort by restricting design alternatives. The use of standards, computer-aided software engineering (CASE) tools, networks, and even computer languages will impact the development effort and affect cost and schedule. These constraints must be captured as an additional source of stakeholder requirements. This recognizes the enterprise and program management team as additional customers who have expectations of their own and are stakeholders in the software development program's success.

External constraints are implied by laws, regulations, or industry policies associated with the problem being solved by the development program. External constraints affect the solution space and must be complied with for the design solution to be politically and socially sound. It is important to identify all possible constraints to the program that will affect the design solution before the requirements are baselined. External constraints are a type of requirement that cannot be deviated from, where software requirements can be changed or negotiated among the software development team, enterprise, and customer.

An example of an external constraint is the public law requiring that the video game industry rate the content of each game in terms of recommended age restrictions based on bloodshed, violence, and sexual content. The Entertainment

Software Rating Board (ESRB) policies are designed to provide accurate and objective information about the content in computer and video games so parents can make an informed purchase decision.[1]

As the game industry's self-regulatory body, ESRB is responsible for the enforcement of its rating system. Every publisher of a game rated by the ESRB is legally bound to disclose all pertinent content when submitting the game for an ESRB rating. After a game is publicly released, ESRB testers review the final product to ensure that all pertinent content was fully disclosed. In the event that material that would have affected the assignment of a rating or content descriptor is found to have not been disclosed, the ESRB is empowered to compel corrective actions and impose a wide range of sanctions, including monetary fines. Corrective actions can include pulling advertising until ratings information can be corrected, restickering packaging with correct ratings information, or recalling the product.

This constraint requires the developers of software games to include a task for obtaining the ESRB rating prior to release of the video game to the market. It requires that the software packaging must clearly display the ratings in accordance with ESRB guidelines. This may affect the release date of the product and must be accounted for in the software development project plan and schedule. In addition, the rating system can have an effect on the design of the game, in terms of the intended audience and the associated content included in the game.

8.1.4 Prioritize stakeholder needs

The project team must condense, prioritize, and summarize the list of stakeholder needs into a manageable collection that will be used to guide the specification of software requirements. Stakeholder needs and expectations must be translated into software requirements for the product (computing environment and software application) and post-development processes. An individual stakeholder need may involve several requirements that the project will be held accountable for achieving. The level of effort and resources necessary to fulfill a stakeholder need must be determined, and the project and technical risks must be included in the cost estimates. The project budget can then be allocated against the prioritized needs. This establishes the initial scope of the software development effort and provides the basis for project and technical planning.

8.2 Operational analysis tasks

The operational analysis tasks involve gathering the detailed information regarding the business or operational processes the software product is intended to facilitate. Characteristics of the business or operational processes should be traced to stakeholder needs. The operational environment should be identified in terms of the

---

[1] See Entertainment Software Rating Board, *http://www.esrb.org/*.

facilities, systems, equipment, data networks, etc. within which the software product will execute. This operational analysis should be described from the perspective of the software product and address its role, functions, and interactions with external systems, personnel, and resource providers (e.g., power, data sources).

During the architecture definition phases, the operational model is elaborated to address the behaviors of the software product within the operational environment. Extension of the operational model is addressed in Chapter 11.

8.2.1 Identify operational concepts

The operational concept for the software product must be documented to describe the characteristics of a proposed software product from the viewpoint of an individual who will use the product. It is used to communicate the software characteristics to all stakeholders. Concepts of operation descriptions usually address the following:

1. Statement of the goals and objectives of the software product.
2. Mission statement that expresses the set of services the product provides.
3. Strategies, policies, and constraints affecting the product.
4. Organizations, activities, and interactions among participants and stakeholders.
5. Clear statement of responsibilities associated with product development and sustainment.
6. Process identification for distributing, training, and sustainment of the product.
7. Milestone decision definitions and authorities.

During software requirements definition, the operational or business process should be modeled to understand the operational activity flows, control flows, and data flows among the elements of the computational environment, associated applications, databases, and users. The operational concept should identify operational threads for each type of transaction that the software application will have to support.

During architecture definition, the operational concepts should address the user interactions associated with installation, operation, distribution, training, and support of the product.

8.2.2 Identify operational scenarios

The operational concept should be expanded to identify the range of the anticipated uses of the software application in terms of operating scenarios. For each operational scenario, the expected interactions with other systems, products, or users should be defined. The business rules for each transaction should be captured and expressed as control decision logic. In addition, each operational scenario should address the possible situations that may prevent a transaction from being completed successfully, and identify the need for transaction rollback procedures. (Note: This represents a derived requirement that may not have been addressed in the original set of requirements.)

Troubleshooting diagnostics threads should be identified given that most computerized systems have some form of automated diagnostics. These troubleshooting threads

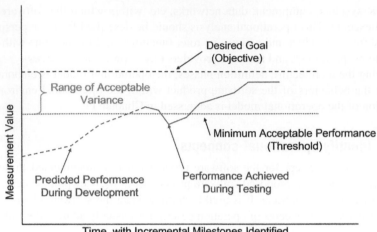

FIGURE 8.2

Elements of a well-defined measure of effectiveness.

should identify the actions that will be taken by the application when failures occur that inhibit specific types of transactions, or when the system is completely degraded.

The measures of effectiveness must be identified for the overall performance of the software solution (combination of the software product and computing environment) in achieving operational objectives. Measures of effectiveness define the desired effectiveness of the solution in terms of its ability to perform its mission as expressed by the operational scenarios. Operational effectiveness is the overall ability of a software solution to achieve mission success considering the total operational environment.[2]

The measures of effectiveness should be specified with a minimally acceptable level (threshold) and desired goal (objective). This provides the range of desired performance against which the computational environment and application can be designed. Figure 8.2 identifies the elements of an effectiveness measure. For an automobile, a measure of effectiveness can be: "The automobile should provide 36 miles per gallon during highway driving." This statement may seem simple, but there are several design factors that affect the achievement of this design goal. The weight, horsepower, fuel efficiency, and drag are some of the design considerations that would have to be managed to achieve the desired measure of effectiveness.

8.2.3 Identify the computing environment characteristics

The computing environment must be identified to establish the scope of the software product's capacity to operate in a networked, collaborative, or multi-user

---

[2](2001). *Systems Engineering Fundamentals*. Defense Acquisition University Press.

environment. Computing environment characteristics should address computing mainframes, servers, workstations, data storage devices, plotters, operating systems, and other application software, such as database management systems. This information is needed as the basis for the definition of the computing development that must be instantiated to support software testing.

It is necessary to identify the computational boundary that may include local, wide area, wireless, and telecommunication networks. Establishing the computational boundary is used to understand how the software product needs to interact with the various elements of the computational environment and other external systems. In the case of an embedded software product, the boundary could be the system it operates within. However, if the system is part of a larger "system of systems," then the computational boundary could be extended beyond the system boundary to other systems, which would indicate the need for external interfaces.

8.2.4 Identify external interfaces

The interfaces to external systems must be identified and the requirements associated with each interface need to be specified. External systems are those systems not being developed as part of the program, but they need to exchange data with the software product being developed. Interface specifications should address not only the physical means of data transfer, but also specify the message formats, data types, units of measures, and precision associated with each data type.

The operational model should be analyzed to specify each of the human–machine interactions for operational, support, and diagnostic actions. In addition, the human–machine interface requirements should address how the application must detect and deal with improper or incorrect manual data inputs. The means of the manual interactions and the interfacing devices, such as keyboard, mouse, touch screen, and card reader, should be identified. The human–machine interface requirements should also address data displayed to the user and the types of output reports that must be generated by the software product.

8.3 Product analysis tasks

The product analysis tasks involve specifying the software product requirements given its role within the operational concepts. The operational concepts and scenarios should be evaluated to identify the functional and performance characteristics associated with the data processing actions that the software product must exhibit. Details concerning the elements that need to be expressed by an operational model are discussed in task 8.3.2, identify functional behaviors (see Figure 8.1).

During architecture definition, the product requirements will be decomposed and allocated to functional and structural units and components. These tasks should be selectively performed to specify the requirements for each element of the software product architecture.

8.3.1 **Identify modes of operation**

Most applications must be designed to operate in different modes that address normal, degraded, maintenance, and training modes. The operational model should be evaluated to identify alternative modes of operation to determine the specific conditions that will transition the application from one mode of operation to another. For example, if an ATM banking machine runs out of cash to dispense, it cannot conduct withdrawal transactions, but it can still process other transaction requests. However, when the ATM machine is undergoing maintenance to replace wornout parts or to refill the cash, receipts, and other consumables, the ATM is taken out of service and no transactions can be conducted.

Separate operational models can be developed for each alternative mode of operation, or the operational model can account for each of the modes of operation. It is sometimes more efficient to initially separate the operational, training, and support models so that each model is given a defined focus. Once they are complete and verified, these models can be integrated or combined into a single model, if desired.

8.3.2 **Identify functional behaviors**

The functional behavior of the software product must be defined and associated with the measures of effectiveness and the previously defined operational threads. The operational behaviors should describe how the organizational elements interact with the software product by performing activities or workflows. The operational model should express the control logic to enforce business rules, policies, and procedures. The exchange of information among organizational elements should be expressed as inputs and outputs of an activity.

An operational model should be developed to depict the operational or business workflow associated with each scenario. During the development of the operational model, the systems that support the operational process should be identified as an actor. Figure 8.3 provides an example of an operational behavioral model. The

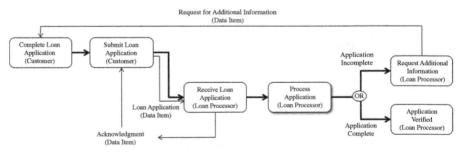

FIGURE 8.3

Example of an operational (behavioral) model.

product behaviors will be explored further in Chapter 11. The operational model should involve the following elements:

1. *Organizational elements* represent the organizations within the business enterprise, or external organizations, such as business partners, vendors, suppliers, and users. Each organizational element represents a role in the operational model, and is used to group the activities each organization must perform. Each organizational element participates in the business process by performing operational activities in a time-sequenced workflow.

2. *Actors* represent a specific organizational role, user type, system, computing equipment item, or application that participates in the operational process. Actors perform activities and exchange information with other actors.

3. *Operational activities* represent the tasks or work that is performed by an actor. An operational activity represents a step in conducting the operational or business process to transform inputs into outputs. Operational activities may require resources to be available to be executed. Operational activities are similar to software functions but are expressed at the operational process perspective and are performed by actors or organizational elements.

4. *Process control mechanisms* are the business rules and control mechanisms that determine which step in the process will be executed next (e.g., If (condition) Then (perform function X) Else (perform function Y)). Control mechanisms may represent a loop condition that repeats previously performed activities one or more times, or conditional branches where each branch involves activities appropriate to respond to an anticipated situation. If a customer applies for credit, then upon an initial credit rating search, the application may be approved, rejected, or subjected to further credit checking. Each result is dependent on the results of the initial credit check and alters the follow-on activities associated with the process.

5. *Data items* are the inputs and outputs of operational activities that represent the exchange of information among the organizational elements and actors who are transmitting or receiving the information exchange. The data flow is important to capture because it may represent one of the following data flow types:

   - *Point-to-point*—an output data item flows from one operational activity to one other operational activity as an input.
   - *Broadcast*—an output data item flows from one operational activity to two or more operational activities as an input.
   - *Trigger*—a point-to-point data item that initiates the receiving operational activity. The receiving operational activity cannot begin to be executed until the triggering data item is received.
   - *Data record*—a data item that is published to or retrieved from a data source, such as a database, file cabinet, or external application. A data record represents useful information that is going to be saved and retrieved in support of business operations.

6. *Duration*—each of the operational activities consumes time and when the operational model is analyzed the operational timeline can be generated to express how long the operational process takes to execute. Since the objective of most automation programs is to make the process more effective, less costly, and conducted more rapidly, it is important to understand the existing process execution time and the improvement in performance expected when the software product is involved.

7. *Resources*—operational activities may require that resources be available for an operational activity to be performed. The unavailability of a needed resource will cause the activity to be placed into a wait-state until the resource is made available. Resources can be of the following types:

   - *Consumable*—a resource that is used up when the operational activity is conducted. Resources that are consumed must have an initial amount that is available, the maximum amount that can be on hand at any one time (inventory capacity), and the amount that is consumed by the activity. An ATM has a supply of money that it can dispense. Each withdrawal transaction decrements the amount of money available to be dispensed as a consumable resource.
   - *Reusable*—a resource that is captured by an operational activity and is released by the activity when it is done executing. A cash register is a reusable type of resource, and only one sales associate can conduct a transaction using a register at a time.

8.3.3 Identify resource utilization needs

The operational model should be analyzed to understand how resource availability impacts the operational or business process. The focus should be on computing environment resources, which involve any physical or virtual component of limited availability. Within the operational model, activities that are performed in parallel may contend for available resources. Contention for resources results in process delays that can be alleviated by increasing the availability of resources. When resources are limited, then scheduling mechanisms may be needed to ensure that high-priority functions are given access to resources before lower-priority functions.

At the operational or business process level, the resource utilization analysis is useful in determining the resources incorporated into the computational environment. At the software product level of analysis, the availability of resources may constrain data processing flow and may identify the need to modify the computing environment definition to incorporate additional computing equipment.

8.3.4 Identify data processing conditional logic

The operational model should be assessed to determine how process control mechanisms need to be addressed by the software product. The process controls that are to be exhibited by the software product must be articulated in a manner that explicitly identifies the conditions to be interrogated, and the follow-on actions to be performed when criterion are met.

8.3.5 Identify data persistence needs

The operational model should be analyzed to identify the data storage and transaction processing requirements. These data persistence requirements should define the computational environment characteristics in terms of the hardware and software selected for database management functions. These requirements must address the database management systems' (DBMS) reliability metrics. Data persistence and storage is an important function for most software applications, and typical DBMSs enable transaction rollback and backup capabilities.

8.3.6 Identify data security needs

The requirements for data security must be specified to ensure that proper data access and control procedures are implemented. The requirements for data security must be evaluated to ensure that business and personal data cannot be compromised. The business rules that govern whom within the business operation can access, modify, or delete data from persistent storage must be specified. The requirements for data access control privileges for each class of users must be specified, as well as specific software requirements for access control monitoring and enforcement.

An important aspect of data security is assigning a security classification identifier for sensitive data elements. The different data security classification levels must be defined and the criteria for data elements to be assigned to each classification level should be specified. Table 8.1 shows some typical security classification levels used in the private and government sectors.

In addition, the need for the application to apply cryptography algorithms to encrypt data before it is stored or transmitted must be specified. Personnel security levels and user classes or roles that may access data must be identified, and the user classes, passwords, and data security administration responsibilities must be identified. How the application is to enforce these responsibilities, provide the

Table 8.1 Typical Private and Government Sector Security Classification Levels

Business Sector	Government Sector
Public	Unclassified
Personal information	Restricted
Sensitive	Confidential
Confidential	Secret
Private	Top secret
Competition sensitive	

administration of the personnel and group accounts, protect personal data, and monitor data access needs to be specified to ensure proper data security.

8.3.7 Identify data storage transactions

The operational model should be analyzed to identify the requirements for each data storage and retrieval transaction. The rules for executing each transaction and the conditions that would necessitate rolling back the transaction should be identified. The selected DBMS should be reviewed to identify causes for transaction deadlock situations. During functional analysis, these potential deadlock situations should be further decomposed to identify how the software product will need to monitor each transaction to detect deadlocks and how these situations should be resolved by cancelling and rolling back the transaction, or the use of other preventative measures that avert deadlock situations from occurring.

8.3.8 Identify measures of performance

During architecture definition, the measures of effectiveness (MOE) should be broken down into multiple measures of performance (MOP) that address how well the software solution is expected to achieve each MOE. Measures of performance should address measures that appraise operational performance characteristics, such as the number of transactions that should be executed within a period of time, accuracy of data transformations, and resource utilization.

8.4 Sustainment analysis tasks

The sustainment analysis tasks address specifying the requirements for product distribution, training, and support. As the software product architecture is developed, the requirements for replication, distribution, training, and sustainment processes must be revisited to ensure that the post-development processes have been adequately specified.

8.4.1 Identify post-development process operational concepts

The software post-development processes must be specified, and eventually designed, implemented, and tested. The primary post-development processes that affect software products are software replication, distribution, training, and sustainment. Software products are unique in that they are a media that can be distributed electronically over the Internet, or packaged and distributed to customers or retail outlets.

The sustainment concept should address how the end users, customers, computing environment, and software product will be supported once the software product is deployed or distributed. Software support involves software modifications that fix reported errors and enhancements of the software product through the addition of new functionalities. System hardware may involve preventive maintenance actions that are necessary to prevent the wear-down of hardware components and replacement of wornout components. The software product operational concepts must identify possible system hardware failure modes and maintenance situations to determine how the application should react. The software product may need to be "state-aware" so that data processing operations can be disabled or suspended while system maintenance actions are being conducted.

The sustainment concepts must be understood to assess the life-cycle costs for the software solution. Since the solution may be part of a business operation, the support costs of the computing environment and software product must be quantifiable and may affect design decisions.

8.4.2 Identify post-development process operational scenarios

The operational concepts should be expanded to identify the range of the anticipated operating scenarios for each post-development process. The scenarios for product distribution should address sales channels, distributors, licensing, product return policies, warranties, and software patch delivery. The scenarios for product training should address tutorials, training exercises and materials, user manuals, classroom instruction materials, and third-party training partners. The scenarios for product sustainment should address help-desk operations, problem reporting, tracking and resolution, and development of software product enhancements.

The measures of effectiveness must be identified for the overall performance of the post-development process solution (software product distribution, training, and sustainment) in achieving sustainment objectives. Measures of effectiveness define the desired effectiveness of the solution in terms of its ability to perform its mission as expressed by the operational scenarios.

8.4.3 Identify post-development process characteristics

The operational model and support concepts should be analyzed to identify and specify the requirements for packaging, distribution, and installation. Software sustainment involves "the processes, procedures, people, material, and information required to support, maintain, and operate the software aspects of a system."[3] These requirements may involve functionality that must be addressed during functional analysis and application design synthesis. In addition, the approach selected for achieving each of these processes may have a schedule impact on product release, as well as product and program costs.

Packaging may be done via external sources and may include media replication (e.g., compact disc duplication), user manuals and installation instruction reproduction, packaging artwork, product packaging, and boxing for shipment.

---

[3] Sustaining Software-Intensive Systems, May 2006, CMU/SEI-2006-TN-008, *http://www.sei.cmu. edu/reports/06tn008.pdf.*

Distribution may be done via in-house shipping resources, external postal services, or through the Internet. Internet distribution will require some effort to prepare, test, and monitor website activity that permits access to the electronic distribution packages, as well as providing electronic payment methods.

Installation may be done at the customer's operational location to properly configure the computing environment to achieve the best software performance, or it may be installed by the organization's network administrator. Commercial software installation packages may be used, and some effort will be required to prepare and verify that the installation package works properly on a variety of computer environments and with a range of operating systems.

Training delivery methods must be determined and specified to incorporate the cost associated with end-user training as part of the software deployment strategy. The common forms of training methods involve: (1) hands-on, instructor-led classroom training, where an instructor shows users how the software works and how to perform common tasks; (2) group demonstration seminars, where an instructor shows users how the software works and how to perform common tasks in a live demonstration; (3) computer-based training (CBT), which allows end users to complete interactive lessons that walk them through the process of performing common tasks, and the interactive software tests them on their performance and understanding; and (4) book-based training, where end users complete workbook lessons in how to perform common tasks, often illustrated with screenshots. Whichever training method or combination is selected, the requirements for product training must be specified. This involves identifying the set of user documentation and training materials that must be developed and available at the software deployment readiness review.

Support processes involve help-desk operations, problem reporting, tracking, resolution, software patch deployment, and software enhancement development. The establishment of the organizational capability to perform each of these processes must be planned and developed to support the software deployment readiness review. This may involve the transition of software development (engineering, implementation, and testing) equipment and CASE tools to the sustainment organization. An inventory of items to be transitioned must be addressed by the software requirements specifications to provide a basis for post-development planning.

8.4.4 Identify architectural guidelines and principles

The architectural guidelines and principles need to be established that will govern the evolution of the software architecture throughout the software product life cycle. These guidelines and principles should address the business and quality objectives for the software product, and should provide governing concepts for the structure of the product and its ability to adapt to changes in the technology components of the computational environment. In addition, these guidelines and principles should address the perspectives of various participants in the software life cycle (user, designer, tester, supporter, etc.). The architecture guidelines and principles must be measurable so that the functional and physical architectures can be evaluated to ensure compliance.

8.5 Project assessment tasks

The sustainment analysis tasks address analysis of the software requirements against project objectives, plans, and resource constraints to ensure that the requirements can be satisfied. Risks that are inherent in the requirements must be considered to provide an acceptable probability of project success.

8.5.1 Assess requirements sensitivity

The software requirements must be evaluated to determine to what extent the viability of the project is influenced by risks. Sensitivity and risk analyses[4] are concerned with factors and combinations of factors that may lead to unfavorable consequences. These factors must be identified in the project framework as risks or assumptions. The set of software requirements may need to be modified to improve the probability of project success.

8.5.2 Identify the software test strategy

The operational model should be evaluated and the initial software test plan should be prepared to establish the strategy and approach to testing the software product against the software requirements and computational environment specifications. The software test plan should identify the software test environment and provide a traceability matrix that relates requirements to the elements of the software test strategy. The software test environment includes the hardware configuration(s), operating systems, and related applications that will be involved in qualifying that the product satisfies the specified requirements.

It is important to begin test planning as the requirements become better understood since testing can consume up to 20% of the schedule and 30% of the development costs.

> *Based on the software developer and user surveys, the national annual costs of an inadequate infrastructure for software testing is estimated to range from $22.2 to $59.5 billion. Over half of these costs are borne by software users in the form of error avoidance and mitigation activities. The remaining costs are borne by software developers and reflect the additional testing resources that are consumed due to inadequate testing tools and methods.*[5]

---

[4] Sensitivity analysis tries to estimate the effect on achieving project objectives if certain assumptions do not, or only partly, materialize. Risk analysis assesses the actual risk that certain assumptions do not, or only partly, occur.

[5] National Institute of Standards & Technology (NIST), Program Office Strategic Planning, and Economic Analysis Group, Planning Report 02-3, The Economic Impacts of Inadequate Infrastructure for Software Testing, May 2002.

	Requirements Analysis	Preliminary Design	Detailed Design	Coding and Unit Testing	Integration and Testing	System Testing
1960s – 1970s	10%			80%	10%	
1980s	20%			60%	20%	
1990s	40%		30%		30%	

FIGURE 8.4

The allocation of effort to software development phases.

Software testing typically is accounted for only during the testing phases, as shown in the NIST report, and reflected in Figure 8.4. However, test planning and the establishment of test cases and procedures occur throughout the early phases of software development. Software testing must be recognized as a significant effort, and its planning must begin at the earliest possible time. While the software requirements are being analyzed, evaluated, and formalized, the challenges to testing and qualifying the software product must be identified. The product qualification section of software specifications identifies the analysis, inspection, demonstration, and test methods that will be used to confirm requirements satisfaction based on test results. The cost of software testing is an important contribution in determining overall software development costs.

8.5.3 Assess proposed changes

Changes to software requirements must be assessed to determine the impact of the change on the project framework against the necessity for the change. If a proposed change is determined to be essential for the software product to satisfy stakeholder needs, then the change may be necessary. However, the project resources may not accommodate the additional work effort necessary to incorporate the proposed change into the software architecture. The approach for performing a change impact assessment involves the following five steps:

1. Define the scope of the change proposed by identifying the work packages that would be affected by authorizing the change.
2. Determine the key differences in the proposed project state to determine the impact on the project's critical path toward achieving milestones and objectives.
3. Determine the ability of the project framework to accommodate the proposed change by adjusting work estimates, as appropriate.
4. Assess the project sensitivity or probability of success assuming the change is authorized.
5. Present the findings and recommendations to the appropriate change control board.

Change proposals should address changes to the requirements baseline once it is established and should involve one or more stakeholders to champion the proposed change. Each change proposal must be authorized by the project-level change control board. Change requests involve a change to the software architecture to facilitate software implementation, testing, or sustainment activities. Change requests must be authorized by the technical-level change control board once the software product architecture is baselined.

Each time the requirements are allowed to be modified the impact of the change on the operational process, functional and physical architectures, specifications, documentation, test plans and procedures, work breakdown structure, and other related items needs to assessed. This leads to application features that weren't originally planned and increases risk to software application quality or development schedule.

8.5.4 Assess project feasibility

The alignment of software requirements to project objectives, work packages, and risks provides the basis for understanding the feasibility of project success. The purpose of this task is to determine if the software solution can be achieved within project cost and schedule constraints. Project feasibility is dependent on the accuracy of the work plan and the technical risks associated with the software solution. Monitoring work progress against plans will confirm whether the project and technical plans accurately reflect the work to be performed. Technical risks may be reduced by initiating prototyping efforts to determine if the solution is viable and can be developed according to plans.

8.6 Establish the requirements baseline

As the requirements evolve and mature, a requirements baseline should be established and maintained to reduce the impact of *requirements creep* or continual changes to the baseline. Requirements creep implies a tendency for product requirements to be modified or supplemented as the solution is being architected and implemented. Requirements creep may be driven by a stakeholder's growing "wish list" or by developers as they recognize opportunities for improving the solution's appeal to users.

The requirements baseline represents the *design-to* set of requirements. The requirements baseline should not be established before the design solution is fairly mature and complete since changes to the requirements baseline will impact project cost projections and schedule timelines. This is why it is necessary to explore the software solution via functional analysis and application design synthesis to ensure that the requirements set is complete, consistent, achievable, and affordable.

Once the software product requirements baseline is established, all recommended changes to the requirements must be formally approved by the project change control board (CCB). Each proposed change should be documented in an engineering change proposal (ECP) with the appropriate specification and documentation change pages included.

Table 8.2 Software Requirements Documentation

Document Title	Type
Software Requirements Specification	Specification
Computational Environment Requirements Specification	Specification
Software Interface Specification	Specification
Operational Model	Design artifact
Functional Behavioral Model	Design artifact
Function Architecture Description	Design document
• Functional Component Specifications	
• Functional Unit Specifications	
• Functional Interface Specifications	
Physical Architecture Description	Design document
• Structural Component Specifications	
• Structural Unit Specifications	
• Software Interface Descriptions	
• Software Integration Strategy	
Requirements Traceability Matrix	Design artifact

As the software architecture evolves and matures, the specification and documentation trees should be updated to identify the requirements specifications, design documents, engineering drawings, and training and user manuals. Table 8.2 provides a list of the typical software requirements documentation items that comprise the software product requirements baseline.

Software Requirements Management

CHAPTER OUTLINE

Managing requirements is an essential practice that contributes to the success of any software development effort. Requirements define the scope of the work the project will execute in an attempt to satisfy stakeholders. The development of a software architecture is enabled by establishing an agreed upon set of software requirements. The software requirements must be controlled to ensure that the software architecture and implementation can satisfactorily pass acceptance testing and configuration audits. If the software requirements are not stabilized early in the project, then the project and technical plans, product architecture, and software implementation will experience continual upheaval attempting to keep up with changing requirements.

The software development must be viewed as a fixed time continuum during which the software solution must evolve from a concept to a deployable product. The software requirements disclose the ingredients for achieving success, while the project and technical plans expose the perils of navigating treacherous territory. Permitting requirements to be superfluous, ambiguous, or erratic will lead the project into a state of chaos. The development of the software architecture cannot be completed until the requirements have been stabilized and baselined.

The primary objective for the software engineering team is to establish symmetry among software requirements, project cost, and schedule objectives. If the software requirements are permitted to be changed constantly throughout the initial phases of development, then the software architecture will be continually in a state of modification. Each change to a software requirement consumes project resources by demanding design rework and replanning. While configuration management practices endeavor to control changes to software requirements, change is inevitable and must be facilitated if the project is to result in a product that is satisfactory to its stakeholders.

This chapter addresses how software engineering practices should be instituted to control requirements instability while establishing the architectural framework necessary to incorporate changes when they are deemed necessary.

9.1 Embracing change

It is not possible to conduct a technology-laden project, such as software development, believing that stakeholder requirements will not be altered from their original articulation. Stakeholders will change their requirements for two fundamental reasons:

1. Their understanding of the software product will improve as they participate in the software development effort.
2. Their business or operational situation will change from the moment the software development project is commissioned.

Change is inevitable and, therefore, must be addressed as an integral element of the development process. To accomplish this, two principles must be instituted to prepare the development team to properly contend with and manage the unavoidable onslaught of change proposals and requests. First, the project team must recognize that time is an adversary, not an ally. Every change that is authorized devours resources and deters progress toward achieving project objectives. Second, because some changes must be authorized, the project structure and product architecture must be adaptable to realize a sophisticated product that will be delivered several years in the future.

9.1.1 Time is a valuable resource

When an organization embarks on a new software development effort, it is imperative that it recognize that its scheduled delivery date is its primary ambition. It is not acceptable to squander its resources performing unnecessary or trivial tasks. Most enterprises place a large burden on development teams with excessive procedures and bureaucracy that distract from the engineering effort. Many organizations favor financial accounting, legal, and administration practices over engineering aptitude. Engineering a quality product, while making the best use of enterprise resources, must be the goal. No amount of administrative oversight will contribute to achieving this end.

Technical planning must account for administrative practices; however, the effort associated with these practices should be incorporated into each of the technical tasks definitions. The work breakdown structure (WBS) and its work packages should focus on the identification of technical effort. Each work package must identify its contribution toward achieving interim development objectives for the software product. Administrative charges must be incorporated into each work package definition and should be restrained as a resource liability and treated as an overhead charge. Documenting technical planning, software design, implementation, and test procedures are not administrative tasks.

The merits of a proposed change to stakeholder needs should be evaluated before much effort is expended on determining its impact on the project framework. Proposals that merit further consideration must be evaluated to understand the importance of the proposed change to the operational concept and the repercussions to the software product architecture and project work load. Proposed changes should be able to be integrated into the architecture without increasing product complexity or risk to achieving project cost and schedule objectives.

The software product architecture involves four primary quality attributes[1]:

1. *Integrity*, which is the ability of separately implemented software elements to work cooperatively together (software implementation).
2. *Modifiability*, which addresses the ease with which the architecture can accommodate changes (product support).
3. *Testability*, which addresses the ease with which the software product can be demonstrated to satisfy its specifications and stakeholder's needs (acceptance testing).
4. *Usability*, which is the ease of use and training of end users (training). Each of these attributes directly impacts a software life-cycle concern and total life-cycle costs.

The evaluation of implementing a desired change proposal must determine the impact of the change on the engineering solution, represented by the software product architecture. If the architecture has been designed to be modifiable, then the effect on the architecture may not be substantial. Assuming the architecture and its documentation have been kept current, then it should be relatively simple to identify the design alterations that must be accomplished to affect the proposed change. This mandates the need for extensive traceability among the software architecture elements and project control mechanisms.

The software architecture and its documentation and relationships to work packages facilitates the incorporation of proposed changes into the software product and plans. However, every change implementation affects the progress of the project as staff effort is diverted from planned activities to revise the product architecture, documentation, and plans. The impact analysis must account for progress

---

[1]See *http://www.softwarearchitectures.com/go/Discipline/DesigningArchitecture/QualityAttributes/tabid/64/Default.aspx*.

regression when assessing the effort required for the incorporation of a change into a partially complete architecture description. Original tasks may need to be revised, rescheduled, or eliminated altogether to accommodate the change. Every change will involve some rework that affects established architectural design documentation, reanalysis of previous architectural decisions, and additional analysis to incorporate the proposed change into the existing architectural framework. This potentially will result in progress being suspended while a change is assimilated into the software architecture to establish a new basis for proceeding toward an architectural conclusion.

In the final analysis, change proposals should not be considered for adoption once the product architecture is nearing completion. Initial planning estimates for the architecture definition phase of development should incorporate adequate resource and schedule leeway to account for requirements changes. With sufficient flexibility planned into the early phases of development, a number of critical change proposals may be accommodated. This preplanned schedule margin should be included in every work package, as a buffer, to ensure the achievement of the critical design review (CDR) milestone and transition to software implementation.

9.1.2 Change impact analysis

Every proposed change must be analyzed to determine if the change should be authorized and incorporated into the development framework. Prior to conducting a detailed impact assessment, the criticality of the proposed change must be established. The critical nature of a proposed change should indicate the necessity of the change from the perspective of software operational suitability. Table 9.1 identifies common industry levels of criticality associated with standard configuration management engineering change proposal priority codes. These criticality levels are intended to establish the relative merits of a change proposal that may improve the return on investment to the enterprise. The decision to initiate a change impact assessment should be based on the perceived importance of the proposed change to stakeholders.

A change impact assessment is a technical cost-benefit analysis where cost addresses the work packages necessary to incorporate the change, while the benefits are those perceived advantages to stakeholders. Intangible benefits may be hard to quantify, but future business opportunities, technical experience, and proficiency gained by undertaking the new requirement and influence on the enterprise reputation all constitute perceived advantages. A change impact assessment involves the following steps:

1. *Change network analysis.* Identification of the related technical tasks that will be affected by the requirement change. The related technical tasks affected by a change to an existing requirement can be identified relatively simply if the requirements traceability associations have been thoroughly identified and maintained. New requirements will need to establish these traceability

Table 9.1 Alignment of Software Change Proposal Criticality Levels

Configuration Management-based Engineering Change Proposal (ECP) Priority Codes	Proposed Software Change Proposal Criticality Levels
Emergency: To affect a change in operational characteristics that, if not accomplished without delay, may seriously compromise national security.	*Emergency:* To affect a change in operational characteristics that, if not implemented without delay, will seriously compromise stakeholder operational effectiveness.
To correct a hazardous condition that may result in fatal or serious injury to personnel or in extensive damage or destruction of equipment.	To correct an unsafe operational situation that may result in serious injury to personnel or in extensive damage or destruction of equipment.
Urgent: To affect a change that, if not accomplished expeditiously, may seriously compromise mission effectiveness of equipment, software, or forces.	*Essential:* To affect a change that, if not implemented, may seriously compromise operational effectiveness of equipment, software, or operational processes.
To correct a potentially hazardous condition that could result in injury to personnel or damage to equipment.	*Decisive:* To affect a change that may be significant to expanding product attractiveness to potential clientele.
To meet significant contractual requirements.	*Compliance:* To meet contractual or agreement requirements.
Routine: When emergency or urgent implementation is not applicable, required, or justified.	*Constructive:* To affect a change that, if not implemented, may be disadvantageous to product feasibility or may be advantageous to expanding product attractiveness to potential clientele.
	Subjective: To affect a change that favors one or more stakeholders' operational processes,

associations to identify the related tasks that must be assessed to determine the impact of a proposed change on the technical plan. New requirements may instigate the inclusion of additional tasks to the work plan. This includes any rework necessary to incorporate a change into the software architecture, documentation, and technical plans (especially the software implementation and testing plans).

2. *Conflict assessment.* Identification of other requirements that may be in conflict with the proposed change. Requirements may impose inconsistent, divergent, or contradictory design objectives that must be resolved before the requirements can be specified. This adjustment to conflicting requirements will impose additional rework of technical tasks and progress recession.

3. *Solution feasibility.* The ability to establish an architectural solution that satisfies the proposed change and associated conflicting design objectives may introduce additional risks to the achievement of project objectives. This typically results in establishing an architectural design that achieves an acceptable compromise among conflicting design objectives. Trade-off analysis and risk assessment of

design alternatives is essential to deriving a feasible and highly advantageous design solution.

4. *Solution cost appraisal*. Identification of the anticipated cost of incorporating the proposed change to the work plan. This includes the modification of existing work packages and inclusion of additional work packages to the work plan. The solution cost appraisal should identify the change in resources required to accomplish the change proposal, as well as modifications to task scheduling and milestone achievement.

5. *Perceived benefit appraisal*. Identification of the anticipated benefits derived from the authorization of the proposed change in terms of stakeholder satisfaction, product viability, market growth potential, potential business capture resulting from the experience gained, etc. In a contracted arrangement, the customer should fund any costs associated for incorporating a change deemed beneficial. If the cost is prohibitive, then the perceived benefits do not exceed the cost of the change.

9.1.3 Adjusting project milestones

The software development schedule should be viewed as a continuum of time in which the software product evolves from concept to operational product. Development milestones represent significant decision points in the product evolution as it transitions from one phase of development to another. At each milestone, the technical accomplishments should be reviewed to ensure that the product development is progressing suitably toward achieving project objectives. Milestones represent a hiatus from technical work to determine if the current product definition is sufficiently complete to justify the initiation of the next phase of development.

The objectives of each phase may be impacted by change proposals that have been authorized. Project milestones should not be delayed by change requests unless the number of changes is deemed excessive. The status of incorporating each change request into the software architecture should be reviewed at each milestone to understand the estimated time to complete the effort. This will result in a delay with milestone completion, and the criteria for completing the milestone should be revised to reflect the need to complete the incorporation of authorized change requests into the software architecture. This effectively extends the planned development phase completion date past the milestone review. Figure 9.1 shows the planned phase-dependent schedule and milestones and the impact authorizing change requests may have on completion criteria.

The relationship between phase completion dates and the associated milestone reviews causes confusion whenever delays occur. Each phase of development is planned by establishing the start data, duration, and planned completion date. A set of criteria must be established to determine when a phase is deemed to be complete. The milestone reviews are typically aligned with the end dates of each phase to permit the technical review of the progress of the development effort. These reviews are intended to represent program decision points on whether the project should

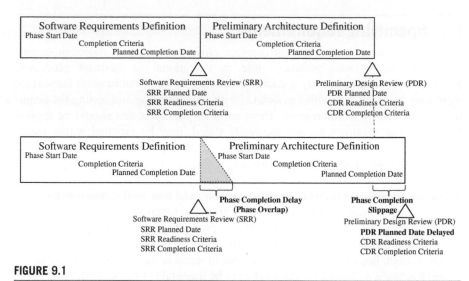

FIGURE 9.1

Phase-dependent schedule and milestones.

begin the next phase of development. Each review should be defined with a set of readiness and completion criteria. Readiness criteria establish the minimum conditions that must be satisfied for the review to be conducted. During the review, many actions may be assigned that affect the current state of the product development effort. Some of these actions must be completed prior to considering the review to be completed. Therefore, a review may not be considered successfully completed until the action items have been satisfied. In most cases, this situation will cause an overlap of two development phases that were initially planned to be conducted in series.

It is important for the project schedule to be driven by progress, not by planning dates. Planned dates for phase initiation may not be dependent on the successful completion of the prior phase or review. There may be large elements of the software architecture that are stable and can be moved into the next phase of development while action items from the milestone reviews are resolved. The challenge is to understand what elements of the architecture are impacted by an action so that effort is not expended defining or designing elements that may be changed as a result of the action.

The plans for ensuing phases of development must be updated to determine the extent of any impact the actions have on phase-dependent work packages. It may be possible to minimize the impact by realigning the work packages to make best use of personnel resources. The objective of this replanning effort is to determine if the planned milestone review dates can be achieved despite change proposals or actions resulting from the reviews.

9.2 Specifying requirements

Specifying software requirements involves close, careful, and thorough examination of the software product's role in operational or business processes. Requirements statements may appear to be straightforward, but beneath the surface there may be many difficulties associated with implementing and testing the conditions stipulated by a requirement. There are nine principles that should be applied to ensure that requirements are accurately stated, may be satisfied within established project constraints, and do not adversely affect post-development processes or life-cycle costs. These principles are:

1. Requirements express what a product must do and how well it must operate. Every requirement should identify an operational function and its associated measures of effectiveness. At the software product echelon, the requirements should address the practical functions the software product is intended to perform. Each function must be measureable in terms of the acceptable range of performance necessary for the product to be acceptable to stakeholders. At lower levels, the requirements should address individual elements of the product design. Lower-level requirements express functions in terms of data processing procedures and must identify the acceptable range of performance necessary for the product to contribute to product execution.

2. Requirements must be unambiguous. Requirements should not be expressed using language that may be vague or unclear. A properly stated requirement should be written in a manner that leads to one, and only one, interpretation. An unambiguous statement is explicit (expressing all details in a clear and obvious way, leaving no doubt as to the intended meaning), unequivocal (allowing for no doubt or misinterpretation), and distinct (clearly different and separate from others). The natural language in which requirements are stated is inherently imprecise with words having more than one meaning or connotation. Therefore, the requirements analysis tasks are intended to ensure that every requirement is properly stated to prohibit misunderstanding or interpretation by being supported with adequate analytical documentation.

3. Use design models to express concepts and eliminate potential confusion. Modeling should be used to express design concepts to stakeholders and members of the development team. Models may be used to express the behavior (functions and performance) of a product and its characteristics. Models may be static (e.g., drawing or diagram) or dynamic (e.g., executable, mock-up or prototype, simulation), and should be used wherever necessary to explain in greater detail the meaning of the requirements.

4. Requirements should not impose unnecessary design or implementation constraints. A constraint limits the freedom of the development team and restricts the solution space. Requirements that enter the realm of the solution should be written as a suggestion to clarify stakeholder desires.

5. Requirements should be challenged if they appear excessive or consequential. Stakeholder needs should be understood by challenging the operational or business demands for a requirement. Such challenges, if substantiated, improve the understanding of the development team and clarify any assumptions that may have been inferred from initial consultations. Stakeholders have grandiose expectations and little appreciation for the intricacy associated with some software gymnastics (i.e., the performance of a series of complex mental or physical operations with great agility and skill). Many requirements may be simplified or diminished when stakeholders are made aware of their exaggerated demands.

6. Requirements impose costs and schedule ramifications. Every requirement involves a cost associated with product development, post-development operations, or product sustainment. Requirements should be analyzed to understand the life-cycle cost implications of each requirement. There may be alternative ways to express a requirement that alleviate software development exposure to risks.

7. Requirements may foster design complexity. Requirements may be stated in a manner that implies or amplifies product complexity. Diminishing the complexity of the product is an imperative principle that reduces product development and sustainment costs, as well as promotes ease of use. Trade-off analysis should be performed to evaluate alternative requirement articulations to determine their impact on design complexity.

8. Requirements should not relinquish control over interface definitions. Whenever a software product must interface with another system, whether it is operational or under development, the software development team must participate in the definition of the interface if it is to be held accountable. Whenever the span of control of the software development team is relinquished, their ability to properly plan the scope of the development effort is impacted. External systems may be aging and in need of technology refreshment or redevelopment. It is important to understand the longevity of the interfacing systems before mandating interface control. Redefining an interface may provide significant improvement in software performance.

9. Risks always originate with the requirements. Requirements should be assessed to identify potential risks to achieving project success. Requirements are the source of all risks and the risks imposed by each requirement should be appraised before the requirement is embraced. Requirements that involve severe risks should be simplified to permit the initial software delivery to be achieved within costs and project constraints. The design and implementation of a risk-burdened requirement can then be pursued in parallel without jeopardizing project success. Requirements should be evaluated by answering the following questions:
   - Can the requirement be satisfied without consuming a disproportionate amount of technical resources?
   - What are the potential consequences that may arise if the requirement cannot be satisfied?

- What are the best-case, probable, and worst-case scenarios associated with an attempt to satisfy a requirement?
- How can the requirement be restated to eliminate or diminish the risks it imposes to project success?

9.3 Requirement decomposition and allocation

Initial software requirements are generally a substantial, complex covenant against which the delivered product is to be qualified. Every requirement must be translated in form from natural language into a set of design features, characteristics, or quality attributes of the software product that can be implemented. This fundamental premise differentiates software engineering, as described in this book, from existing software development methodologies or practices. The translation of a requirement into a design requires the application of software engineering practices to design, plan, implement, and sustain software products. Beginning with software requirements, the technical organizations must collaborate to establish a software product architecture that can be implemented, tested, and sustained. Requirements must be able to be traced throughout the product architectural design, test cases and procedures, technical plans, and control mechanisms. This traceability facilitates the technical team's responsiveness to proposed changes to stakeholder needs, software requirements, or design challenges. Figure 9.2 identifies the requirement decomposition and allocation flow.

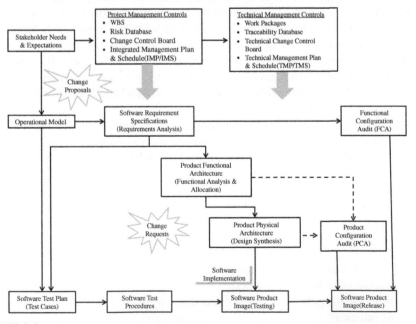

FIGURE 9.2

Requirement decomposition and allocation flow.

Requirements are decomposed to identify lower-level functional and performance requirements that are necessary to satisfy the original requirements. Decomposition provides a basis for identifying, in increasing levels of detail, how the software product will perform its operational functions. Requirements decomposition must be performed to break large, complex functions into elementary functions that can be used to develop structural design concepts. Requirements decomposition is necessary to examine the problem space addressed by a requirement and to determine the sequential or concurrent functions that must be performed to provide an adequate software solution to that requirement.

9.3.1 **Functional analysis**

It is not possible to decompose operational or business requirements directly into software structural elements, such as classes. Requirements must be decomposed into subrequirements for which design solutions are straightforward, uncomplicated, and unproblematic. Therefore, the operational requirements for the software product must first be decomposed to identify the intermediary and root functions (components and units) that the software product must accomplish.

Functional analysis is the software engineering practice by which operational functions, expressed by the software requirements, are decomposed into transitional (functional component) and rudimentary (functional unit) functions. The resulting functional architecture identifies and specifies the complete set of functions that the design solution must comprise. This practice emphasizes a top-down methodology for breaking the problem down into a complete set of functions that the design solution must exhibit. However, the practice involves iterating up and down the functional hierarchy to resolve functional complexity challenges.

9.3.2 **Performance allocation**

The performance associated with the operational requirements must be satisfied by the combination of functions. Therefore, the functional solution must satisfy the operational performance characteristics established by the operational requirements. The functional timing and resource utilization of the functional solution must resolve the performance requirements specified for the software product.

Performance allocation involves the establishment of performance budgets as the operational functions are decomposed. Root functions must then be analyzed to determine the range of execution performance measures utilizing computer science, mathematics, and knowledge of the computing environment performance characteristics. Functional performance budgets must be revised to establish the functional specifications for each element of the functional architecture. The functional architecture is declared to be complete when the functional specifications for functional components and units can be verified to satisfy the software product requirements.

The allocation of performance requirements throughout the functional architecture establishes the basis for achieving software product performance requirements. The objective of software performance engineering is to achieve response time, throughput, and resource utilization levels that meet specified performance objectives. Software performance is dependent on the characteristics of the computing environment. Computing environment characteristics that must be considered during software architecture definition include, but are not limited to, the following:

1. Execution time
2. Memory utilization
   a. Primary memory (random-access memory, RAM) consumption
   b. Virtual memory (secondary storage) consumption
3. Swap time (virtual memory management read and write latency)
4. Data storage latency (the time it takes to access a particular location in storage)
5. Data storage throughput (the rate at which information can be read from or written to the storage)
6. Interrupt latency (the time between the generation of an interrupt by a device and the servicing of the device)

9.3.3 Structural unit synthesis

Design synthesis is the software engineering practice that establishes the structural units of the design solution or physical architecture. Structural units represent the building blocks of the software product and are specified to facilitate software implementation (coding and testing). Structural units are derived by combining similar functional units and resolving differences among the functional specifications. This results in an integrated specification for each structural unit. During software implementation, the majority of the coding is accomplished at the unit level of development.

9.3.4 Structural component synthesis

Structural components are determined by identifying structural units that need to be integrated to provide intermediary structural assemblies. Structural components represent the incremental assembly, integration, and testing of the software product providing successive levels of functionality. Structural components establish the strategy for software component integration and testing to be accomplished during software implementation.

Structural components are specified by identifying the functional and performance characteristics that arise as a result of the integration of lower-level structural components or units. During software implementation, structural components may require additional code to be generated to administer execution control logic. This will result in the recognition of internal and external interfaces that must be exercised during component integration and testing.

9.4 Requirement traceability

Software product requirements must be traceable throughout the functional and physical architectures to facilitate stakeholder change proposals, design change

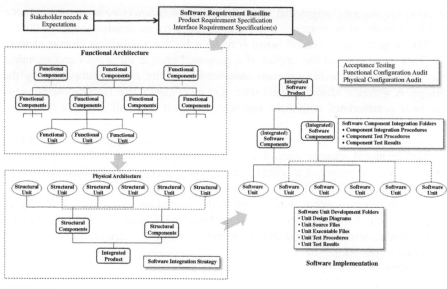

FIGURE 9.3

Traceability within the software product architecture.

requests, and product configuration audits. These architectural perspectives (functional and physical architectures) establish the software *product* design (referred to as the *architectural design*), which is distinctly different from the structural unit programmatic design devised during software implementation. During software implementation, each structural unit specification is transformed into an explicit design utilizing computing language–specific constructs. This programmatic design is utilized to implement software units in computing language instructions that are particular to the implementation language (e.g., Java, C+). Figure 9.3 shows how requirements must be traced from stakeholder needs to software implementation units and components.

It is necessary to establish traceability among the stakeholder needs, software requirements, architecture, implementation, and test artifacts to enable the development teams to be responsive to proposed changes. Traceability provides the ability to assess the potential impact of proposed changes and is critical to ensuring that the software development project can achieve its objectives.

9.4.1 Change control

Within a software development project there are formal and informal configuration management practices that affect the manner in which change requests and proposals are processed. To simplify the concept of change control, a change proposal should be considered for proposed changes that require additional project resources (costs and schedule) to be incorporated into project and technical plans. Change requests are design changes that affect the software architecture or implementation and are considered necessary to achieve specified software requirements.

The project change control board is responsible for authorizing change proposals. This mandates that the impact of a proposed change on project and technical plans be socialized with important stakeholders whom may be impacted by the change. A technical change impact statement must ensure that the proposed change can be accommodated within the augmented project cost and schedule resources. It may be possible to negotiate the elimination or adjustment to other software requirements if the project cost and schedule objectives are to remain unchanged.

The technical change control board is responsible for authorizing change requests that are proposed to affect a change in a previously specified element of the software product architecture. A change request represents suggested modifications to the software architecture definition that remediate obstacles, complexity, or obscurity with elements of the software architecture. Change requests should simplify software implementation and test efforts or resolve architectural specification flaws and imprecision.

9.4.2 Configuration audits

Ultimately, requirements traceability is critical to supporting the functional and physical configuration audit. The software architecture provides the mapping of the software product configuration to its implementation, test results, and documentation artifacts. Configuration audits are performed prior to software deployment or distribution to confirm that the final software product:

- Satisfies the specified software requirements.
- Incorporates authorized change proposals and requests.
- Is ready for software sustainment with accurate design documentation, operational manuals, and source files under configuration control.

Formulating the Functional Architecture

10

This chapter describes the functional architecture and its various forms of representation. It also provides guidance by which the functional architecture is derived. Chapter 11 establishes a set of detailed tasks for the functional analysis and allocation practice necessary to transform the software requirements specifications into the functional architecture. The functional architecture provides a basis for deriving the structural configuration and physical architecture for the software product. The physical architecture involves the documentation, drawings, diagrams, etc. that express the structural configuration of the software product. Among these tasks are points of departure that identify linkages to other software engineering tasks, such as requirement verification, software analysis to assess design complexity and risks, software design synthesis, and architecture control. These links are identified within the detailed task descriptions provided in Chapter 11.

10.1 **Motivation for the functional architecture**

The functional architecture provides a working view of the software product with no physical or structural features. It is derived from the operational or business model from which the software requirements were specified. At the uppermost layer it identifies the principal software functions that interact with external entities to describe the software response to external stimuli. The principal functions are decomposed to provide additional details concerning the data processing services that the software product must provide. Figure 10.1 addresses the role of the functional architecture as the initial step in the translation of software requirements into a design for the software product.

The functional architecture expresses the purpose or use of the software product for which it is to be structurally designed. While the operational model describes the role of the software product in executing a business or operational process, the functional architecture explains the data processing actions the software product must perform. The functional architecture must ultimately be decomposed into elementary functions that yield a single result when invoked. Elementary functions are labeled functional units and must be specified to support the structural design of the software product.

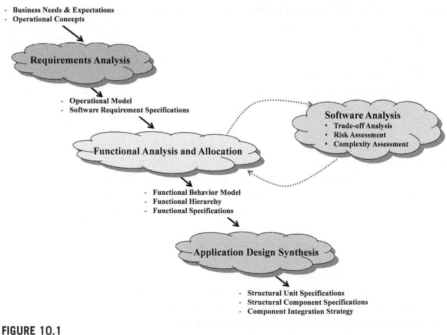

FIGURE 10.1

Role of the functional architecture.

The functional analysis and allocation practice provides an approach for transforming software requirements into the functional transactions that the software product must enable. The functional architecture represents a comprehensive, integrated set of data processing transactions. Functional analysis and allocation is employed to achieve the following six fundamental design challenges confronting software product quality.

1. *Elaborating a solution.* The design solution involves many individual software elements that must work together to support the business or operational process. This encompasses numerous data processing transactions, services, or threads of behavior. Software data processing transactions involve many analytical combinations and permutations that are difficult to comprehend. Functional analysis provides the means for identifying the myriad of possible data processing sequences the software must facilitate. The functional analysis and allocation practice systematically identifies and investigates discrete transactional threads to completely specify a functional solution.
2. *Clarifying ambiguity.* Language, which is used to communicate and express requirements, involves imprecise, vague, unclear, ill-defined, inexact, nebulous words and expressions. Functional analysis ensures that every function is clearly specified so that no misunderstanding exists in the description of the functional solution.
3. *Resolving assumptions.* All assumptions must be resolved with stakeholders before a solution can be finalized. Assumptions that are not challenged and resolved may result in a software product that does not effectively satisfy customer needs and expectations. Functional analysis can be used to speculate about and evaluate assumptions, thereby eliminating judgment or opinions as the basis for product design. Functional analysis accentuates the existence of incomplete or inconclusive information to draw attention to suppositions that are not substantiated.
4. *Achieving performance objectives.* Specified performance requirements or objectives must be comprehended and the software product designed to achieve these criteria. Software design techniques, drawings, and models must be utilized that exhibit software performance characteristics. Performance measures at the software product level must be allocated to provide lower-level design aspirations. Initial performance budgets must be established against which design strategies can be assessed. Performance requirements can then be allocated and specified for the design elements once the solution has been appraised to be suitable.
5. *Determining resource utilization.* Data processing efficiency and effectiveness depends on the regulation of computing resource utilization. The functional architecture must model resource utilization to permit the design to be optimized for efficient and effective execution. The software design must be sensitive to the impact of resource utilization on performance objectives.
6. *Simplifying the solution.* Complexity is never a desirable characteristic of any software product. The user interface design and user interactions must not be

convoluted. This will require extensive user training and may dissuade potential customers from adopting the software product as an institutional standard. Design complexity directly translates into code intricacy and obscurity. Software sustainment costs will increase in proportion to the complexity of the design. The functional architecture provides the initial design paradigm where complexity can be regulated.

The objective of functional analysis and allocation is to formulate a complete, consistent, and verified functional architecture that conforms to the specified software requirements. The software architecture must identify every data processing task, including failure detection, remediation actions, and consequential degraded modes of operation. The functional architecture is complete when every functional component, unit, and interface has been specified. Functional units and interfaces are the "building blocks" used to derive the physical architecture for the software product. The physical architecture identifies and specifies the structural software elements that will be elaborated (designed, coded, integrated, and tested) during software implementation. Chapter 12 describes the physical architecture and how it is derived from the functional architecture.

10.2 Functional architecture ontology

This section identifies the nomenclature used to describe a functional architecture. According to Dictionary.com, an ontology is "the hierarchical structuring of knowledge about things by subcategorizing them according to their essential qualities." Therefore, the following "things" are entities used in describing and documenting the functional architecture. The labels are not specific to software engineering and are applicable to describe the functionality of any human-made product.

10.2.1 Functional component

A functional component represents a complex task the software product must perform. A functional component is activated when control is transferred to the component for execution. Every function transforms one or more data items, in the form of an input or global or local variables, into an output data item or processed variable. Functional complexity is apparent when any of the following conditions exists:

- A function involves several data transformation actions and at least one action has no clear, uncomplicated solution.
- A function involves distinguishable conditional responses.
- A function involves multiple interfaces with other functions or external systems, users, or other software applications, such as databases.

Functional complexity compels the solution to be further decomposed into less complex functional components. Decomposition requires that a functional component be broken down into two or more subfunctions. The designation of a function as a component indicates that it involves a lower level of functional detail to unambiguously express the manner by which the data processing or transformation is performed. Several layers of decomposition may be necessary to establish a noncomplex solution.

10.2.2 Functional unit

Functional units represent elements at the lowest level of the hierarchy. A functional unit signifies that no further decomposition is necessary to unambiguously express the solution. Functional units can be recognized when the design or implementation of the function can be easily comprehended. Functional units should perform a single, noncomplex task; should receive data items as input from a limited number of sources; and should output data processing results to a limited number of receiving functions or external elements.

10.2.3 Data item

Data items represent information that must be processed by the software product. Data items may be complex in nature and may need to be decomposed to express the specific data elements involved with the data processing. For example, a debit card is encoded with account information that is read by an automated teller machine's (ATM) card reader. The initial data item may be generalized as "account information." However, it is important to be precise in expressing the various pieces of information encoded on the debit card. Typical customer information may include customer name, card expiration date, bank routing number, checking account number, and savings account number. Each of these information elements must be identified as a data item at some level of the functional decomposition to express the data specification.

Data items involve characteristics that may affect the performance of the software product. Data has a size attribute expressing the amount of information represented by the data item, which may affect storage, retrieval, and transmission rates. Transmission rates affect the time it takes to transfer a data item between functions, which is constrained by the computing environment's internal bus subsystem that transfers data between components inside a computer or between computers via an external interface. The capacity of an external interface also affects the transmission rate of data from the host computing device to external systems.

10.2.4 Functional interface

Data that is exchanged between functions represents a functional interface. A functional interface identifies a requirement for data to be exchanged. The functional interface provides the initial basis for establishing a functional interface specification. It should identify and characterize the data elements being communicated among the interacting software functions internal to the software product.

10.2.5 **External interface**

Information that is exchanged between the software product and external systems, devices, users, or other software applications represents an external interface. External interfaces should have been specified during the software requirements analysis and addressed by the functional architecture to support interface design.

10.2.6 **Control structures**

Control structures provide the means for guiding execution flow to perform a data processing task accounting for the conditional treatment of data processing intermediate results. From the operational model perspective, control structures represent business rules or operational procedures that determine how a process should be executed. Within the functional architecture, control structures represent the decision or computational logic that determines how the data processing execution should proceed. The general control structures are as follows:

- *Branch*—a path of execution involving a sequence of data processing tasks or functions.
- *Concurrency*—enables multiple threads of behavior or branches to be initiated and executed in parallel.
- *Selection*—enables one thread of behavior to be initiated based on some conditional argument.
- *Iteration*—enables a thread of behavior to be repeated one or more times.
- *Trigger*—activates an action, process, or series of events.

These control structures have comparable constructs implemented by most computer languages. However, for the purposes of establishing the functional architecture, it is not desirable to adhere to the implementation-specific control constructs. A concurrency is analogous to task synchronization in the Ada and C++ programming languages. A selection represents an If (If…Goto, If … Then, If … Then … Else) or Case statements in most programming languages. Iteration represents a loop mechanism similar to For … Next, Do While, Do Until, or ForEach (collection control loop) in most programming languages.

10.2.7 **Resource**

A resource represents any quantifiable entity of which the availability may impact the performance of the software product. Resource utilization influences the performance assessment of the software product and typically involves a dynamic random behavior. Resources can be used to understand the computing environment characteristics that affect execution timing, or other assets that impede data processing effectiveness. Resources have several characteristics that affect software performance:

- *Inventory capacity.* The volumetric quantity that identifies the maximum number of units that can be present at any time.

- *Inventory stock.* The amount of a resource that is available to the support data processing needs of the software product.
- *Amount consumed.* Functions may consume a resource drawing down the inventory stock, thereby reducing the amount of the resource available to other functions. Functions may replenish a resource representing the restocking of the inventory.
- *Amount capture.* A function may acquire a reuseable resource to support its execution and release the resource when the function has finished executing.
- *Resupply amount.* The amount of a consumable resource that is replenished by a function.

10.2.8 Data Store

A data store is a repository that retains digital data and supports data preservation or persistence. Data stores support data storage and retrieval functions that involve transactions to search and manipulate data records. Issues surrounding data store transactions that affect software performance include data store availability, transaction processing and rollback, data model definition, data security and access control, and database query optimization.

10.3 Conceiving the functional architecture

The functional architecture involves answering the question, "What functions (data processing tasks) must the software product perform to satisfy the specified software requirements?" This is a process of exploring the solution space from available information without addressing the structural arrangement of modules, subroutines, objects, or other physical forms of software delineation. This should be achieved by establishing successive layers of refinement or decomposition of functional, data, and control flows, which results in two necessary perspectives: the functional hierarchy and the behavioral models.

The behavioral model provides a more precise description of the software functionality than the functional hierarchy. Complex functions identified in the behavioral model should be decomposed into individual models that describe how each function should be performed. The decomposition of functions from a behavioral perspective can be used to generate the functional hierarchy. However, it is not necessary to begin functional analysis activity with the behavioral modeling practice. Functions derived from the software requirements can be methodically decomposed to create the functional hierarchy before analyzing functional behaviors. The two practices—decomposition and behavioral modeling—are complementary and should be applied to explicitly describe the functional solution.

The approach to preparing the functional architecture involves five steps:

1. *Derive the primary functions.* The software requirements must be analyzed to identify the primary functions the software product must perform. Since the

software requirements describe the software product from an operational or business process perspective, the identification of primary functions may not correspond to or coincide with the requirements. This may be reflective of the terminology used to describe the operational or business process. The software requirements must be translated into software functions that reflect semantics associated with the appropriate software domain. A software domain reflects a field of study that defines a set of common requirements, terminology, and functionality for any software program constructed to solve a problem in that field.

2. *Decompose primary functions.* The primary functions can be assumed to be complex since they have been derived from the operational or business process descriptions. Each complex function represents a software task of which the solution is too extensive or challenging to comprehend. Functional decomposition involves reducing complexity by investigating the problem space to improve the understanding from which a design solution can be conceived.

   - *Functional decomposition.* Functional decomposition identifies the procedural operations by which a complex function will be performed. In most cases, there are multiple approaches by which a complex function can be accomplished, and each design approach or alternative will exhibit different performance and architectural quality characteristics.

   - *Model functional behaviors.* Construct a model of how the function behaves by identifying the functional sequences, data items, and control mechanism necessary to perform the source function. The performance characteristics and resource utilization criteria specified for the source function must be budgeted or allocated among subfunctions.

   - *Evaluate alternative approaches.* Every functional decomposition or behavioral model involves design alternatives. Contending alternatives should utilize the software analysis activity to evaluate, prioritize, and select a preferred solution. Each solution should be assessed to understand its effectiveness, suitability, and risks in terms of satisfying the specified performance requirements and desired software quality characteristics.

   - *Identify implied behaviors.* Functional solutions should be evaluated to identify inferred, complementary, or supplementary behaviors that enhance the data processing thoroughness. It should be assumed that the specification is incomplete and has converged on a suitable expression of the data processing actions. The functional solution must be meticulously evaluated to identify behaviors needed to contend with every possible situation that may arise during data processing.

   - *Optimize the functional solution.* The functional solution should be evaluated to identify aspects that have the largest influence on software performance and resource utilization. Important aspects of the initial functional solution should be refined to increase the effectiveness of the solution, such as data integrity, possible causes of failure conditions, input/output data item definitions, and the precision of data transformation algorithms.

3. *Specify the solution.* The elements of the functional solution resulting from the decomposition of a complex function must be specified. The requirements for each element must establish the performance and resource utilization objectives for each subfunction. Data persistence transaction characteristics, failure detection and recovery actions, and data item properties must be quantified. Specification of the functional solution provides the basis for further decomposition, behavioral analysis, and specification of the remaining complex functions.

4. *Assess functional complexity.* The functional solution must be assessed to determine if further functional analysis and allocation is necessary.
   - If a function is determined to be complicated, then repeat steps 2 and 3 for each complex function.
   - If a function is determined to be noncomplex, then its specifications and hierarchical and behavioral diagrams must be placed under technical configuration control.

5. *Simplify the functional architecture.* As the functional architecture evolves, it is prudent to review the functional configuration to identify opportunities by which the architecture can be simplified.

10.4 Documenting the functional architecture

The functional architecture involves a set of software engineering artifacts (diagrams, models, and specifications) that must be prepared to document the functional architecture. While many software methodologies prescribe a wide variety of diagrams, the number of fragmented representations fails to provide a complete, cohesive view of the software architecture. This challenges the ability of stakeholders and members of the software development effort to perceive the "wholeness" of the solution.

Two principle representations of the functional architecture are necessary to express the entirety of the solution: functional hierarchy and behavioral model. In addition, there are four additional representations that support the analysis and specification of the functional solution: functional timeline, resource utilization profile, functional specifications, and requirement allocation sheets. The following subsections describe each of these engineering artifacts in terms of its purpose and features.

10.4.1 Functional hierarchy

The functional hierarchy conveys the transformation of software specifications into the essential functions (functional units) that the software product must perform to execute the operational or business processes. It provides traceability of the software requirements to the initial software product design configuration.

The functional hierarchy provides a gage of the software product complexity in three manners:

- The number of levels of decomposition.
- The breadth of each level of decomposition.
- The number of fundamental functional elements (functional units) from which the structural design is to be derived.

The number of levels of decomposition will not be consistent throughout the functional hierarchy. The number of layers involved with the decomposition of a primary function is a good indication of the complexity of the data processing transaction being executed. The breadth of each level of decomposition implies the complexity that will be encountered during software component integration and testing. The number of functional units provides an initial indication of the scope of the software unit design, code, and testing activity. However, this indicator will be firmly established as a result of the software design synthesis activity. During software design synthesis, common or closely coupled functional units may be combined into a single structural unit, thereby reducing the anticipated workload for software unit design, coding, and testing.

10.4.2 Behavior model

The behavior model provides decisive information that supports the specification of functional components and units. It expresses a complete, precise representation of the software behavior in a notation that eliminates conjecture, assumptions, or speculation. The behavior model may be a static or dynamic model of the software product execution of data processing transactions and identifies the responses to potential data transformation results, operator errors, and hardware malfunctions.

The behavior model is essential to the software engineering activity because it provides an unambiguous expression of the various data processing transactions that must be performed. The behavior model forms the basis for software design, enabling design alternatives to be evaluated and resolved. It provides the design framework from which the functional timeline and resource utilization profile are formulated. The functional behavior model describes the:

- Sequence of functions that must be performed (functional flow).
- Data flow among the software product and external systems, applications, or operators (data flow).
- Data flow among functions or functional interfaces (data flow).
- Business rules or control logic that determine the execution flow among conditional functional sequences (control flow).
- Resources necessary to accomplish each function (resource utilization).

Control logic can be associated with the result of a function and is modeled as a function that terminates with a selection among multiple functional flow sequences. The selection of which behavioral path to proceed to execute may be deterministic to force the selection of a desired sequence, or probabilistic to randomly select a sequence to execute. The behavioral model may include a probability distribution equation to represent the random selection. The following is a list of common probability distribution functions:

- Bernoulli distribution
- Binomial distribution
- Uniform (discrete) distribution
- Poisson binomial distribution
- Geometric distribution
- Logarithmic distribution
- Exponential distribution
- Pareto distribution
- Chi-square distribution
- Weibull distribution

An executable behavior model can be utilized to support design trade-off analysis, an element of the software analysis practice (see Chapter 14). Rather than relying on abstract diagrams, an executable model provides a working prototype of the software product. Competing design alternatives can be compared to determine which design approach performs best under anticipated operational conditions. A Monte Carlo simulation can be achieved by enclosing the model in a looping control structure and conducting repeated analysis of functional timing and resource utilization. This enables the probabilistic identification of critical paths through the model that can be used to guide the development of software test cases. The executable model also is valuable in verifying that the functional architecture satisfies the specified software requirements.

10.4.3 Functional timeline

The functional timeline provides an assessment of the time required to execute each operational scenario or behavioral thread. The timeline depicts the duration for every action that occurs during execution and enables the analysis of time-critical design requirements. Variability of execution duration can be provided with the generation of random outcomes that affect business rules or control logic. Execution timeline analysis is used to determine if the software performance will satisfy the specified requirements and can highlight behavioral deficiencies with the current functional architecture. Trade-off analysis can be used to mitigate software performance impediments and resolve resource contention issues that result in deadlock or thrashing situations.

10.4.4 Resource utilization profile

The resource utilization profile depicts the percentage of a resource that is actually occupied, as compared with the total time that the component is available for use. Resource availability may have significant impact on the performance of the software product during peak load situations. The availability of a resource can be assessed to be restrictive if it is overused and impacts transaction processing. These results may be used to modify the software functional architecture or to modify the computing environment definition to enhance resource availability.

10.4.5 Functional specifications

A specification must be developed for each functional component and unit. These specifications provide the traceability among elements in the functional hierarchy to the specified software requirements. The functional unit specifications are utilized during software design synthesis to establish structural unit specification (see Chapter 13). A fundamental principle of engineering is the specification of every part or component involved in the design of the product. Functional specifications are also necessary to support software reusability. The selection of reusable software components is predicated on how well a commercially available (commercial off the shelf, COTS) or previously developed (nondevelopmental item, NDI) software component satisfies the required functionality and performance.

10.4.6 Requirement allocation sheet

The requirements allocation sheet (RAS) identifies the elements of the software architecture and computing environment that contribute to the achievement of software requirements. The RAS provides the detailed information concerning the manner in which the software functions, coupled with the computing environment characteristics, satisfy the specified software requirements. It provides traceability to trade-study results and design decision memorandums from which the resulting allocation was derived. The RAS must be aligned with the requirements traceability matrix, which provides additional traceability among the software engineering design artifacts for each software requirement.

Functional Analysis and Allocation Practice

Functional analysis and allocation is the practice that transforms the software requirements into a functional architecture. Functional analysis is the first step in exploring the customers' problem domain and deriving a design solution. The operational activities assigned to the software product represent complex functions that need to be decomposed for which a structural design solution is pursued. The functional analysis technique involves the following fundamental tasks:

1. *Complexity analysis*—evaluation of a function to determine if it warrants further simplification by decomposing the function into subfunctions. The decomposition of a function results in the identification of smaller, less-complex functions

for which a design solution can be unambiguously distinguished. The result of the functional decomposition is a functional hierarchy that depicts the manner in which complex functions have been simplified, clarified, and specified.

2. *Behavioral analysis*—involves an integrated modeling approach to postulate how the software product will execute a sequence of functions to perform operational transactions or data processing actions. Behavioral analysis results in integrated behavioral models that involve functional flows, control flows, data flows, and resource utilization.

3. *Performance allocation*—allocates software performance requirements among the functional elements of the behavioral model and computing environment. Software product performance is reliant on the computing environment performance characteristics that may need to be augmented as a result of the functional analysis activity.

4. *Architectural assessment*—review of the evolving functional architecture to ensure that the software requirements are being satisfied, the projected software performance will tolerate anticipated utilization loads, and the functional architecture is noncomplex and will facilitate product sustainment and enhancement throughout its life cycle.

The functional behavior model represents the decomposition of the operational model with a focus on comprehending the software product's functional and performance qualities. The behavior model is derived to explicitly specify the software response to a variety of stimuli and inputs. As the software behaviors are explored, the specified software requirements may need to be revised to reflect the level of performance that can be achieved given the limitation of the computing environment. Behavioral alternatives should be investigated before embracing a solution with which to proceed into design synthesis. Competing alternatives should be evaluated via trade-off analysis and risk assessments to aid the selection of the optimal alternative in terms of life-cycle costs, risks, and performance.

Functional analysis identifies data processing operations or *what* the software product is expected to do to support the operational or business process. Functional analysis should not impose structural design or implementation details. This implies that it is not necessary to completely specify computational constructs, data structures, or resource characteristics. The software design synthesis practice establishes the structural composition, arrangement, and design specifications for the elements of the physical architecture. Software design synthesis configures the physical architecture that identifies *how* the software product will be structured to provide the specified functionality.

The approach to functional analysis and allocation described in this chapter has been adapted from the systems engineering discipline. It has been modified to address the unique challenges associated with the design of software products independent of the implementation language. However, key software implementation personnel should participate in the functional analysis activity to ensure that the functional architecture can be realized given the implementation language constraints. Figure 11.1 depicts the tasks that contribute to software functional analysis and allocation.

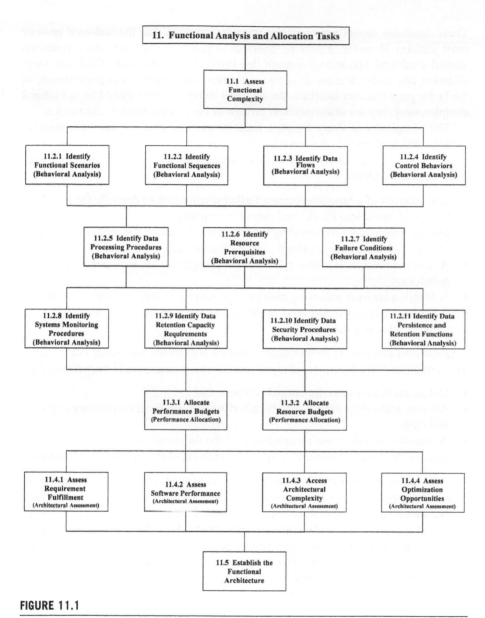

FIGURE 11.1

Functional analysis and allocation tasks.

11.1 Assess functional complexity

Functional analysis and allocation is performed at every level of the functional architecture. The initial set of functions that form the top layer of the functional hierarchy are derived from the specified software requirements or operational model.

These functions should represent the primary functions that the software product must perform. However, it may be desirable to group and organize these functions around a software operational concept that involves some form of initial user identification and authentication or software application initiation and presentation of the home graphical user interface. At this level, every function should be considered complex since they are at the business process or operational level of abstraction.

The complexity of every function must be assessed to determine if it necessitates further decomposition to provide an uncomplicated, unambiguous functional depiction. Functional complexity may be recognized when any of the following conditions are evident:

- The behavior of a function requires further clarification to describe the transformation of inputs into the desired output or response.
- Multiple approaches to providing the functionality can be conceptualized and the most advantageous approach must be determined.
- A function involves business rules or control logic that are ambiguous or nebulous.
- A function involves accessing multiple data storage or retrieval transactions.
- A function involves inputs from multiple sources, such as users, external systems, or other functions.

Functions that require further decomposition are labeled functional components. The remainder of the functional analysis and allocation tasks should be performed to:

- Define the behaviors of functional components.
- Allocate software performance characteristics among functional components and units.
- Assess the suitability and completeness of the functional architecture.
- Specify the design requirements for every element of the functional architecture.

As a rule of thumb, functional analysis continues until a function is recognized of which the implementation is noncomplex and its behavior can be specified without further investigation. These noncomplex functional elements are labeled functional units and represent the fundamental features from which the physical architecture will be configured. The number of levels of decomposition will vary throughout the functional hierarchy due to the uneven complexity associated with a functional problem and its solution. It is not necessary to strive to have a uniform leveling throughout the functional hierarchy. The intent is to ensure that the behavior of each function is well understood and that each functional unit can be unambiguously specified and implemented. Several guidelines apply to functional decomposition:

1. A function cannot be decomposed into a single function. Decomposition warrants the identification of at least two subfunctions.
2. The need for further decomposition is driven by functional complexity, and therefore the functional hierarchy will not be horizontally symmetrical or vertically consistent in depth.

3. No further decomposition is necessary when a function's design solution can be comprehended or exists as a reusable software module.
4. Functions that involve several data transformation steps may not require further decomposition if the design solution is considered manageable.
5. If a function involves data transformation steps that are common with other functions, then decomposing the function represents an opportunity for establishing common subroutines that can reduce software complexity by eliminating duplication.
6. Avoid identifying a function that generates more than one output or product. With some deliberation it should be possible to identify an abstract function which can then be decomposed into subfunctions which generate alternative outputs or products.

11.2 Behavioral analysis

Behavioral analysis involves a set of tasks that are intended to fully explore the functional solution space. The objective is to describe how the software product must respond to user inputs or computing environment state change or failure conditions. Behavioral analysis tasks construct functional design models of data processing transactions. The intent is to explicitly design how each transaction will be conducted, including any possible error condition or computing environment failure or degraded mode of operation.

The behavior model depicts how a complex function will be executed. The behavior of the software product must be specified in sufficient detail to unambiguously express how each function will be performed to enable the operational process to be accomplished. The behavior modeling technique may produce static (nonexecutable) or dynamic (executable) models. Dynamic models are preferred since they provide an analytical verification of the design adequacy and may be used to support trade-off analysis. Therefore, the behavior model must address the following elements:

1. *Organizations or actors*—the business or operational organizations or personnel roles that interact with the software product.
2. *External systems*—the elements of the computing environment, external systems, and other software applications that interface with the software product.
3. *Data stores*—the abstract data repositories that support data storage and retrieval transactions.
4. *Functional sequences*—the sequential flow of data processing actions. Parallel threads of behavior can be used to model concurrency or conditional execution (selection of execution flow based on business or control rules) of functional sequences (see task 11.2.2).
5. *Data items*—the information elements that represent inputs and outputs of functions (see task 11.2.3).

6. *Control mechanisms*—the enforcement of business or control rules to decide which conditional branch is to be executed. Loops provide a control mechanism that causes a segment of the functional sequence to be reexecuted one or more times. (*Note:* A loop may be continuous (neverending) or terminated based on the achievement of a conditional criteria (e.g., Do...Until)) (see task 11.2.4).

7. *Computing resources*—the consumable or reusable assets provided by the computing environment, such as memory, data storage, and communication interface bandwidth (see task 11.2.6).

11.2.1 Identify functional scenarios

The software products support many operational scenarios that should have been identified by the software requirements specification. The functional scenarios represent abstract sequences of data processing actions that are necessary to enable the software product to facilitate the business or operational process. Each operational scenario should be evaluated to identify the assortment of functional scenarios that must be designed for. For example, an automated teller machine (ATM) supports several distinct banking (business) transactions. Each banking transaction must be evaluated to identify the various situations that would trigger a separate functional scenario. These situations include: (1) the bank account is inactive due to customer closure, (2) the bank account is suspended due to inappropriate account activity, (3) the bank account contains insufficient funds to support the requested transaction, and (4) the bank account has sufficient funds to support the requested transaction. Each of these situations represents a functional scenario the software product must be designed to support.

11.2.2 Identify functional sequences

Each of the functional scenarios must be expressed in terms of the sequence of functional actions that are necessary to accomplish the scenario. The functional sequence is represented by a functional flow block diagram (FFBD). If further situations warrant the identification of alternative functional solutions, then the sequence should branch into multiple sequences. The control rules and criteria for each alternative branch must be specified.

The FFBD notation is a proven technique for depicting a sequence of functional actions. However, it may need to be enhanced to permit the expression of control rules and alternative branching within the sequence of functions. It is necessary to express the control decision logic and branch selection criteria as an integral description of the functional flow sequence diagram. An example of a simple FFBD is presented in Figure 11.2 to depict the decomposition of the process application operational activity identified in Figure 8.3 in Chapter 8.

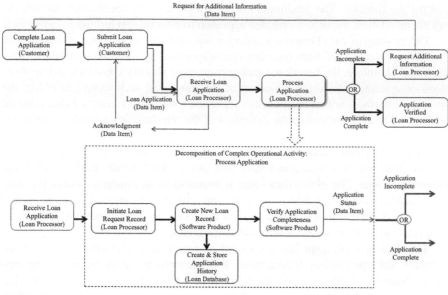

FIGURE 11.2

Example of an FFBD.

11.2.3 **Identify data flows**

The purpose of most software functions is to transform inputs into an output or product. However, some functions will receive control flow instead of an input. Examples of functions that receive only control flow include: (1) the action to present graphical user informational screens, messages, or dialog screens; (2) take action on global data values; and (3) take action when a state variable (e.g., computing environment health indication or software procedural status) has changed or needs to be assessed (e.g., obtain the status of the default printer). While functions that do not directly process data may not satisfy computer language specific or mathematical criteria, they do perform significant actions within the software engineering field of study.

Data items represent the information that flows among functions. The passing of data between software functions represents a functional interface, such as a subroutine invocation or "call" statement. The controlling function passes a variable to another function that is processed and the result returned to the controlling function. For example, a function may invoke a temperature conversion function by passing a temperature value in Fahrenheit. The receiving function converts the Fahrenheit temperature value to Celsius and returns the resulting value to the controlling function. The functional interface represents the mechanism for achieving encapsulation, the object-oriented approach to information hiding.

The passing of data between a software function and an external application or system represents a software interface that is specified by a software interface specification. Therefore, the functional architecture must identify these external applications or systems outside the boundary of the functional architecture to reflect the software interface. Software interfaces represent a multiparty contract that must be conformed to as it pertains to the definition of the interface design and implementation characteristics.

Global data items represent data that is accessible to any function. This type of data item does not represent a data flow due to the "global" availability of the parametric value. The global data value is available to all functions within the software architecture. Local data items represent variable or constant parameters that are declared internal to a function and not accessible to other functions. Therefore, access to local data items does not represent a data flow.

The data flow diagram has been used to represent a data-centric view of the software data processing transactions. It represents the data items as the primary elements of interests and the functions as the connectors or transformation agents between data item states. The behavior model combines the functional flow sequences with the data flows to provide a more general and complete representation of the software data processing scenarios. A software data dictionary (nomenclature document) must be produced to ensure that each data item is uniquely identified and their characterization is available to all members of the software development team.

11.2.4 Identify control behaviors

The control behaviors must be identified to disclose the decision logic and criteria that govern data processing control flows. Control behaviors must account for all possible conditions that may be encountered throughout a functional scenario. Control behaviors dictate which functional sequence will be enabled among the possible courses of action. For example, when a loan application is being evaluated by a bank officer, the loan may be approved, disapproved, or deferred until further information is provided. The operational or business model should have identified the business rules that guide this transaction. The control behaviors must identify how the software will interrogate data items to enforce the business rules.

The control behaviors represent the decision logic that must be captured at a detailed level so that the software development team understands the precise nature of how data processing control flow choices will be affected and the selection criteria that govern which branch of functional execution to enable. The following are typical control logic constructs used to describe control behaviors:

AND—used to describe a parallel condition where two or more sequences of data processing functional behavior (branches or processes) are executed concurrently.

OR—used to describe a selection condition where only one sequence of functional behavior will be performed. The logical path of execution is determined by the state of data item or resource and the conditional selection criteria.

LOOP—used to repeat a sequence of functional behaviors until a condition is met that terminates the repetitive behavior, and the subsequent function in sequence beyond the LOOP is executed.

LOOP EXIT—used to evaluate if the condition has been satisfied to cause the LOOP behavior to terminate.

ITERATE—similar to a LOOP, used to repeat a sequence of functional behaviors a specified number of times. When the specified number of iterations has be achieved, the looping behavior terminates, and the subsequent function in sequence beyond the ITERATE is executed.

11.2.5 Identify data processing procedures

Each function must be specified by identifying the data transformation procedures necessary to transform inputs into the desired outputs, response messages, or state information. Response information pertains to situational awareness concerning issues encountered during data processing, such as data record not found or input data out of range. State information pertains to internal variables that represent the status of a transaction or computing environment asset. The data processing procedures should address the algorithms or computational logic by which the desired outputs are generated.

It is not sufficient to verbally describe the data processing procedures to be performed. The procedures should establish the transformational sequence of steps that must be accomplished to execute the function. For example, the ATM personal identification number (PIN) verification function may involve the following transformational steps:

1. Format the PIN verification request message.
2. Transmit the PIN verification request message to the central bank account management system.
3. Receive the verification response form the central bank account management system.
4. Establish the PIN verification success or failure.
5. Notify the customer of the PIN verification results by one of the following:
   - Display customer welcome ccreen.
   - Display incorrect PIN notification screen and request the customer to reenter a PIN or cancel the transaction.

The complexity of the data processing procedures should be reassessed (per task 11.1, assess functional complexity) to determine if further functional decomposition is warranted. The challenge of the functional complexity assessment is to determine whether the data processing procedures represent an uncomplicated, straightforward action that can be satisfactorily designed, implemented, and tested by a competent software professional.

11.2.6 Identify resource prerequisites

The resources that are necessary for each function to execute must be identified. A resource represents an item that enables a function to be performed properly. When a resource is unavailable, the data processing transactions may be suspended, delayed until the resource is made available, or performed inefficiently. Resources can be thought of as the computing resources or intermediary data items that need to be present for the function to fulfill its purpose.

There are two types of resources that must be addressed to support behavioral analysis. The first type of resource is one that is consumable. A resource that is consumed represents an inventory stock that may be incrementally utilized until the inventory is empty or of insufficient quantity to support further data processing actions. A function that requires a consumable resource must wait until the inventory stock has been replenished before it can be executed. An example of a consumable resource is a printer with its paper supply. As long as there is paper available within the tray, the printing function can be performed. However, when the paper supply is empty, the printing function is suspended until the paper supply is restocked.

The second type of resource represents a reusable item, such as memory. Each function is loaded into memory for execution, and unloaded from memory when the function is no longer necessary to be resident in memory. The amount of memory is fixed and is temporarily decremented by the amount consumed by resident functions. When a function is removed from memory it frees up space for other functions that may require the memory for execution purposes. Understanding the amount of available memory at any point in time is crucial to software performance and is dictated by the computer's memory management scheme.

Resource utilization is a critical aspect of overall software performance. The time associated with resource management and delays imposed by limited resources may adversely affect processing time. Therefore, resource allocation and management contribute directly to the establishment of a functional architecture that satisfies stringent performance requirements. Therefore, task 11.3.2, allocate resource budgets, involves an assessment of the functional resource availability and utilization and management scheme, and establishes the approach to software performance requirements allocation among elements of the functional architecture.

11.2.7 Identify failure conditions

Every functional transaction must be evaluated to identify situations or conditions that may cause failure conditions. Identified failure states must be resolved by stipulating the data integrity criterion that must be interrogated to determine a failure state, and the actions to be taken when a certain state arises to complete the data processing transaction.

Some failure conditions may result in a state that cannot be resolved via automation and requires human intervention. The functional analysis effort must then address the manner by which the software will continue to operate in a degraded mode, if possible. For example, if an ATM's supply of money has been depleted, then the withdrawal function must be temporarily suspended until the money supply if restocked. The software functions for detecting failure conditions and operating in a degraded mode must be included within the functional architecture. This includes identifying how the software product can be "informed" of the current state of data processing or system resources and how the state indicators are managed.

Potential data processing failure modes and effects must be analyzed to determine how the software product should behave in response to each failure condition. Failure modes and effects analysis (FMEA) is an engineering procedure that enables the design team to classify potential failure modes by the severity (consequences) and likelihood of the failures resulting with improved product quality and dependability. *Dependability* is a term that is better suited for software products than reliability. Throughout the engineering community, reliability deals with predicting the mean time between failure (MTBF) of hardware components during normal operation and provides an estimate of the expected duration life expectancy for the component. Software does not breakdown or wear out over time with use. Therefore, dependability refers to a software component's ability to perform its function as expected under all circumstances. Dependability is a more suitable term to be used for software products due to the nature of the material of which it is comprised. If a software component fails, it is due to the software design inability to be resilient to unexpected circumstances or situations.

Software FMEA should be used to identify potential failure modes, determine their effects on the operation of the system or business process, and design response mechanisms that prevent the failure from occurring or mitigate the impact of the failure on operational performance. While anticipating every failure mode may not be possible, the development team should formulate an extensive list of potential failure modes in the following manner:

1. Develop software product requirements that minimize the likelihood of potential operational failures from arising.
2. Evaluate the requirements obtained from stakeholders in the software performance and post-development processes to ensure that those requirements do not introduce complicated failure conditions or situations.
3. Identify design characteristics that contribute to failure detection and minimize failure propagation throughout a data processing transaction.
4. Develop software test scenarios and procedures designed to exercise the software behaviors associated with failure detection, isolation, and recovery.
5. Identify, track, and manage potential design risks to ensure that product dependability is predictable and substantiated via the software test effort
6. Ensure that any failures that could occur will not result in personal injury or seriously impact the operation of the system or operational processes.

Properly used, the software FMEA provides the development team several benefits, including:

1. Improved software dependability and quality.
2. Increased customer and stakeholder satisfaction.
3. Identifies and eliminates potential software failure modes early in the development process when such design challenges can be cost-effectively regulated.
4. Emphasized failure detection and preventive measures.
5. Provides a focus for improved software test coverage.
6. Minimizes late design changes and their associated cost and schedule impacts.
7. Improves teamwork and idea exchange among development team members.

A complete FMEA for a software product should contend with failures arising from the computing environment hardware, external systems, and data processing transactions, and their effects on the final system or operational processes. The software FMEA procedures should adhere to the following steps, adapted from IEC 60812[1]:

1. Define the software boundaries for analysis (accomplished during computational requirements analysis).
2. Understand the software requirements, functionality, and performance.
3. Develop the functional architecture representations (hierarchical decomposition and behavioral views).
4. Identify functional failure modes and summarize failure effects.
5. Develop criteria for successful failure detection, isolation, and recovery.
6. Report findings.

11.2.8 Identify systems monitoring procedures

If the software product involves control or monitoring of mechanical or other types of equipment, then the software FMEA should have identified the situations that must be regulated. The systems monitoring, status notification, and corrective action functionality must be identified. The systems monitoring and control behaviors should be highlighted throughout the behavioral model and functional hierarchy so that they may be emphasized during software implementation and testing. As the software architecture evolves, changes to systems monitoring and control behaviors should be evaluated thoroughly due to the important nature of these functions.

The systems states must be identified and the periodicity of software monitoring functions specified. The behaviors associated with the software response to systems state changes must be incorporated into the functional architecture. Real-time or near-real-time monitoring should provide for detection of the health status of the systems and establish the software response to a degraded system's operational

---

[1] Analysis Techniques for Systems Reliability—Procedure for Failure Mode and Effects Analysis (FMEA), International Electrotechnical Commission, Jan. 25, 2006.

situations. Safety-critical systems state changes must be modeled or prototyped to ensure that the software properly detects and executes corrective actions necessary to properly safeguard systems operational conditions.

11.2.9 Identify data retention capacity requirements

The data storage capacity requirements for long-term data retention records must be specified. The operational or business model should be evaluated to determine the anticipated most-excessive amount of data records that would need to be supported for a given time period. Operational projections should be used to determine the periodic demand for data storage capacity. Factors that must be considered when preforming capacity planning are location of data storage facilities, data record retention duration, recovery of deleted data record storage space, and periodic demand for new data record creation. The data retention capacity requirements will affect the software interaction with a database management system, as well as directly impact the configuration of the computing environment.

11.2.10 Identify data security procedures

Data security functions and procedures must be identified that protect confidential or classified information. Information security is a profession that addresses a broader range of computer security and information assurance challenges. Data security represents a subset of the information security capabilities that will be performed by the software product. Information security means protecting information and information systems from unauthorized access, use, disclosure, disruption, modification, perusal, inspection, recording, or destruction. Software engineering involves the establishment of logical controls that monitor and regulate access to sensitive (confidential or classified) information. Information security functions must be identified and the appropriate procedures defined for:

- *Access control*, including user account administration, identification, authentication, and authorization. Access control protects information by restricting the individuals who are authorized to access sensitive information.
- *Information security classification*, involving the identification of different data classification levels, the criteria for data to be assigned a particular level, and the required controls to govern the access to each level of sensitive information.
- *Cryptography*, including information encryption and decryption.

11.2.11 Identify data persistence and retention functions

The data elements must be evaluated to identify requirements for temporary transaction persistence and long-term retention. Temporary data persistence is needed if there is an intention to capture the state of a transaction to support undoing or reversing transaction steps to return the operational state to a previous condition. Long-term retention is needed when historical records must be maintained to support transaction recordkeeping, statistical analysis, or other business functions. Data persistence and retention requirements must be specified to support the definition of the data retention mechanisms needed to support the software operations.

Additional functions should be integrated into the behavioral model and functional hierarchy that address the need for data persistence actions. Data storage and retrieval transactions may need to handle database reliability issues, data verification procedures, or possible transaction deadlock situations. As the functional architecture matures, data storage and retrieval functions may be grouped, specified, and documented in a database transaction document. A database transaction block diagram should identify the data records, data types, and definitions that are necessary to the design of a database to support the operational or business data retention requirements.

11.3 Performance allocation

It is imperative that the software performance requirements be allocated among the elements of the functional architecture. This allocation must address the duration of each software function, and the accuracy and precision associated with mathematical calculations. The software functional performance should only address the execution time associated with carrying out software tasks. The performance associated with user input and output and interfacing with external systems and other software products should be included in the determination of the performance of the operational or business process.

Software performance *is* dependent on the execution of the computing technology and the availability of adequate hardware resources. Performance bottlenecks may arise when access to shared resources becomes contentious and delay functional execution or extend the time for a function to be performed.

> A bottleneck is a phenomenon where the performance or capacity of an entire system is limited by a single or limited number of components or resources. The term bottleneck is taken from the "assets are water" metaphor. As water is poured out of a bottle, the rate of outflow is limited by the width of the conduit of exit—that is, bottleneck. By increasing the width of the bottleneck one can increase the rate at which the water flows out of the neck at different frequencies. Such limiting components of a system are sometimes referred to as bottleneck points.[2]

Therefore, software performance requirements must be allocated among the elements of the functional architecture. This involves addressing software execution or timing, as well as resource utilization to avoid resource-imposed performance degradation.

---

[2]See *http://en.wikipedia.org/wiki/Bottleneck*

11.3.1 **Allocate performance budgets**

The execution performance of each function must be specified and allocated among its constituent subfunctions. Execution performance addresses the time that a software function will take to be executed on the specified computing environment. The duration of software functions should not account for any delay associated with external users or systems interactions. The initial allocation of performance requirements should be considered budgets until the design of the software functional architecture is complete. The resulting functional specifications must then establish the performance requirements associated with every software function. While the functional architecture is evolving, the performance budgets may undergo continual change as the software implementation subject-matter experts refine their expectations associated with what can be achieved and delivered.

Functional timing may be specified as a constant or variable duration. Constant durations should be used when functional timing will be relatively consistent. Variable duration specifications should utilize probability distribution functions to represent the random execution duration of a function.

Analysis of the behavioral model may provide insight into the critical path of functional execution. Critical-path analysis is a powerful approach for identifying bottlenecks in highly concurrent systems, but typically requires detailed domain knowledge to construct the required event graph that identifies the dependencies and timing among events in the software behavioral model. The criticality of a particular function can be determined as the ratio of the duration of the function to the total time of the critical path. This metric gives a quick summary of the most important functions within a data processing sequence and contributes to the critical path. This analysis identifies the areas within the functional architecture that offer the largest opportunities for improving overall software performance.

11.3.2 **Allocate resource budgets**

Analysis of the behavioral model should be conducted to balance resource utilization among the software functions. Resources become constrained when data processing functions execute concurrently and require access to or control of limited resource assets. A resource that is unavailable to a function responds with a denial-of-service response, which may place the function in a wait state (i.e., waiting for resource availability). Some resources can be managed by queuing or organizing functional requests for service. Prioritization of resource requests provides a basis for managing resources and ensuring that data processing actions are accomplished in the most efficient manner.

Initial resource allocations should be considered budgets that will be adjusted as the software design and implementation are finalized. Performance budgets represent desired objectives for each element of the physical architecture. Structural element specifications should identify performance requirements for implementation, however, these specifications may be adjusted to reflect the actual performance achieved during implementation. The software implementation and test activities should be conducted to establish performance characteristics and permit the optimization of resource utilization strategies.

11.4 Architectural assessment

The emerging functional architecture must be continually assessed to ensure that it will satisfy the software specifications and is not overly complex so as not to impact software sustainment costs. These architectural assessment tasks provide the software engineering team reassurance that the functional architecture represents an efficient and effective foundation for software product life-cycle sustainment and will facilitate future enhancements and extensions.

11.4.1 Assess requirement fulfillment

As the functional architecture is advanced, the architecture must be continually be assessed to ensure that it will satisfy the software. The set of functional specifications should be traceable to the software requirements specifications and stakeholder needs and expectations. The adequacy of the evolving functional architecture is primarily determined by ensuring that the software functional decomposition is noncomplex and that software requirements specifications have been realized.

11.4.2 Assess software performance

The software behavior must be assessed and adjusted to ensure that the performance requirements will be satisfied. Functional timing and resource utilization tactics should be synchronized to provide adequate software response to data processing requests.

11.4.3 Assess architectural complexity

The functional architecture must be assessed to ensure that the behavioral complexity will not adversely preclude future software enhancements. The software behaviors must efficiently and effectively satisfy operational or business processes.

11.4.4 Assess optimization opportunities

The functional architecture must be assessed to identify opportunities for improvement. The cost of optimizing the functional design (decomposition and behaviors) must be justified by a significant gain in performance or reduction in design complexity.

11.5 Establish the functional architecture

The functional architecture should be placed under technical configuration control to establish a functional design baseline for software design synthesis. The

Table 11.1 Design Documentation for Functional Architecture

Document Title	Document Description
1. Functional Decomposition Description	This document describes the manner by which the software functionality has been decomposed into subfunctions. The functional hierarchy diagrams present the levels of functional breakdown of functional requirements to components and units.
2. Functional Component Specifications	Software functional and performance specifications for compound elements of the software functional configuration. These specifications represent the subrequirements necessary to support the achievement of higher-level functional components or software product requirements.
3. Functional Unit Specifications	Software functional, performance, and design specifications for the basic elements of the software functional configuration. These specifications represent the subrequirements necessary to support the achievement of a lowest-level functional component.
4. Functional Interface Specifications	Technical description of each software functional interface. Identifies the purpose of the interface and provides the general information concerning the type of information exchanged by the interface.
5. Software Behavioral Models	The behavioral models describe the functional sequences, control, and data flows for complex functions. The behavioral models establish the software performance and resource utilization specifications for each thread of behavior. Failure modes and effects are described, and fault detection, isolation, and recovery procedures should be described.
6. Data Persistence Specifications	Documents the requirements for data persistence, including the data storage capacity requirements and data storage and retrieval transactions.
7. Requirements Traceability Matrix	Documents how each requirement in the software specifications has been satisfied by the elements of the functional architecture.
8. Software Nomenclature Document	Documents the characteristics of every function, data item, and resource identified in the functional architecture to provide a consistent glossary of named elements.

functional architecture must be complete and traceable to software specifications. The software engineering team representatives from software implementation and test and evaluation organizations must endorse the functional architecture and revise their technical plans and schedules to align organizational resources with anticipated task assignments.

The functional architecture must be documented to provide the diagrams, drawings, models, and specifications against which software design synthesis can be performed and evaluated. Functional architecture includes the design documentation shown in Table 11.1.

Configuring the Physical Architecture

12

This chapter addresses how the software physical architecture is derived and configured from the functional architecture. The software functional solution was analyzed, specified, and simplified during functional analysis and allocation. During software design synthesis, the structural elements of the product are identified and the manner in which these elements are arranged, assembled, and integrated is established. The result of software design synthesis is the structural configuration of the software product, which along with its documentation comprises the physical architecture. The complete software design solution is comprised of the functional and physical architecture. The software product architecture is comprised of the software product specifications, the functional and physical architectures, and the computing environment architecture. The complete software architecture involves the software product architecture and the post-development process architectures. Figure 12.1 shows the relationships among the various architecture configurations.

The physical architecture captures the structural representation of the design solution, as well as the engineering drawings, diagrams, and models from which

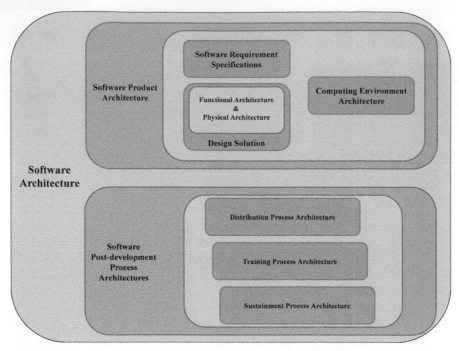

FIGURE 12.1

Relationships among the software architecture configurations.

the solution was devised. It specifies the fundamental building blocks (structural units) from which the software product will be implemented. During the initial implementation phase of software implementation, these structural unit specifications communicate how software units are designed, coded, and tested. How structural units are identified and specified during software design synthesis is discussed further in this chapter. The software integration strategy addresses the software assembly, integration, and testing scheme that results in a fully integrated product configuration. Finally, the use of modeling and simulation methodologies as an aid in deciding on the preferred design solution is discussed.

The physical architecture is comprised of the technical drawings, diagrams, specifications, and models that document the structural design solution. The structural design solution addresses the configuration of structural units and components, as well as how they are assembled and integrated into a single product. Structural unit and component specifications provide the basis for software implementation, which involves software unit design, coding, and testing, as well as software component integration and testing. Therefore, the physical architecture results in the software product technical data package that provides the necessary structural design documentation to enable software implementation. The content of the technical data package is discussed later in the "Preparing the Software Technical Data Package" section.

The biggest challenge to software engineering is determining how to transform the functional architecture into the physical architecture. The functional architecture establishes the fundamental data processing tasks, data flows, logical controls, and resource allocations for the software design solution. The physical architecture represents the software structural design solution in terms of the software modules or structural units and how these units interact and integrate into software components. Therefore, this chapter discusses the following challenges to developing the physical architecture:

1. How are the structural units identified and specified?
2. How is the software integration strategy devised?
3. How is the structural design configuration simplified to reduce complexity and sustainment costs?
4. How is the structural design solution transitioned to software implementation?

12.1 Structural design solution

The structural design solution establishes the arrangement and integration relationships of structural units and components for the software product configuration items. A software product may be composed of one or more configuration items, as needed. A client/server–based software product will involve a client configuration item and a server configuration item. The structural design solution also identifies the interfaces between the software product configuration items and elements of the computing environment, external systems, and other software applications, such as a database management system (DBMS). The block diagram for a conceptual software product design solution is depicted in Figure 12.2. This block diagram shows the integration relationships among the elements of the software product configuration, as well as the interface relationships between the software product and external entities. The elements identified in Figure 12.2 are:

1. *Software structural design solution*—identifies the software product configuration, structural assemblages, software integration strategy, and interfaces that characterize the software design. The design artifacts (drawing, diagrams, models, specifications, and documentation) that describe the product configuration comprise the software product technical data package (TDP).
   - *Software product configuration*—identifies the structural units and components that are assembled and integrated to form the software product.
   - *Structural unit*—represents the fundamental design elements or software building blocks from which structural components are assembled. Typical terms used to refer to a structural unit include module, routine, procedure, function, and object.
   - *Structural component*—represents compound software building blocks comprised of two or more structural units or lower-level components.

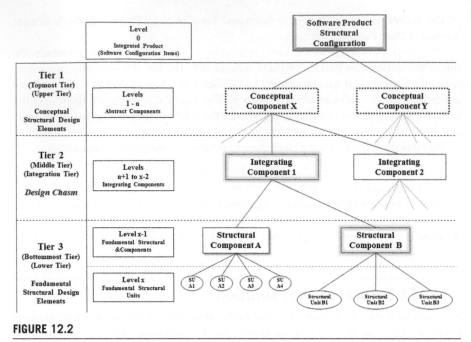

FIGURE 12.2

The software structural design solution.

2. *Software integration strategy*—identifies the sequence of assembly and integration tasks by which larger, more complex structural components are combined into the final software product configuration.
   - *Structural assemblages*—represent the assembly and integration tasks that generate a structural component and the test stubs needed to support engineering test and evaluation.
   - *Graphical user interface assemblage (example)*—a common example of a structural assemblage that is composed of only the graphical-based display screens, menus, icons, and pointing device interface structural units and components.
3. *Software operational environment*—identifies the computing equipment, external systems, and related software applications the software product under development is intended to execute within so that it may collaboratively perform its tasks.
   - *Computing environment*—the set of computing technology resources that the software product is designed to operate in combination with.
   - *Interface relationships*—identifies the agreement and commitment for the software product to exchange data with other systems, equipment items, or software applications. An interface may involve a flow of data in one

direction with one source of information and one destination; it may be bidi-rectional with multiple sources and destinations of shared data; or it may be a broadcast-type interface in which a source broadly transmits data to any and all qualified receivers.

- *External interfaces*—identifies the data exchange protocol and format for data shared among interfacing (communicating) systems and applications. An interface is a formal agreement among system developers that commits both sides to conform to the interface control document that describes the interface.

  a. *External systems*—an external system or software application that the software product under development must interface with to collabora-tively achieve some purpose.

  b. *Database management system (example)* —a common example of an external software application with which a software product may be designed to operate and interface.

The software product configuration is comprised of a number of structural units that are combined and integrated into structural components. Structural com-ponents are larger configuration elements that are comprised of a set of integrated structural units and/or components. The integrated set of structural components is used to describe the software product configuration that is intended to be delivered to customers, stakeholders, or consumers. Structural units and components are the product elements that will be implemented, tested, and managed throughout the software life cycle.

It may be necessary to create assembly configurations (structural assemblages) to support software integration and testing. A structural assemblage represents an intermediary engineering structure that involves additional software (test stubs) that supports software integration and testing (e.g., test harness in the hardware manu-facturing vernacular).

Structural assemblages identify the structural units, components, and test stubs that will be assembled and integrated to support software testing. Structural units do not appear in the structural assemblage configuration since they are integrated into structural components as the first level of assembly and integration. Any test stubs necessary to support structural unit test and evaluation are not relevant to the structural assemblage configuration since they have outlived their usefulness at the structural assemblage level of integration and testing.

12.1.1 Designating structural units

Structural units are identified from the set of functional units specified by the func-tional architecture. It is not efficient to resolve the collection of structural units as a one-to-one alignment with functional units. The objective of designating structural units is to establish a minimal but complete set of structural units from which the software product can be configured. Structural units will ultimately be the focus of the initial software implementation effort to design, code, and test individual software modules, routines, or objects. Therefore, the designation of each structural unit must consider the scope of functionality it is assigned, the need for interaction with other structural elements, and the effort necessary to achieve the integrated and interoperable functional performance.

The functional architecture must be evaluated to identify a set of common or tightly coupled functional units that may be designated a structural unit. This does not prohibit a single functional unit from being designated a structural unit. However, the challenge of this engineering practice is to organize the specified functionality in a practical manner that provides an efficient and effective solution. Several factors must be considered that affect the ability to evolve the design solution over time:

1. The potential for future extension or enhancement to the software functionality.
2. The ability to adopt or adapt to changes in the computing environment.
3. The ability of the software product to be modified to repair design or coding deficiencies.
4. The sequence of software integration and test activities necessary to assemble the software product.

Structural units should be classified by key functional categories, such as user interface, database transaction processing, business process function, user administration, resource management, error handling, and data security. Criteria for identifying structural units include:

- A single functional unit stands alone in the action it performs and there are no similar functional units with which it should be combined.
- A single functional unit is problematic, risky, or requires special engineering attention to warrant designating it a structural unit.
- A single functional unit requires significant modeling, simulation, or testing effort to warrant a dedicated prototyping effort and designation as a structural unit.
- Multiple functions perform similar data processing actions and can be combined without increasing structural complexity or exceeding structural unit size guidelines.
- Multiple functions perform data transformation on a common data set and the grouping of these functions aligns well within the overall structural configuration.
- The structural complexity of the design solution will benefit from the combining of similar functional units regardless of the structural size guidelines.
- The combining of similar functional units would adversely affect software component integration and testing.
- The combining of similar functional units would impact post-development software support associated with the incorporation of changes or preplanned product enhancements.

The set of structural units will be itemized on the software bill of material (BOM).[1] The software BOM establishes the hierarchy of structural components and units that form the software product configuration. It is used to support the software build process where source code files are converted into executable code, linked together in the proper order, until a complete set of executable files is generated. The software build process utilizes the software BOM with knowledge of the dependencies among the source code files to link the executable files into a complete software product configuration.

12.1.2 Prepare structural unit specifications

Each designated structural unit must be specified to support software implementation. Structural units that are allocated multiple functional units are specified by combining and assimilating the set of functional unit specifications in a manner so as to eliminate duplication, resolve conflicting requirements, and aggregate performance parameters. For structural units that correspond to a single functional unit, the structural specification inherits the requirements contained in the functional unit specification. In both cases, the structural unit specifications must be enhanced to address structural requirements, which include:

- Source lines of code (software size) estimates
- Memory utilization and resource utilization estimates
- Internal interface definitions (software-to-software interfaces)
- External interface definitions
- Computing environment interactions and diagnostics
- Real-time execution constraints
- Synchronous data processing execution and scheduling

12.1.3 Establishing the software integration strategy

The initial level of structural components should be identified based on the need to combine common structural units into larger, more complex assemblages. The structural components at this initial level may be labeled as *fundamental* structural components due to their composition consisting of only structural units. Each fundamental structural component represents a task to assemble and integrate a set of structural units into a single executable file for integration-level testing.

---

[1] See *http://en.wikipedia.org/wiki/Bill_of_materials*. A bill of materials is a list of the raw materials, subassemblies, intermediate assemblies, subcomponents, components, parts, and the quantities of each needed to manufacture an end item. A BOM can define products as they are designed (engineering BOM), as they are built (manufacturing BOM), or as they are maintained (service BOM). The different types of BOMs depend on the business need and use for which they are intended. BOMs are hierarchical in nature with the top level representing the finished product. BOMs that describe the subassemblies are referred to as modular BOMs.

Successive levels of structural components should be identified that combine structural subcomponents and/or units into larger components. These central structural components in the integration hierarchy may be labeled *intermediate* structural components. The integration of structural subcomponents and/or units into intermediate structural components should continue until the topmost components are recognized. This should result in a final set of *primary* structural components from which the software product configuration will be assembled.

Each structural component must be specified by combining and assimilating the specifications of the integrated elements. These structural component specifications should not address the functionality exhibited by an individual substructural element (component or unit), but should address functionality or transaction processing, which is realized or provided as a result of the integration effort.

The individual component integration test strategy must ensure that the integrated component performs satisfactorily. However, the main focus of the integration test strategy should be to ensure that the component requirements that are most affected by the integration are stressed. Structural component requirements that are not impacted as a result of the integration may be assumed to be satisfied by the subcomponent or unit-level testing.

The number of levels in the component integration hierarchy provides a gage into the overall complexity of the software design solution. Therefore, the formulation of the software integration strategy should be guided by the following guidelines:

1. Each structural component must be independently testable against its component integration specification.
2. Structural components should provide a significantly more capable element in the structural integration hierarchy. Therefore, each structural component should be able to be traced to a significant task within the operational or business process, or should satisfy one or more of the software requirements.
3. Structural components should be able to be tested as a "black box" with an emphasis on ensuring the internal interfaces among integrated subcomponents and/or units, and the measurement of component performance. Black box testing does not evaluate the internal logic, behaviors, or algorithms of integrated elements. It should focus on exercising the integrated functionality and performance of the structural component that results from the integration effort.
4. The number of integration tasks involved with the software integration strategy should be condensed as much as possible. Excessive integration tasks will increase software development costs and extend the software development schedule. The burden associated with software integration and testing will occur many times throughout the software product life cycle with each update or new release of the product. Therefore, each integration task should be scrutinized to ensure that it represents a necessary and cost-effective integration activity.

12.1.4 **Designating engineering assemblages**

Each structural component identified in the integration hierarchy should be evaluated to determine if the component needs additional software drivers or stubs to be tested. The need for additional test drivers or stubs needs to be identified and incorporated into the scope of software implementation planning. This is recorded within the physical architecture as an engineering assemblage that is associated with the structural component that needs the expanded implementation content to support software integration and testing. The engineering assemblage must identify the test drivers and stubs, and an engineering specification must be developed to express the requirements for the additional software implementation tasks.

12.1.5 **Preparing the software technical data package**

The software TDP must be prepared to document each structural unit, component, and engineering assemblage that must be developed during software implementation. The software TDP consists of the technical documentation (diagrams, drawings, specifications, data definitions, and software integration strategy) associated with structural units and components. The software TDP provides the formal representation of the software physical architecture necessary for the software implementation stage of development. Software implementation involves the design, coding, and testing of structural units, and the assembly, integration, and testing of structural components. The effort associated with software implementation and testing will be made significantly more efficient and effective with a coherent, thoroughly specified and documented software physical architecture.

The software TDP is the technical description of the software product necessary for software implementation, acceptance testing, and post-development software sustainment. Therefore, the TDP must be consistent with the evolving software product architecture, as well as compatible with all authorized change requests and proposals. The software TDP, together with software development folders, acceptance test results, and authorized change proposal, deviations, and waivers provide the basis for the software functional configuration and physical configuration audits (FCA/PCA).

12.2 **Structural design considerations**

Software products provide a vast array of technical solutions for a variety of industries. Therefore, configuring the physical architecture will be dependent on the type of design solution being pursued. This section provides general guidelines or suggestions to be considered when establishing software design policies, procedures, and approaches.

12.2.1 **Structural design guidelines**

Several software engineering principles apply to all software products, regardless of the type of application being developed. The software engineering process is based on a de facto top-down approach to establishing the software functional architecture. However, configuring the physical architecture is essentially a bottom-up methodology. The manner by which the structural design is devised must account for the following basic tenets concerning the manner in which the software architecture is crafted:

1. Functional analysis attempts to resolve unknown information about the problem and solution in a methodical manner. Because it involves analysis of the problem and solution space it implies a top-down methodology by which a large, incomprehensible problem or situation is reduced to smaller, more coherent design challenges.
2. Functional analysis attempts to resolve complex tasks by decomposing each task until a set of simpler, less complex functions are perceived.
3. The comprehension achieved by applying the functional analysis methodology incites a natural need to iterate upward to reconsider the problem bolstered with a new appreciation of the problem and solution space.
4. The physical architecture is derived via design synthesis that strives to combine software elements into a new, larger, more complex software element that contributes effectively and efficiently to the overall design solution.
5. The default methodology for applying design synthesis is to begin with the smallest parts and to progress toward a design solution by assembling and integrating structural units and components into larger, more complex structural components. However, engineering analysis involves identifying the design challenges that entail the most risks and to seek a design resolution that involves less risk. Then, the remainder of the design can be worked out utilizing the less risky design solution as its centerpiece.
6. The desire to generate a suitable and competent design solution defies a strict top-down functional and bottom-up design synthesis practice. Design efficiency and effectiveness supersede the adherence to any design approach that dictates a strict architectural design stratagem.
7. Software engineering blends the top-down analytical and bottom-up synthesis techniques with an understanding that the structural design must evolve in an abstract top-down manner. However, the abstract structural design is only representational until it is refined by the thorough application of the bottom-up design synthesis practice.

Software products are not bound by any scientific, technological, engineering, or mathematical principles that provide design reference models for other products. The vast majorities of products in the market today are based on existing products with only minor innovative variations. The architectural design of many software products does not have a conventional legacy from which to initiate their design. Software reference architectures may be established with a domain or software product line. However, stakeholder requirements and advancements in computer technology often render these reference architectures ineffective and inefficient. Therefore, most software products begin the design effort with a clean slate from which to being deriving a design solution. The following set of software design guidelines are provided as a suggested approach to establishing the structural design configuration:

1. Evaluate the top levels of the functional architecture as it is being formulated to distinguish the central elements of the software product structural configuration. This involves searching for common themes among the functional components from which abstract structural elements can be identified to provide an organizational, supervisory, or monitoring construct. Since all software products perform a form of data processing, the challenge is to establish an abstract design configuration of top-level structural components that will be used to partition and apportion the product functionality. The organizational, supervisory, and monitoring constructs are addressed here to provide additional guidance in the establishment of the abstract software design configuration.
   - An organizational-based design draws its configuration from the manner by which the operational or business process is performed. This can result in a process-oriented, task-oriented, or role-based design configuration.
   - A supervisory-based design draws its configuration from the need to provide guidance concerning the interaction of the user/operator with the execution of software functionality. An example of this would be a word-processing or CAD/CAM/CAE[2] application that provides a set of dropdown menus from which the product's main functionality is accessed.
   - A monitoring-based design draws its configuration from the need to observe the status of process-control systems and equipment items, and to take corrective action when a deviation in system performance is recognized. The major structural components may be organized around the real-time process being controlled, the system or equipment items being monitored, or the types of failures that may occur and corrective actions to be taken by operators of the computer-based monitoring system.

2. As the functional architecture evolves, the abstract structural design configuration can be extended to encompass the improved knowledge of the functionality associated with each structural component. This involves the identification of abstract subcomponents to organize the lower level functions. This can be done in parallel with the functional analysis practice to account for the evolving understanding of the functional architecture. When the functional architecture is complete, the functional units must be grouped and allocated to structural units as the building blocks or parts from which the software product will be assembled. The structural units must be aligned with the abstract structural components to complete the initial structural design configuration. This is where the design effort applies both a top-down and bottom-up orientation with an objective of establishing a comprehensive structural configuration for the physical architecture.

---

[2]CAD/CAM/CAE are acronyms for computer-aided design, computer-aided manufacturing, and computer-aided engineering, respectively.

3. Evaluate the structural configuration to refine the design to optimize performance, reduce software integration and testing efforts, and simplify the configuration.
4. Establish the software integration strategy by identifying intermediary structural components that form logical collections of structural components for the purpose of assembling the final software product configuration. These intermediary structural components are subcomponents of abstract structural components. There may be rationale to restructure the structural configuration based on this task, and abstract components may be eliminated altogether or rescoped to accommodate a broader functional responsibility. The final software integration strategy should identify the manner by which structural units and components will be assembled, integrated, and tested during software implementation. The software build process will be patterned after this integration strategy but without the need for the intermediary structural integration testing.

These software design guidelines emphasize the application of functional analysis and design synthesis in a manner that harmonizes the structural configuration with the functional architecture. Functional analysis establishes the functional and performance characteristics of the software product. It provides a well-defined, organized approach to explore the problem space and gain in-depth understanding of the operational features and attributes that may have been ambiguously implied by the stakeholder needs and software requirements specifications.

Design synthesis enables the software engineering team to deduce a conceptual design framework while the functional architecture is still being elaborated. The conceptual design should focus on the skeletal structure of the software product configuration upon which additional structural components can be affixed. The conceptual design framework is devised by abstracting dominant functional concepts into a set of top-level abstract structural components.

Upon the completion of the functional architecture, the design synthesis practice is used to group and organize functional units into a complete set of structural units that form the building block of the structural configuration. Structural unit specifications result from the consolidation of functional unit specifications into an integrated set of requirements. The software integration strategy is established to identify structural assemblages and intermediary structural components that bridge the design space between structural units and the conceptual design framework. Structural assemblages represent intermediary structural components that involve additional test stubs and drivers to support component integration and testing. The complete structural configuration resulting from design synthesis must be completely specified and documented to provide the software technical data package that is delivered to the software implementation team. The software physical architecture refers to the complete structural design as documented by the software TDP.

12.2.2 **Use of modeling and simulation**

The purpose of all engineering disciplines is to design a solution to a problem utilizing mathematics or scientific principles to design, plan, construct, or maintain products. A product design is almost always shown in the form of models that express the design characteristics of the product on a smaller scale than the original. Engineering diagrams and drawings are forms of static models that express manufacturing, assembly, construction, maintenance, or engineering details. Simulations are dynamic models that are used to support the conduct of experiments to gather information concerning the product or process design. The results of modeling and simulation are used to refine the engineering characteristics and design to improve product performance, dependability,[3] and life-cycle sustainment qualities of the product.

Modeling and simulation is the use of models, including emulators, prototypes, simulators, and stimulators, either statically or over time, to develop data as a basis for making architectural decisions. The terms *modeling* and *simulation* are often used interchangeably.[4] Models are static representations of the product or process being designed, while simulations are dynamic representations.

Models and simulations are engineering tools used to:

1. Convey to stakeholders the characteristics of the product.
2. Prove the achievement of challenging engineering and design characteristics, such as performance, interoperability, user input acceptability, and usability.
3. Evaluate competing design alternatives from a variety of engineering trades, such as cost-benefit analysis, feasibility, supportability, and resource utilization.
4. Provide engineering representations (drawings, diagrams, executable models) of the product design configuration, interfaces, behaviors, and integration and test procedures.
5. Support user training and education on the proper use or exploitation of the product.
6. Express a process definition in support of process analysis, design, and evaluation.

Engineering models take many forms and may be constructed in a number of materials and media formats, such as paper, clay, wood, spreadsheets, drawings, diagrams, and CAD/CAM/CAE-based computer representations. Engineering simulations are dynamic models that are used to evaluate design characteristics under operational and environmental conditions.

---

[3]*Dependability* refers to the trustworthiness of a product to perform suitably under a variety of operational environments. It is a term that is better suited for software-based products than reliability, availability, and maintainability, which apply to hardware-based products.
[4]Department of Defense Modeling and Simulation (M&S) Glossary, DoD 5000.59-M, U.S. Department of Defense, 1998.

Models and simulations may be utilized to support many tasks throughout the software engineering practices to represent design concepts, evaluate design competencies and quality factors, and to gather feedback on the effectiveness of the software product or a post-development process design. This feedback fortifies the software engineering team's understanding and knowledge of stakeholder needs, wants, and desires. The following sections discuss the primary uses of modeling and simulation within the software engineering practices.

12.2.3 Behavioral analysis

Behavioral modeling and simulation support the functional analysis and design synthesis practices by providing a comprehensive, integrated representation of the software architecture (product and process architectural representations). Behavioral models capture the relationships among the elements of the architecture that provide traceability from design elements, characteristics, and features back to stakeholder requirements and software specifications. Behavioral models should represent the software architecture via the following design representations or model perspectives:

1. *Functional decomposition diagram*—a depiction of the functional hierarchy that captures decomposition bidirectional relationships among functional components and units.
2. *Operational model*—a depiction of the operational or business process represented as an integrated view of functional, data, and control flows. The operational model is a composite view of a functional flow block, data flow, and control flow diagrams.
3. *Execution timeline*—a depiction of the software product or process execution timeline that identifies functional sequencing, data exchange durations, and resource utilization graphs. The operational models should provide a simulation capability that can automatically generate the execution timeline.
4. *Entity-relationship diagram*—a depiction of a single element of the software architecture and its established relationships to other elements of the architecture.
5. *Interface block diagram*—a depiction of the physical interfaces an element of the structural configuration has with other structural elements, external systems, or applications.
6. *Structural configuration diagram*—a depiction of the structural elements that comprise the software product structural configuration, structural assemblage, or component. It identifies the decomposition of the software product or a structural component into lower-level structural elements (components or units). (*Note:* When viewed in a bottom-up manner, this diagram should identify the software integration strategy.)
7. *Engineering assembly diagram*—a variation of the structural configuration diagram that identifies the structural subelements, test stubs, or drivers that are

necessary to assemble, integrate, and test a structural component or the software product configuration.

8. *Software integration diagram*—a variation of a structural configuration diagram that identifies the version, file name, location, etc. of each structural element that will be involved in the assembly, integration, and testing of a structural component.

Figure 12.3 provides a sense of the behavioral analysis design representations for the software product architecture. The design representations identified for the software product architecture are applicable to the architectures for each of the post-development processes. (*Reminder:* The integrated product and process development, or IPPD, philosophy states that the software engineering practices apply to the design of the software product and post-development processes.)

12.2.4 Structural trade-off analysis

A trade study is any information-gathering exercise where two or more design alternatives are analyzed to assess the response of the design to the same operational or environmental situation and conditions. The competing design alternatives must be evaluated to understand a wide variety of product characteristics and support engineering decision making. A design trade-off will typically involve key performance, operational, and sustainment cost factors that affect product suitability, as well as the attainment of product sustainment and development project objectives.

To derive a reasonable design solution it is necessary to consider a variety of physical design alternatives to satisfy the functional architecture. These design alternatives must be analyzed and assessed to determine which alternative provides the best compromise of product and project characteristics in terms of satisfying stakeholder requirements, needs, and objectives.

The software analysis practice is an integral element of software engineering that supports the trade-off analysis and risk assessments associated with software requirements analysis, functional analysis and allocation, and design synthesis. Software analysis will be discussed in Chapter 14.

12.2.5 Software product performance evaluations

Ultimately, the software product design solution will be judged on how effectively and efficiently it performs data processing tasks. Software engineering involves continual assessment of product responsiveness to stimulus (user and external interfaces), its dependability to respond to a variety of operational situations and conditions, and how well it utilizes and conserves computing resources. The following sections discuss the challenges involved with these critical performance investigations.

12.2.5.1 Design responsiveness

Software design responsiveness involves the timeliness of the software product's response to user inputs, external interface stimuli, or interactions with elements of

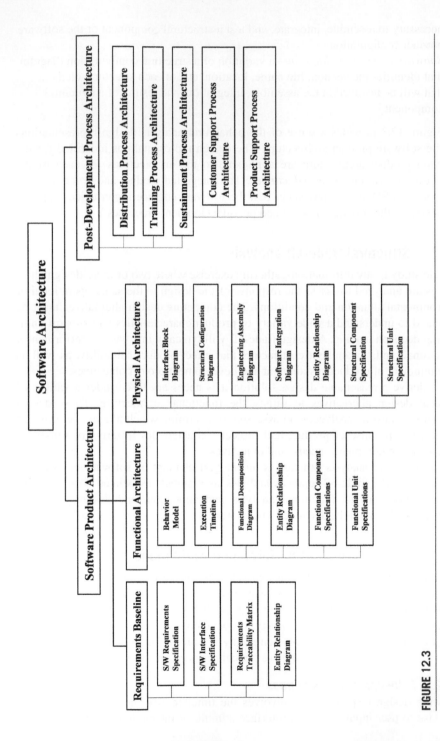

FIGURE 12.3

Behavioral analysis design representations.

the computing environment. The software structural design must be evaluated to determine if the design can be enhanced to improve the software product's responsiveness to requested actions. The following guidelines are provided that address enhancing the software responsiveness to user-based requests[5] :

1. Provide timely feedback concerning the requested action:
   * Promptly acknowledge a user input.
   * Provide data processing progress indicators for actions taking a significant amount of time.
   * Respond initially by providing the most important information then disclosing additional information when it becomes available.
   * Alert the user concerning the anticipated delay needed to respond to complicated requests.
2. Prioritize data processing actions:
   * Postpone low-priority data processing actions until computing resources are available.
   * Anticipate data processing needs and perform actions in advance, when possible.
3. Optimize task queue backlog:
   * Reorder the task queue based on priority.
   * Flush tasks that are overtaken by events or may no longer be needed.
4. Multitasking performance supervision:
   * Monitor multitasking progress and adjust resource allocations to optimize task execution and termination.
   * Balance task duration and resource commitments.
   * Predict task durations and determine task discreteness, concurrency, and synchronization tactics.
   * Establish resource monitoring and intercession supervision procedures by anticipating resource conflicts and deadlock situations.

12.2.5.2 Design dependability

Software dependably can only be provided by extensive design evaluation of every failure mode that may be possible. This demands that every data processing action be examined to consider what conditions, stimuli, or user inputs could potentially cause the data processing action to result in a faulty outcome. This involves incidents that may occur within the computing environment; prevent access to external systems or applications that are critical to the data processing action; or the receipt of faulty data being provided by an interfacing system or application.

The Failure Mode and Effects Analysis (FMEA) performed during functional analysis and allocation (see Chapter 11) should provide a basis for determining how the software can be designed to be resilient to potential faults. There are two primary methods of ensuring software fault resilience: fault prevention and fault tolerance.

---

[5]See *http://blogs.msdn.com/b/zainala/archive/2008/08/21/tips-for-improving-software-responsiveness. aspx*

Fault prevention involves establishing mechanisms intended to prevent faulty inputs or conditions from occurring. Fault prevention directly affects the design of the structural solution to ensure that all data introduced into a data processing transaction is within the acceptable, anticipated boundary for the data definition. This includes ensuring that all data entry and user interface interactions are supervised to prevent the introduction of improper data values.

Fault tolerance involves the detection of a faulty condition and selects a recovery course of action. The fault recovery approach may return the software state to a previously saved state (backward recovery). Another fault recovery approach involves multiple functionally equivalent processes in a primary backup scheme where results are compared and the preferred result is selected with which to proceed (forward recovery). If three or more redundant processes are involved, then the comparison of intermediate results (voting) can determine which result is most likely incorrect and the dominant result can be selected to proceed with the data processing transaction (masking the incorrect result).

During software design synthesis it is important to address the need for fault detection and recovery in the specification of the structural solution. Fault prevention will affect the individual specifications of structural units. Fault tolerance will impact the structural design solution to a greater extent to accommodate redundant, parallel data processing operations. Fault tolerance is a common engineering design concept for hardware products with redundant components working in parallel to ensure continued operational performance should one component fail.

12.2.5.3 Resource utilization

The software design solution must provide for the efficient rationing and utilization of scarce computing resources. During software design synthesis it is important to establish resource utilization budgets against which structural specifications can be established. This budget should provide an understanding of anticipated resource consumption profiles for each thread of behavior. Further resource budgets can be established for individual structural components and units, if desirable. Engineering assemblies may be needed to establish resource monitoring stubs to capture actual resource consumption profiles and provide a basis for resource utilization optimization. Figure 12.4 identifies the software architectural design and implementation flow to ensure that resource utilization budgets are successfully realized.

Software engineering involves a number of design strategies associated with resource utilization that must be considered to establish an efficient and effective design solution. During functional analysis and allocation, the software behaviors should involve the resource allocations among functional threads and individual components and units. Resource supervision behaviors should be incorporated into the behavioral models to evaluate multitasking scheduling, task prioritization, and resource queuing strategies. During design synthesis these results should be incorporated into the specifications of structural components and units. Resource critical structural components should be identified as engineering assemblies that specify the resource utilization stubs needed for a performance evaluation.

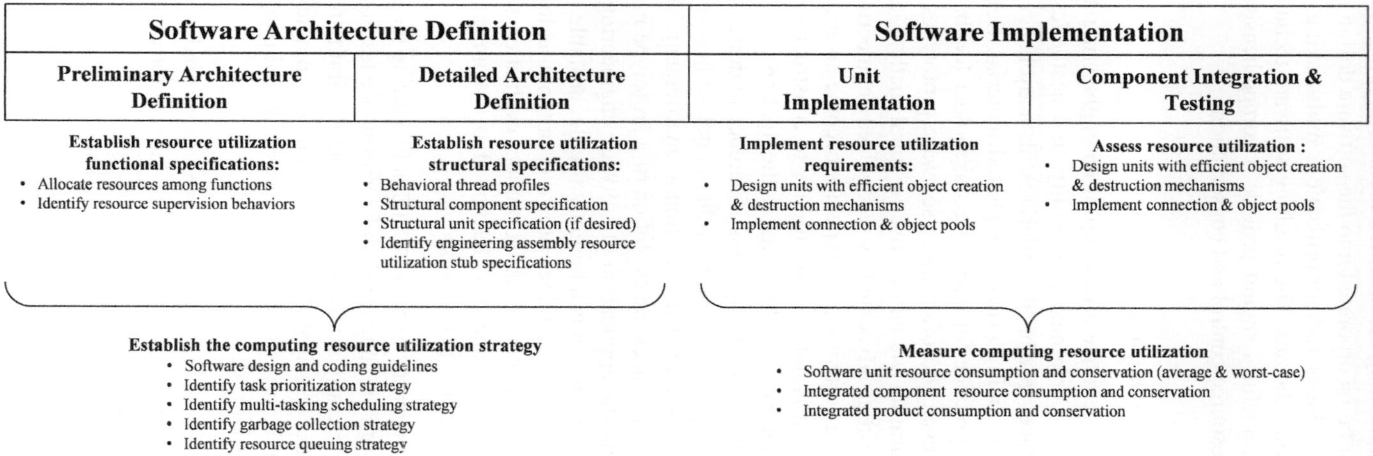

Software Architecture Definition		Software Implementation	
Preliminary Architecture Definition	**Detailed Architecture Definition**	**Unit Implementation**	**Component Integration & Testing**
Establish resource utilization functional specifications: • Allocate resources among functions • Identify resource supervision behaviors	**Establish resource utilization structural specifications:** • Behavioral thread profiles • Structural component specification • Structural unit specification (if desired) • Identify engineering assembly resource utilization stub specifications	**Implement resource utilization requirements:** • Design units with efficient object creation & destruction mechanisms • Implement connection & object pools	**Assess resource utilization :** • Design units with efficient object creation & destruction mechanisms • Implement connection & object pools

Establish the computing resource utilization strategy
- Software design and coding guidelines
- Identify task prioritization strategy
- Identify multi-tasking scheduling strategy
- Identify garbage collection strategy
- Identify resource queuing strategy

Measure computing resource utilization
- Software unit resource consumption and conservation (average & worst-case)
- Integrated component resource consumption and conservation
- Integrated product consumption and conservation

FIGURE 12.4

Software resource utilization realization.

As a result of establishing the software architecture, the computing resource utilization strategy must be incorporated into the software design and coding standards, as applicable. This includes task prioritization, multitasking scheduling, queuing, and garbage collection schemes. The resulting software technical data package and design and coding guidelines should provide a comprehensive blueprint for treatment of computing resource control and conservation.

12.2.6 Software prototyping

Prototyping is used to generate a mockup of an engineering assembly for the purpose of evaluating the performance, usability, and aesthetics associated with the graphical user interface, graphical renderings, data exchange throughput, or data presentation forms, including printed or plotted material. Software prototyping is a generally accepted practice for gathering stakeholder feedback on partial product configurations. However, too often these software prototypes are evolved into the final product configuration via an iterative or spiral methodology. This is a misuse of the prototyping practice advocated by recognized engineering disciplines.

The generation of a software prototype has become an accepted software development practice since it is not cost-prohibitive to construct a software prototype in the same manner and computing language as the final product. However, prototypes are often rapidly created without rigorous adherence to design and coding practices. This results in a prototype configuration that is not sufficiently conceived to withstand the demands of the intended operational environment. Thus, when a software development strategy embraces the evolution of a prototype into a deliverable product it is circumventing the application of software engineering practices. The result is a structural configuration that is inherently fragile, unstable, and unmaintainable.

Traditional engineering disciplines utilize prototypes as test articles or a proof-of-concept archetype generated to assist product evaluation in terms of "form, fit, and function." The product concept is fashioned as a representative model that aids the evaluation of the product in terms of:

- Determining the materials to be used in manufacturing the product.
- Verifying the design via functional and performance testing.
- Qualifying commercially available component feasibility to satisfy engineering specifications under anticipated operational and environmental conditions.
- Confirming manufacturing (fabrication, assembly, and integration) procedures.
- Optimizing the product design features.

There are many forms of models and prototypes used in the engineering of a product. A prototype represents an accurate fabrication of the product design in preparation for manufacturing, construction, or implementation. Prototypes are never finished products and many wind up in display cases, museums, or scrapyards due to the devastating nature of the test and evaluation effort.

Software prototyping must be a focused endeavor for the purpose of reconciling critical design challenges that cannot be resolved with other types of models, simulations, or engineering problem-solving techniques. Software prototyping has evolved into a scandalous practice that subverts formal software engineering practices in favor of incremental product development strategies. Current software prototyping strategies involve four primary forms of prototyping[6] :

1. *Rapid prototyping*—creating a working model of various parts of the software product at a very early stage, after a relatively short investigation. The approach used in constructing the prototype is usually quite informal, the most important factor being the speed with which the prototype is completed. The model then becomes the starting point from which users can reexamine their expectations and clarify their requirements. When this has been achieved, the prototype model is thrown away, and the system is formally developed based on the refined requirements.

2. *Evolutionary prototyping*—creating a very robust prototype in a structured manner and constantly refine it. The evolutionary prototype forms the foundation of the software product. This permits the software team to modify and extend the prototype in a manner that could not be conceived during the requirements and design activities. Evolutionary prototypes may be deployed and evolved through use in its intended operational environment. The software product is never "finished" and is "matured" as the operational environment changes.

3. *Incremental prototyping*—the final product is built as separate prototypes that are integrated into an overall product configuration.

4. *Extreme prototyping*—Extreme prototyping is used for developing web applications. It establishes a series of three incremental software builds. The first phase is a static prototype that consists of HTML pages to portray the page layout design. In the second phase, the HTML pages are dynamic to permit website navigation. In the third phase, the transaction processing functionality is implemented.

The misconception surrounding these software prototyping strategies is the suggestion that this resembles engineering. While software prototypes serve a useful purpose in conventional software development approaches, the software industry has embraced an amateurish, evolutionary prototyping approach to software product design and development. This prolongs customer engagements as the product is evolved over time, results in failed or cancelled projects due to cost overruns and extensive schedule delays, and provides job security for many unqualified, undisciplined software specialists. Using, or perhaps misusing, prototyping has its disadvantages:

- *Faulty assumptions.* The focus on a limited prototype can distract software analysts from addressing the complete scope of the problem space. This can lead to overlooking alternative design solutions, preparation of incomplete specifications, and a general lack of appreciation by the analysts for the complexity of the software problem space.

---

[6] See *http://en.wikipedia.org/wiki/Software_prototyping#Types_of_prototyping*

- *Prototypes fail to scale.* Since a prototype is limited in functionality, the design it characterizes may not scale well when extended to solve the original customer requirements. In many cases, the fragile structural framework upon which the prototype was developed will not be capable of being enhanced in a manner to provide a stable, long-term design solution.
- *Users mistake the prototype as a nearly finished product.* Customers view a software prototype as a nearly complete, final product that merely needs to be enhanced and fine-tuned. This leads customers to form misconceptions concerning the readiness of the development team to deliver the final product. Customers may demand that the prototype be introduced into an operational situation well before the product is ready for such a trial.
- *Developers become attached to the prototype.* Developers become loyal to prototypes they have spent a great deal of effort producing. This can lead to attempts to renovate a limited prototype into a final system even though the prototype is not founded upon a durable, underlying design architecture. (This suggests that throwaway prototyping, rather than evolutionary prototyping, is the preferred approach.)
- *Excessive development time dedicated to the prototype.* A key property to prototyping is the fact that it is supposed to be done quickly. If the developers lose sight of this fact, they very well may try to develop a prototype that is too complex and too costly.
- *Expense of implementing a prototype.* The costs for constructing a software prototype may exceed the benefits gained from its existence. The original purpose of a prototype is to be evaluated to resolve engineering design challenges. However, as a prototype consumes an increasingly large amount of the software development budget it becomes a significant investment that may be difficult to scrap.

There are situations for which a software prototype development effort should be commissioned. Each assessment of the structural solution may reveal a technical challenge or risk that can best be reconciled by prototyping a software-based solution. When considering the development of a software prototype, the following considerations must be factored into the scope of the effort:

1. Each commissioned software prototype is an engineering step toward solving a more significant problem. The commitment of resources to the development of a prototype must provide a return on investment in terms of clarifying customer needs and requirements or providing a resolution to design challenges or risks.
2. Software prototypes must be "engineered" in a similar manner as the deliverable software product. The prototype must be undertaken with the understanding that certain features and characteristics envisioned for the final product will not be incorporated or addressed by the prototype. The scope of the prototype must be dedicated to the engineering problem for which answers are being sought. However, the prototype must be sufficiently crafted based on software engineering practices to tolerate demanding test conditions.

3. The prototype development effort must not be held accountable for complying with software design, coding, and other quality-related practices, which do not add value to the prototyping effort. This empowers the prototyping team to eliminate practices or procedures of which the intent will only impede the prototype development effort without providing meaningful advantages.

4. The prototype must be properly specified and tested to ensure that it was designed and implemented in a manner that will substantiate the results of the prototype evaluation. Testing of the prototype should focus on confirming that the prototype properly manifests the design characteristics it was envisioned to represent. The intent of prototype testing is to ensure that the prototype will provide the data necessary to solve the problem the prototype was intended to resolve.

Software Design Synthesis Practice

CHAPTER OUTLINE

This chapter identifies the design synthesis tasks that are performed to establish the software structural configuration and physical architecture. The structural configuration identifies the structural components and units that comprise the integrated software product. The physical architecture represents the structural configuration with its associated assemblages, engineering drawings, models, and documentation. The term *architecting* is not used; however, architectural design guidelines must be established to guide the formulation of the structural configuration. The physical architecture results from the application of software design synthesis in an iterative manner in concert with the other software engineering principles and practices. Therefore, software engineering is the discipline by which a complete, consistent, and practical software product architecture is formulated.

Software design synthesis, as discussed within this chapter, addresses the tasks necessary to establish the software product structural configuration and physical architecture. This software engineering version of design synthesis has been adapted from the systems engineering discipline to address the unique characteristics of software products. The systems engineering version of design synthesis should be applied to the design of the computing environment and software post-development processes. However, both versions of design synthesis are very consistent and either can be used for nonsoftware product or process design efforts. Figure 13.1 identifies the software design synthesis tasks as they apply to the definition of the software product configuration, and its structural units, components, and engineering assemblies. This presentation of the software design synthesis tasks is not intended to suggest a prescribed sequence by which these tasks are performed. They are organized into logical groupings for the purpose of discussing the major design activities within which these tasks correspond. The major software design synthesis activities include the following:

1. *Design conceptualization*—the establishment of initial structural design concepts derived from the ongoing functional analysis. Structural design concepts originate from brainstorming and inspirational collaborations that suggest structural design patterns that range from typical to progressive, radical, innovative, pioneering, and revolutionary. This involves the identification of abstract structural components and user interface mechanisms, and their arrangement and interactions that form the upper tier of the structural configuration.
2. *Design resolution*—the continual evaluation and refinement of the physical architecture focused on elaborating the structural configuration. Design resolution facilitates the balancing of software design features, functionality, and performance characteristics as the design solution emerges via extrapolation (drawing conclusions or inferences). This includes the identification of structural units and components that represent the building blocks or material from which the lower tier of the structural configuration will be crafted.
3. *Design assessment*—the evaluation of the evolving structural design solution to determine its suitability and completeness. These design assessments are intended to identify any challenges associated with the design solution's ability to be implemented and its resilience to endure enhancements and extensions sustained throughout its anticipated life cycle. Performance engineering assessments should provide a calculated appraisal of the design solution's conformance with performance benchmarks.
4. *Design correlation*—results in the identification of integrated structural components that bridge the design chasm and form the integration tier of the structural configuration.
5. *Design manifestation*—concludes the search for a design solution and endorses the structural configuration. Identifies structural assemblages that represent structural components and additional software test stubs to support integration testing. Finalizes the engineering drawings, diagrams, and documentation

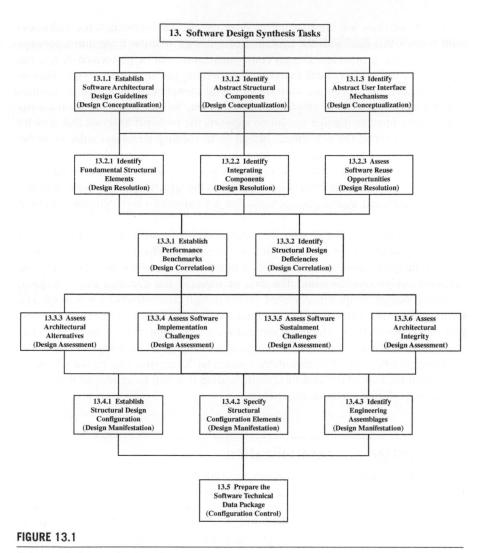

FIGURE 13.1

Software design synthesis tasks.

associated with each element of the design in preparation for the transition to software implementation.

6. *Configuration control*—the technical documentation for the software product configuration is placed under configuration control and the technical data package (TDP) is prepared. The TDP contains the specifications, drawings, diagrams, and associated documentation that will be delivered to the software implementation team to convey the design characteristics for each software configuration element.

These activities are intended to organize the design synthesis tasks into common themes that deal with the evolution of a design solution from initial concept to resolved and manifested. Design conceptualization can be performed during the early execution of functional analysis. This permits the structural design solution to be roughed out to capture abstract structural components in a natural, instinctive manner. This activity implies an imaginative, artistic treatment of the software design practice. Design resolution supports the trade-off analyses that may be performed to refine the conceptual design or to identify structural units from the completed functional architecture. This results in a design in which the conceptual design and structural units must be aligned by the identification of integrating structural components. Design correlation establishes the structural associations between structural units and abstract components that are enforced via integrating structural components.

The remainder of this chapter discusses each of the software design synthesis tasks and provides some guidance on how the software structural design is formulated. Principally, these tasks establish a three-tiered paradigm for describing the software design configuration. The first or topmost tier captures the conceptual structural design components derived via the design conceptualization activity. The third or bottommost tier identifies the fundamental structural design elements (units and components) from which the structural configuration will be fabricated. The second or middle tier provides the design chasm that must be bridged to unify the fundamental structural elements with the conceptual design structure. Figure 13.2 identifies the three tiers of the structural configuration that will be employed throughout the software design synthesis discussion.

13.1 Design conceptualization

Design conceptualization encompasses the initial design tasks that contribute to establishing the overarching structural configuration. These tasks can be performed after the initial layers of the functional architecture have been fashioned. Developing a conceptual design involves the identification of abstract structural elements to devise broad design strategies intended to resolve pivotal design challenges. It is not crucial to stipulate the conceptual design elements meticulously at this time since the concept will be modified and refined as the functional architecture continues to evolve and provide additional technical insights. It may be desirable to defer embracing design interpretations that are founded on speculative or deductive conclusions. It is advisable to maintain the conceptual design solutions nebulous until technical evidence corroborates the selection of a preferred design arrangement.

13.1.1 Establish software architectural design guidelines

The software architectural guidelines must be established to address how the structural configuration will be devised or constrained to promote an effective, efficient, and

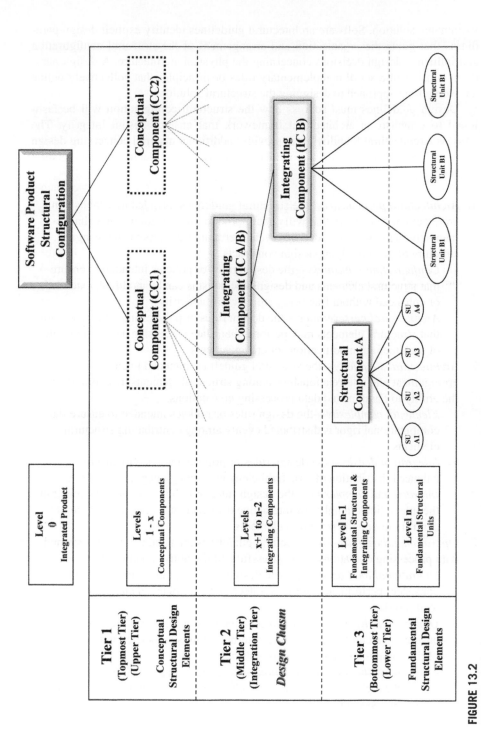

FIGURE 13.2

The software structural design three-tiered paradigm.

sustainable solution. Software architectural guidelines identify explicit design paradigms that guide the organization and arrangement of the structural configuration and influence design decisions concerning the physical architecture. A design paradigm consists of a set of complementary rules or principles that collectively define an overarching approach to designing the structural solution.

Design guidelines must address how the structural configuration will be fashioned to establish an architectural framework that ensures design integrity. The "Assess Architectural Stability" task provides additional material concerning design integrity. The following criteria should be considered when identifying architectural guidelines:

1. *Architectural permanence*—the structural guidelines intended to establish an architectural framework that will endure product modifications and enhancements throughout its intended life cycle. Permanence infers the unchanging structure of the underlying design constructs.
   - *Configuration robustness*—the design rules or policies intended to ensure that structural elements and design mechanisms can be modified, extended, or enhanced without fracturing architectural integrity.
   - *Architectural perseverance*—the design rules or policies intended to ensure that structural elements may perform their data processing actions regardless of architectural modifications or enhancements.
2. *Architectural simplicity*—the structural guidelines intended to ensure the arrangement and interrelationships among structural elements that complicate the ability to comprehend data processing conventions.
   - *Elemental complexity*—the design rules or policies intended to ensure that computational rigor is distributed evenly among contributing structural elements.
   - *Integration density*—the design rules or policies intended to ensure a balanced distribution of structural elements among integration tasks.
   - *Interactional complexity*— the design rules or policies intended to constrain the interactions (number of interactive data exchanges or transference of control) among the structural elements.
3. *Operational durability*—the structural guidelines intended to ensure sustained data processing operations under stressful and disruptive conditions.
   - *Operational load resilience*—the design rules or policies intended to ensure consistent performance of the architecture under planned and extreme workload profiles.
   - *Operational disruption acclimation*—the design rules or policies intended to ensure the architecture to endure external failures associated with elements of the computing environment or external systems.
   - *Computer technology assimilation*—the design rules or policies intended to ensure the architecture is resilient to changes in the computing environment equipment, systems, or applications.

13.1.2 **Identify abstract structural components**

Developing a conceptual design begins with the identification of abstract structural components. The top level of abstract components represents major containers for software functionality. These abstract components will provide the foundational elements upon which the design concept can be expressed, analyzed, and debated. Deliberation concerning the suitability of the design concept may result in the concept evolving into a more appropriate design concept. As functional analysis proceeds, the initial design concept must be reevaluated to determine if it continues to embody the operational nature of the software product.

Abstract structural components should be labeled for their role in carrying out the principal threads of operational behaviors. An abstract component should provide a single, focused role within the structural design concept. However, there are no restrictions on how many roles an abstract component may assume responsibility for. When considering how to label an abstract component, the primary focus should be placed on how the assortment of abstract structural components should be arranged to facilitate their interaction while diminishing structural complexity.

The conceptual design layers should be captured as a software block diagram to depict the arrangement of abstract structural components and their interfaces (internal and external). Since the software configuration does not embody any physical dimension, the structural layout of abstract components should be based on the relative prominence of each component within the design concept. An abstract interface should be identified to initially represent the data exchange relationships among abstract components and with external systems. The software block diagram should present the conceptual design at various levels of deliberation to contend with the most decisive design challenges.

In the early stages of forming conceptual design it is not necessary to include every conceivable abstract component. The conceptual design is merely a device for organizing the structural configuration to reflect the emerging perception gained from the functional solution. It is beneficial to formulate several design concepts that accentuate different architectural solutions to determine the preferred conceptual design configuration. Alternative conceptual configurations must be evaluated to identify the most balanced solution regarding the functional architecture, stakeholder requirements, and project cost and schedule constraints.

13.1.3 **Identify abstract user interface mechanisms**

The user interface mechanisms, in the form of screens, windows, and display gadgets, often form a focal point for the software conceptual design configuration. The software design concept may involve the identification of abstract user interface mechanisms that may be regarded as structural components. User interface mechanisms typically provide access to, and activation of, software functionality. However, user interface mechanisms, such as windows, screens, dialog boxes, or drop-down menus or buttons, are structural design widgets of which the behavior facilitates user interactions with the software product.

During the conceptualization of the design solution user interface mechanisms should be abstract in nature to provide a placeholder for further design delineation. The conceptual design solution should not invoke user interface drawings, mock-ups, or prototyping since it may be premature to elect design preferences. The user interface mechanisms must be fashioned to facilitate user interactions with the software product, and therefore necessitates the application of human factors and ergonomic[1] analysis (physical, cognitive, organizational, and environmental) to devise appropriate human–software interactions.

As the structural design solution advances, the user interface may need to be accentuated to promote stakeholder consensus as to the suitability of the mechanisms, their arrangement, and appearances. Prototyping the user interface should be the last course of action taken in an attempt to garner stakeholder acceptance of a proposed user interface design solution. Developing a user interface prototype is a considerable undertaking that results in a tangible, observable mockup or visual representation of the graphical display mechanisms. Every prototype represents a significant investment by the project that may be extravagant given the availability of alternative approaches to portraying the user interface design solution. Prototyping is analogous to software development in terms of the effort to specify the scope of the prototype, design the it architecturally, and implement (design, code, test, and integrate) it.

The following types of design representation should be considered before electing to develop a costly, time-consuming user interface prototyping effort:

1. *Illustrating*, which establishes illustrated or computer-generated graphical representations of the individual user interface (UI) mechanisms.
2. Content mapping, which identifies the relationships and manner of traversing among UI mechanisms. Extremely useful in representing information display and data input form layouts.
3. *Storyboarding*, which is used to express the progressive UI screens that the software will render to demonstrate the user experience. Storyboards can be used to sketch UI design concepts that correspond to individual operational processes.
4. *Modeling*, which is the generation of UI mechanisms or screens within automated design tools to enable UI graphics to be rapidly generated and modified. These UI models can be used to capture stakeholder feedback at a reasonable cost, which contributes to the specification of UI design mechanisms. The final UI design documentation and diagrams can be generated by the automated toolset.

---

[1] See *http://en.wikipedia.org/wiki/Human_factors_and_ergonomics* for more on human–system/ human–computer interactions as forms of cognitive economics. The term *human–software interaction* is used here to address the factors that affect the design of software products.

13.2 **Design resolution**

Design resolution encompasses the identification of the fundamental structural design elements and configuration alternatives to investigate the characteristics of each structural design solution. Utilizing the nearly complete functional architecture, structural units and components must be identified and specified. Structural units provide the "material" or building blocks necessary to perform specified functional behaviors and form a structural design solution.

13.2.1 **Identify fundamental structural elements**

The fundamental structural design elements must be identified to establish the bottom tier of the structural design solution. The fundamental structural design elements include structural units and components that are depicted in Figure 13.2 within the bottom tier of the software structural design paradigm. Structural units are established and synthesized by grouping and combining similar, compatible, or complementary functional units into a single structural design element. Structural components identified within the bottommost tier represent more complex functional units of which the behavioral solution was understood and required no further decomposition. These structural components may need to be decomposed into two or more structural units to provide an efficient, effective design solution.

This task results in the identification of the bottom-tier structural design elements. It is desirable for the bottom tier to involve no more than two level of elements, with the lower level consisting of structural units and the upper level organizing structural components. These fundamental structural elements represent the software modules—procedures or objects that will be specified and conveyed to the software implementation team for programming (detailed design, coding, testing, and integrating).

Structural units are distinguished by sorting, correlating, and combining functional units into a cohesive, synthesized design element. This is accomplished by

- Unifying the functional unit specifications into a single structural unit specification.
- Resolving contradictory, incongruous characteristics within the unified specification.
- Refining the performance attributes against which the structural unit will be implemented.
- Incorporating any necessary supervisory or administrative behavior into the specification.

The resulting structural unit specification should entail the requirements that address the cohesive behaviors for the structural unit.

Structural components are resolved by analyzing the functional component specification and ascertaining the prerequisite structural mechanisms necessary to satisfy functional component behaviors. This should result in the identification of two or more structural units that, when integrated together, will comply with the functional component specification.

13.2.2 Identify integrating components

At this juncture in the design synthesis practice the upper and lower tiers of the design solution have been resolved with a conceptual and fundamental arrangement of structural design elements. Between these two tiers emerges the *design chasm*, which must be bridged to unite the conceptual design layers with the structural design layers. This design chasm can only be traversed by identifying integrative structural components that either:

- Progressively extend the structural design layers toward the conceptual design components.
- Progressively decompose the conceptual design components to envelop the elements of the structural design layers.

Integrating components enable the conceptual and structural design layers to coalesce into a comprehensive, unified structural design solution. Integrating components should be recognizable as conceptual mechanisms of which the purpose is to provide an assembly packaging apparatus. The integration tier provides one or more layers of integrating components that align the lower-tier structural components with upper-tier conceptual components. The following guidelines suggest some principles for determining how to identify integrating components:

- Integrating components should provide an intuitive adaptation in the transition from the structural to conceptual design layer.
- Each integrating component should represent a significant assembly and integration action and should form a perceptible element within the structural configuration.
- Integrating components should provide a judicious progression of the software integration and testing strategy. The result of each integration and testing endeavor should be a self-contained, proven structural component with verified interfaces.
- Minor, incremental integration actions should be avoided unless they are deliberately devised to mitigate risks.

Every integrating component is a higher-level structural component. The rationale for distinguishing between the structural and integrating components is the level within the structural configuration in which they are stationed or located. Structural components are situated in the top level of the bottommost tier and were derived unambiguously from the functional architecture as large, complex functional units.

13.2.3 Assess software reuse opportunities

As the structural configuration matures it may be advantageous to investigate opportunities for reusing existing software packages. Existing software packages may be available from other companies or exist within the enterprise's proprietary software repository. To determine if an existing software package is beneficial to be incorporated into the software product configuration, an engineering cost-benefit analysis must be conducted. This is sometimes referred to as a "make-or-buy" analysis to support design decision making. The make-or-buy analysis assesses the viability of utilizing a software nondevelopmental item (NDI) in lieu of incurring the expense of developing a new software package (structural component or unit). A make-or-buy analysis is a form of trade-off analysis that will be discussed in Chapter 14.

A software make-or-buy analysis evaluates the advantages of incorporating an existing software package into the design structure. The following factors should be addressed by this analytical deliberation:

1. *Availability of a suitable NDI solution.* Software packages may bear many superficial characteristics in common with the structural element definition. However, there are several industrial practices that may negate an existing software package from consideration, including:
   - What is the maturity of the NDI software package? How dependable is the software package based on its operational experience? How stable is the NDI software package in terms of problem reports and fixes?
   - Is the provider or supplier of the software package able to continue to support the package if it were incorporated into the software product configuration?
   - Can the source code and documentation be purchased to enable continued sustainment should the provider/supplier go out of business?
   - Are there licensing or proprietary right issues with distributing the NDI software package as an element of the software product configuration?
2. *NDI package technical characteristics.* While an NDI software package may appear suitable at first glance at the specifications, there are performance-related details that must be addressed:
   - Will the NDI package execute properly within the specified computing environment?
   - What are the performance benchmarks for the package on a computing environment that is similarly configured to the target computing environment?
   - How efficiently does the package utilize computing resources?
   - What is the precision of the data value resulting from the data processing calculation?
   - What language was the NDI software implemented? Can an alternate language be assimilated and integrated into the overall software product configuration? Can the NDI package be assembled and complied with the software product configuration or does it need to be linked at build time?
   - Are the NDI package external interface and associated software interfaces adequately documented to facilitate integrating the package into the software product structural configuration?

For each candidate NDI package the software engineering team must gather the information concerning its availability and suitability for incorporation into the software design configuration. This information is used to conduct a software reuse trade-off analysis. The candidate NDI costs and benefits, performance, and risks will be evaluated against the projected implementation and testing costs associated with further development of the targeted software structural unit or component. The use of commercially off-the-shelf (COTS) database management systems (DBMS) or similarly available COTS packages should not warrant a make-or-buy analysis. These packages are widely used to support software application development and have proven their adaptability to a variety of data persistence tasks.

13.3 Design correlation

Design correlation involves the application of software engineering practices to fine-tune the structural configuration to bring the design solution within specification. The cohesive structural design exhibits collaborative technical and performance characteristics that must be gauged against the functional architecture and software requirements specifications. Aspects of the design solution that fall short of these prerequisites must be adjusted to bring the structural design into compliance. The design refinement actions should be guided by the conduct of an engineering trade-off analysis.

13.3.1 Establish performance benchmarks

The performance characteristics (benchmarks) of prominent design mechanisms should be established for the bottom tier of the structural design solution. Prominent design mechanisms involve structural elements of which the notional data structures, data transformation algorithms, data integrity assurance, and data transference procedures are computationally demanding or challenging. Performance benchmarks establish estimated data processing efficiencies and effectiveness of design mechanisms within the boundary of the structural design. Performance benchmarks establish the design goals for structural elements against which software implementation can be evaluated. Performance benchmarks are derived from the structural specifications accounting for the distribution of data processing functionality among structural units and components identified within the bottom tier of the structural configuration.

It is necessary to establish the performance benchmarks for the bottom-tier structural elements since they represent the building block that will be implemented (designed, coded, and tested) against the structural specifications. The performance benchmarks must establish the performance requirements to be specified for the lower-tier structural units and components.

The performance of the integrated software product is a result of the sequential integration of the structural elements, through several levels of integration. Software performance engineering must account for the effect of any encumbrance the assimilation burden may have at the integrated component or product levels.

The progressive assimilation through the levels of integration must be accounted for to establish accurate structural element performance specifications.

Computing resource–intensive processes may perform adequately when initially evaluated, before any integration has occurred. However, the integration detracts from individual structural element performance as computing resources must be shared with other data process threads. The intent is to understand the implications of apportioning computing resources among interrelated, interdependent, and isolated design elements. This suggests that software execution profiles must be analyzed within the context of the computing system execution framework. This permits the software performance benchmarks to account for resource sharing, multi-user workloads, and other conditions that may be encountered during software product operations.

Software performance benchmarks should establish the computational durations and resource utilization requirements for the structural elements throughout the structural configuration. These benchmarks must extrapolate structural design mechanism performance to account for the integrated product's execution profile constrained by the shared computing system's resource demand and allocation strategy. These performance benchmarks provide an engineering approximation of the performance characteristics derived from the functional architecture specifications.

The intent of this practice is to ensure that software product performance is designed into the structural configuration. It is not acceptable to delay focus on performance to software testing. By that time, the structural architectural decisions have established a design configuration that impedes performance satisfaction. Software performance must be an integral design consideration throughout the engineering of the software product. Establishing software performance benchmarks addresses understanding how structural design elements provide constructive, collaborative data processing mechanisms to satisfy performance objectives. Performance is realized by aggregating performance-related measures from the bottom-tier design elements up through the structural configuration.

13.3.2 Identify structural design deficiencies

The structural configuration should be evaluated to identify design challenges and impediments that hinder the establishment of a complete, coherent design solution. The identified structural elements involve abstract design mechanisms that may not adequately support the operational data processing transactions effectively or efficiently. These abstract design mechanisms must be fortified or replaced with design mechanisms that will perform their actions properly under all operational scenarios and conditions. Identified design issues should be evaluated and prioritized to distinguish them in terms of their:

1. Technical imperative or necessity to be resolved.
2. Scope associated with their relevance to the overall design solution.
3. Consequences or impact if the deficiency is not resolved.

Prioritization of design issues focuses the attention of the software engineering team on design issues that have the most significant impact on the design solution. Many design challenges may be considered a risk to project success. A risk involves any aspect of the structural design that could potentially impact one or more of the following project success factors:

- The software development project's budget, resources, and schedule adequacy to afford a high level of confidence for successful execution.
- The product suitability and dependability in regard to satisfying stakeholders' needs and expectations. For consumer products, this addresses the viability of the product to capture sufficient market share to generate the anticipated return on investment.
- The availability of technical skills and expertise within the software development team to implement and test the structural design mechanisms successfully.
- The structural design provides an effective basis for software product sustainment (post-development). This involves the structural configuration and its design mechanization's ability to facilitate: (1) identification, isolation, and resolution of design deficiencies (bug fixes); and (2) the incorporation of pre-planned product improvements (P^3I).

The prioritized design deficiencies must be evaluated to determine which design issues will be investigated to work toward a restorative design solution. There are four principle areas that are addressed here as a way to present a simplified categorization of software design influences. A description of these principle areas is provided below to introduce the subsequent design synthesis tasks:

1. *Product design preferences*. The evaluation of design alternatives in terms of their performance characteristics. The focus of this task is to assess each proposed design strategy in terms of the effectiveness, efficiency, and simplicity. The result of this task is a set of viable alternatives ranked in terms of technical inclination.
2. *Product implementation implications*. The evaluation of design alternatives in terms of the software implementation and testing organizations' ability to execute and integrate the abstract design mechanisms into the structural design solution.
3. *Product sustainment implications*. The evaluation of design alternatives in terms of the software sustainment organization's ability to repair, extend (increase in scope), and augment (incorporate additional functionality or data processing variations) the structural design solution given the inclusion of abstract design mechanisms.
4. *Product design integrity*. The evaluation of the architectural-level structure in terms of the structural integrity and integrity (adherence to design principles and standards) associated with integrating abstract design mechanisms within the structural design solution.

13.3.3 Assess architectural alternatives

Architectural alternatives identify distinctive abstract design mechanisms intended to perform demanding data processing transactions. It may be difficult to resolve convoluted design situations flawlessly without sufficient design analysis. Brainstorming can be used to identify potential design alternatives that lead to innovative solutions. However, design decisions must be made with sufficient comprehension of the merits and inadequacies associated with each design paradigm or mechanism. The preferred architectural approach should be determined to be one that is balanced in terms of design effectiveness, efficiency, scalability, and simplicity. Establishing the relative importance of architectural quality factors or preferences is often where the design of software products is mistaken as an artistic practice. The term *architecture* embraces the unification of art and science within the construction engineering discipline. It is of no consequence for a software product to exhibit a stunningly attractive user interface if the product's performance cannot satisfy the demands of the customer's operational or business environment.

Trade studies should be conducted to gain an appreciation for the best architectural approach to adopt among competing alternatives. Each trade study originates with the identification of two or more approaches to an identified technical obstacle. These competing design alternatives must be defined and adequately characterized to support a thorough trade-off analysis (see Chapter 14).

13.3.4 Assess software implementation challenges

The software engineering team involves representatives of the software implementation team to ensure that the structural configuration and assemblages provide a context for software implementation. The software implementation representatives must sanction the structural design solution declaring that it may be achieved within established implementation plans, resources, and schedule constraints. The software implementation team must evaluate the scope of the workload implied by the architectural solution. Several factors must be considered to appreciate the software implementation workload:

1. The skills and experience of the software implementation personnel to design, code, test, and integrate the structural elements into a complete software product configuration.
2. The data manipulation dexterity of the programming language constructs (statements, semantics, evocation, extensibility, etc.) to enable software units to be effectively and efficiently designed and coded.
3. The appropriateness and suitability of structural specifications to commence implementation.
4. The availability of project resources (personnel, equipment, facilities, funding, schedule, etc.) apportioned to the software implementation tasks.

Software implementation challenges must be resolved prior to the critical design review (CDR). The CDR represents a project milestone that signifies the architectural solution is sufficient to begin the software implementation phase of the software development project. The software implementation team should endorse the architectural solution prior to the conduct of the CDR. Any lingering issues the software implementation team has with the architectural solution should be deemed inconsequential to delay the project review of the architectural solution.

Programming language selection is often done for reasons other than the technical challenges inherent with the architectural solution. Frequently, the programming language is driven by the availability of experienced and skilled staff members. However, the programming language selection may impose significant challenges associated with implementing the architectural solution. The following factors must be considered when making a programming language selection:

1. *Programming language technical capabilities.* Does the language support the data processing characteristics challenges inherent with the architectural solution?
2. *Programmer productivity.* Does the software implementation team have the proficiency in the programming language to design, code, test, and integrate the architectural solution?
3. *Availability of programming language tools, training, and consultative services.* Is the programming language supported with adequate educational and technical services to facilitate staff knowledge acquisition and automated tool support. Programming language tools include compilers, assemblers, programmatic design, code generation, debugging, and documentation applications.

13.3.5 Assess software sustainment challenges

The software engineering team involves representatives of the software sustainment team to ensure that the architectural configuration and design mechanisms provide a context for customer and product support. The software sustainment representatives must sanction the structural design solution declaring it may be maintained, within established sustainment plans, resources, and schedule constraints.

The baseline work plan for software product sustainment may include the effort to provide customer support, help-desk operations, design deficiency resolution and P^3I. Once the initial software development effort is completed, the software sustainment team may be augmented by authoritative software engineering and implementation personnel to supervise significant software product enhancements.

13.3.6 Assess architectural integrity

The integrity of the physical architecture must be evaluated to determine its ability to adapt to future changes and conformance with established architectural guidelines. The following are some suggested assessment definitions based on the guidelines suggested by task 13.1.1, establish architectural design guidelines:

1. *Architectural permanence*—an assessment of the ability of the architectural framework to endure product modifications and enhancements throughout its intended life cycle.

- Configuration robustness—the ability of structural elements and design mechanisms to be modified, extended, or enhanced without violating architectural guidelines.
- Elemental perseverance—the ability of structural elements to perform their data processing actions regardless of architectural modifications or enhancements.

2. *Architectural simplicity*— – an assessment of the arrangement and interrelationships among structural elements that complicate the ability to comprehend data processing conventions.
   - Elemental complexity—an assessment of the distribution of computational rigor among contributing structural elements.
   - Integration density—an assessment of the balanced distribution of structural elements involved in integration tasks.
   - Interactional complexity—an assessment of the number of interactive data exchanges or transference of control among structural elements.

3. *Operational durability*— – the ability of the architecture to sustain data processing operations under stressful and disruptive conditions.
   - Operational load resilience—an assessment of the consistency of performance by the architecture under planned and extreme workload profiles.
   - Operational disruption acclimation—an assessment of the ability of the architecture to endure external failures associated with elements of the computing environment or external systems.
   - Computer technology assimilation—the ability of the architecture to adapt to changes in the computing environment equipment, systems, or applications.

These architectural assessments focus on three primary aspects of the structural configuration's ability to endure enhancement and refurbishment resulting from varying operational needs, technological advances, or the resolution of design defects. Architectural permanence and simplicity address the positive qualities that permeate the structural configuration and enable it to endure post-development turmoil (product operations and sustainment). Simplicity of design is the inverse of complexity and results from the use of a small number of uncomplicated elements to maximum effect. This is achieved by striving for a minimalist approach to architectural attainment. Permanence of design addresses the enduring nature of the structural foundation on which the product design is based. The inverse of permanence is transience, which infers that the architecture will endure only a short time and cannot remain unchanged for an extended period of time. Architectural permanence and simplicity are design principles that must be pursued to establish a stable architectural configuration.

Operational durability addresses the ability of the product architecture to adapt to anticipated operational situations and changes in computing technology. These operational durability measures address the ability of the software architecture to make adjustments in response to a change in the operational environment or status. The objective is to maintain software performance within acceptable levels despite the variable, sometimes erratic, operational conditions a software product must tolerate.

13.4 Design manifestation

Design manifestation is the preparation of architecture diagrams, drawings, and documentation that detail the structural configuration. This includes the specification of every element of the structural design, external and internal interfaces, and associated data structures. Structural configuration items that need software stubs to support software integration testing should be identified as engineering assemblies and these test stubs specified.

13.4.1 Establish the structural design configuration

The structural design configuration should be placed under technical configuration control to prevent the introduction of inadvertent changes. Every element of the structural configuration should be uniquely identified per approved software configuration control procedures. From this point forward, only change requests or proposals that have been approved by the software change control board (CCB) should be integrated into the structural configuration.

13.4.2 Specify structural configuration elements

Each element of the structural configuration must be specified to support software implementation. These specifications represent the technical requirements for the design, code generation, testing, and integration of structural units and components. Each structural element specification, diagram, and drawing should be placed under technical configuration control before being included in the software technical data package.

13.4.3 Identify engineering assemblages

Engineering assemblies should be identified and the additional test stubs specified. The identification of engineering assemblies provides the complete scope of work necessary for the software implementation team to plan and execute software integration and testing. Engineering assemblies involve the integration of structural components and the associated test stubs needed to verify integration success.

13.5 Prepare the software technical data package

The software technical data package (TDP) must be finalized in preparation for the CDR. At this stage of development, the software technical data package is marked *engineering* to distinguish it from the *release* version that supports the software build and product replication processes. The software TDP contains the software bill of material (BOM) for the software implementation phase of development. It identifies the software architecture material that describes the software product under development. This TDP involves the complete set of drawings, diagrams, documentation, and models that describe the software product to be implemented. The TDP involves a software BOM and the complete set of software product documentation material or a reference to the authorized version of each material item. Material items that are being hosted electronically must be identified by a file identifier and location where they are stored within an engineering data management facility (or software product data management (PDM) application).

The following material must be identified within the software BOM:

1. Software Product Identification
    1.1. Nomenclature
    1.2. Product Identifier
2. Software Requirements Baseline Material
    2.1. Software Requirements Specifications
    2.2. Software Interface Specifications
    2.3. Operational Models
        2.3.1. Operational Scenario A
        2.3.2. Operational Scenario B
    2.4. Operational Environment Description
3. Software Functional Architecture Material
    3.1. Functional Hierarchy
    3.2. Behavioral Models
    3.3. Functional Specifications (Optional[*])
4. Software Physical Architecture Material
    4.1. Architectural Guidelines and Principles
    4.2. Structural Configuration—Tier 1 (Abstract Components)
    4.3. Structural Configuration—Tier 2-N (Integration Components)
    4.4. Structural Configuration—Tier N (Structural Components)
    4.5. Structural Configuration—Tier M (Structural Units)
5. External Interface Design
    5.1. DBMS Design Document
        5.1.1. Table Descriptions
        5.1.2. Query Descriptions
    5.2. (External System) Interface Description Document
6. Outstanding Change Requests and Proposals
7. Computing Environment Description
8. Notes

---

[*]*Note:* The functional architecture has been included in this software BOM to provide a complete description of the software product architecture. The functional unit specifications are incorporated into the structural configuration element specifications. Therefore, it is not necessary for them to be included in the software BOM, although they will be required to support software configuration audits.

Software Analysis Practice 14

CHAPTER OUTLINE

The software analysis practice stage involves the analytical tasks for performing a variety of engineering trade studies to assist in making architecture-based design decisions. Software analysis trade studies address compound situations that involve an array of factors concerning the software product and its life cycle, and the software development project. This distinguishes software analysis trade studies from other types of analysis techniques that may only focus on establishing software product characteristics.

Software analysis trade studies may be referred to as trade-off analysis, which is a technical form of cost-benefit analysis. An engineering trade study is more complicated than a cost-benefit analysis since it is intended to achieve a balance among a broader range of competing product characteristics, technical and project-related risk factors, as well as considerations for life-cycle cost implications. Software architectural design alternatives must be expressed in terms of the level of stakeholder satisfaction, projected software product life-cycle costs (development and post-development processes operations), and anticipated benefits to the enterprise over time. Software engineering trade studies are devised to be holistic by considering a full range of factors in the decision-making process.

Trade studies must be established in a manner that provides a "value" assessment for competing architectural alternatives. Architectural decisions should contribute to establishing an enduring structural framework (composition, organization, arrangement, and structure) for the software product that can withstand extreme operational situations, adapt to changing computer technology, and accommodate future enhancements and improvements. Software architectural alternatives must be evaluated in a manner that permits the analysts to gather information concerning a variety of design repercussions, including:

- Software product features and functionality
- Product performance
- Aesthetics or user interface "look and feel"
- Difficulty to implement
- Difficulty to test and evaluate
- Impact on software replication (reproduce the executables on distribution media) and distribution
- Impact on user training and comprehension
- Impact on customer support processes
- Impact on product support processes
- Impact on product enhancement and scalability
- Alignment with organizational objectives, such as product lines, component reuse, and product frameworks.

Software analysis involves 16 tasks that are organized within six general themes. These themes identify a typical flow for conducting a trade study. However, the tasks within a theme may be conducted in any order or sequence suitable to the trade-study situation. The trade-study themes and tasks are identified in Figure 14.1. The six themes are:

1. Defining the trade study
2. Preparing the trade-study environment
3. Conducting the evaluation
4. Assessing project repercussions
5. Evaluating trade-study results
6. Decision assimilation

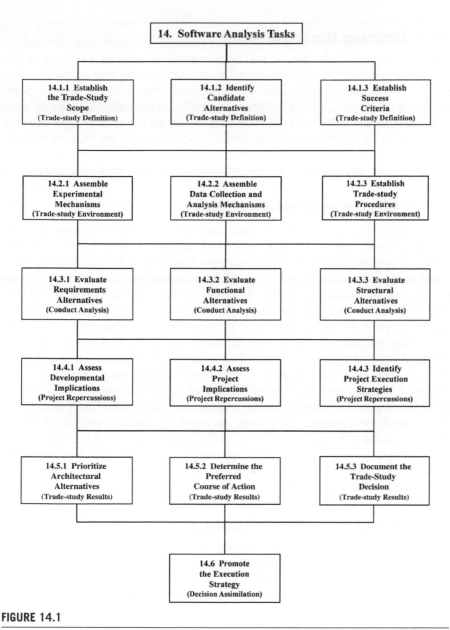

FIGURE 14.1

Software analysis tasks.

14.1 Defining the trade study

Every architectural trade study should be formally authorized by the leader of the software engineering team. Architectural trade studies imply that an architectural function, differentiating characteristic, or performance objective represents a decisive opportunity to impact product performance, quality, or durability. The design decision should not be left to a single individual due to the repercussions the decision may have on the product throughout its life cycle. Therefore, the decision must be derived by a consensus vote of the software engineering team, and may involve other members of the project management team, customers, or important stakeholders.

14.1.1 Establish the trade-study scope

Trade studies originate from architectural challenges affecting the software product definition. These areas of concern involve: (1) the establishment of an achievable software requirements baseline, (2) formulating the functional architecture and its representative behavioral models, and (3) establishing a robust structural configuration for the physical architecture. Each area of concern represents a distinct type of architectural decision that can potentially affect other aspects of the architectural solution.

The scope of each trade study must be defined to restrain the investigation and ensure that the analysis will provide the data necessary to facilitate an informed, impartial design decision. Therefore, the manner in which the trade study is defined deserves thoughtful consideration. Establishing the trade-study scope should be driven by the data required to be collected and analyzed to support the architectural assessment. The problem under investigation may present itself as a stakeholder need, performance, behavioral, structural, or quality concern. However, every architectural decision may entail complications associated with other aspects of the product definition and life-cycle processes. No architectural decision should be taken casually. Conversely, the rigors applied in conducting the trade study must be tempered to the significance of the architectural problem being evaluated.

14.1.2 Identify the candidate alternatives

For each architectural challenge there may be a vast number of alternatives that complicates the selection of viable alternatives. The candidate solutions that will be considered during the trade study only include those of which the potential for enhancing the software architecture are significant. The list of possible solutions must be trimmed to a small set of viable candidates. Candidates should be assessed to surmise the anticipated benefits and consequences of incorporating the solution into the software architecture. The following questions should be contemplated when attempting to appraise the viability of candidate solutions:

1. What are the important technical characteristics associated with the solution?
2. How should the solution contribute to the architectural integrity (adherence to architectural principles) of the software product architecture?

3. How should the proposed solution affect the performance characteristics of the integrated software solution?
4. What is an acceptable level of difficulty associated with implementing and testing the solution?
5. How should the solution impact software operational and sustainment processes?

These questions and others should be used to establish the trade-study entrance criteria for candidate solutions. Entrance criteria provide the prerequisite conditions that must be satisfied for a candidate solution to be included in the list of viable candidates. Viable candidates may be prioritized to establish an authoritative ranking among the alternatives prior to the conduct of the trade-off analysis. The list of prioritized alternatives should be presented to stakeholder representatives at the trade-study kick-off meeting. Stakeholders should be canvassed to identify any further factors that may contribute to a candidate solution from being considered or ranked differently.

14.1.3 Establish the success criteria

The success criteria must be established, against which candidate alternatives will be assessed. Success criteria establish the minimally acceptable and objective factors that characterize the ideal solution. This provides a range of values for each success factor within which an alternative should be deemed acceptable. The alternative that is determined to be best suited to be adopted into the software architecture should conform to a majority of the success criteria.

Success criteria must address an assortment of software life-cycle factors, including performance, technical difficulty to implement, usability, effect on the enduring properties of the software architecture, and risks to project success. These criteria should be weighted to prove a balanced appraisal of an alternative. The success criteria and weighting scheme should ensure that all success factors influence the determination of the preferred solution.

A radar or spider chart provides a diagrammatic means of expressing the success criteria and rating the alternatives. A radar chart is a graphical method of displaying multivariate data in the form of a two-dimensional plot of three or more quantitative variables. Each variable or success factor is measured on an axis that extends from a center point similar to a spoke on a wheel. The innermost ring of values represents the minimal value for each success factor and the outermost ring of values represents the objective values. When an alternative's measurement falls below the innermost ring, touching the center point, it has not met the minimally acceptable criteria. If the measurement extends beyond the outermost ring, it has exceeded the objective criteria. Multiple alternatives can be plotted on the diagram to provide a comparison among them in a simple manner. Figure 14.2 provides an example of the radar chart.

14.2 Establish the trade-study environment

The environment in which the trade study will be conducted must be established and qualified that it is suitable to perform the investigations. The trade-study

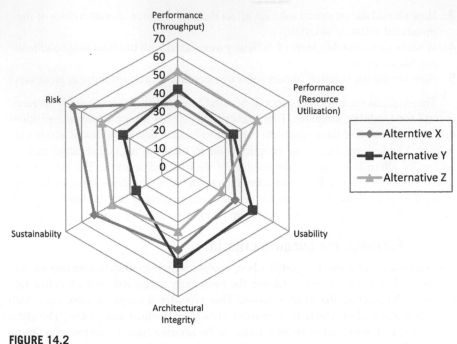

FIGURE 14.2

Radar or spider chart example.

environment involves the mechanisms (tools, equipment, and scenarios), data collection and analysis tools, and procedures that define how the trade study will be performed.

There are a variety of approaches to conducting a trade study. However, the "design of experiments" involves a formal, scientific approach to gather data under controlled conditions. The term *experiment* implies an efficient approach to gathering engineering data that enables conclusions to be drawn. To establish a "controlled" experiment, it is necessary to ensure that the experimental environment can be controlled in a manner that provides consistent, repeatable results. The trade-study methodology must ensure the accuracy and nonbiased assessment of competing architectural alternatives.

14.2.1 Assemble the experimental mechanisms

The trade-study definition should provide sufficient information concerning the investigation to determine the tools, models, or simulations that are needed to support the trade study. These experimental mechanisms must be assembled and qualified. Trade-study tools and models should provide abstract representations of each architectural alternative. A computer-based simulation provides dynamic modeling mechanisms that emulate expected operational or behavioral responses of a design representation to stimuli and conditional situations. Experimental mechanisms should be defined in a manner that enables each architectural alternative to be evaluated under the same conditions to ensure the consistency of the data collected.

The experimental mechanisms should express the architectural alternatives at a level of engineering detail that reflects the maturity of the overall software architecture. The mechanisms must exhibit the design characteristics needed to assess the competing alternatives against the evaluation success criteria. Experimental techniques must address the scenarios that will be used to exercise the alternatives and generate the data required for comparative analysis. Scenarios should identify the preconditions and sequence of events under which the experiment will be conducted. Unlike a test case, it is not necessary to establish the expected outcomes for a scenario. The results of the experiment are to be captured and analyzed to determine how the architectural alternatives reacted to each scenario.

14.2.2 Assemble the data collection and analysis mechanisms

The purpose of a trade study is to establish the relative value proposition of each competing architectural alternative. To accomplish this, the ability to gather and analyze the proper data is influential toward the relevance and suitability of conclusions drawn from the data sets. Data collection tools, instruments, and appendages are directly predisposed by the selected experimental mechanisms. Therefore, data collection and analysis mechanisms must be considered during the identification of the experimental mechanisms defined in the "Assemble Experimental Mechanisms" task.

There are a variety of approaches to collecting and analyzing experimental data sets dependent on the experimental approach utilized. Table 14.1 provides a list of data collection mechanisms available and the types of analytical techniques that support their analysis. When computer-based models and simulations are employed it may be necessary to assess the fidelity of each model to capture and preserve the pertinent data elements. The precision of the model parameters must be harmonized to ensure a consistent data set for analysis. The data files resulting from the experimentation should be backed up and controlled to provide an historical record of the trade-study outcomes. The data analysis techniques represented in Table 14.1 are defined as follows:

1. *Time series analysis*—the analysis of a sequence of data points, measured typically at successive time instants spaced at uniform time intervals. The analysis of time series data for the purpose of extracting meaningful statistics and other characteristics from the data.
2. *Data mining*—a technique that attempts to discover patterns in large data sets or databases.
3. *Sensitivity analysis*—an assessment of how the output of a model can be attributed to the input to support what-if analysis exploring the impact of varying input assumptions and scenarios.

Table 14.1 Data Collection Mechanisms and Analysis Techniques

Data Collection Mechanism	Description	Data Analysis Techniques							
		Time Series	Data Mining	Sensitivity Analysis	Structural Analysis	Behavioral Analysis	Quantitative Analysis	Qualitative Analysis	Simulation
Survey	Used when there is a need for a particular class of people to provide expert opinion in the area of concern.	X	X						
Interviews	Used when there is a need to gain first-hand information from stakeholders, users, or other experts. It is unsuitable in cases where there is a need to gather data form a large number of individuals.	X	X						
Group consensus	Used to obtain the consolidated opinions of a select group of individuals and to sort out personal opinions or prejudices.	X				X		X	
Engineering judgment	The application of professional engineering knowledge to work out a solution or render a course of action.	X	X	X		X		X	
Scientific experimentation	A test under controlled conditions to demonstrate a known truth, examine the validity of a hypothesis, or determine the efficacy of something previously untried.	X		X	X	X	X	X	X
Physical models	A conceptual, graphical, or mathematical representation of a real-world product or process being studied. Physical models are typically used when it is either impossible or impractical to create experimental conditions in which scientific experimentation can directly measure outcomes. A model is also a way in which the human thought process can be amplified or assumptions can be clarified.	X		X	X		X	X	
Computer-based models	The development of a software-based model of a product or process for the purpose of obtaining an understanding of anticipated or unanticipated behaviors or results.	X		X	X	X	X	X	X

4. *Structural analysis*—a determination of the effects of physical or environmental loads on physical structures and their components. Structures subject to this type of analysis include buildings, bridges, vehicles, machinery, furniture, etc. The results of the analysis are used to verify a structure's fitness for use, often eliminating the need for physical stress testing.

5. *Behavioral analysis*—Reproduces the required behavior of the modeled system in terms of functional, control, and data flows; resource utilization; execution duration; and interface data transmission rates.

6. *Quantitative analysis*—improves the overall quality of decision making through the use of complex mathematical and statistical modeling, measurement, and research. These techniques are most commonly used in functional or behavioral models, decision trees, and simulations.

7. *Qualitative analysis*—provides a subjective way of analyzing data without using mathematics or statistics. It is used to investigate behaviors exhibited by a system to understand the design mechanisms that govern such behavior.

8. *Simulation*—the imitation of the behavior of a real-world process or system over time. Simulation is used with engineering modeling of natural or human-made systems to gain insight into their performance and behavior under various operational conditions.

14.2.3 Establish trade-study procedures

Trade studies are controlled experiments and involve adhering to a consistent set of procedures for each trial. The procedures must permit a consistent application of experimental conditions and stimuli for each alternative being evaluated. The trade-study procedures must be prepared so that they address the following stages of trade-study progression:

1. *Environment setup*—the preparation of the experiment for each candidate alternative.

2. *Initialization*—the loading of scenario data sets and preparation of data collection mechanisms to capture and record the experimental data.

3. *Execution*—the carrying out of actions, such as operator inputs during the trial scenario.

4. *Termination*—the actions necessary to end the trial and place the environmental and data collection mechanisms into an inactive state.

5. *Analysis*—the consistent approach to examining the captured data sets to identify the level of accomplishment achieved by each candidate alternative evaluated.

14.3 Conduct the analysis

The software analysis practice distinguishes between three types of trade studies that apply to the definition of the software architecture: requirements-oriented studies, functional architecture–oriented studies, and physical architecture studies. Each of these elements of the software architecture has unique characteristics that must be considered when conducting a trade study. Therefore, each of these analysis areas will be addressed separately in the following sections.

14.3.1 Evaluate requirement alternatives

Requirement trade studies should be conducted in the area of requirements to ensure that stakeholders and the software engineering team comprehend the implications of every requirement. There are several motivations for conducting a trade study within the requirements domain:

1. *Requirements as a communication mechanism.* The language used to express a requirement is ambiguous by design. Language is inherently ambiguous to permit the context in which a term is used to define its meaning. Whenever there are formal expectations concerning a product or service, the agreement that specifies the deliverable must not be ambiguous. Thus, establishing a clear understanding of stakeholder needs and expectations is vital to establishing an achievable software requirements baseline.
2. *Stakeholder needs and expectations may involve conflicting demands.* Stakeholders become absorbed with their particular needs and must be made to understand how individual demands conflict with other's needs. To resolve stakeholder conflicting demands, it may be necessary to conduct experiments to derive a proper balance among stakeholder needs.
3. *Software products automate business and operational processes.* While stakeholders may be familiar with their processes, the semantics used by stakeholders to describe a process may be overloaded with industrial terminology unfamiliar to software personnel. Operational models provide a mechanism to encapsulate and translate these process descriptions into a representation comprehensible to software-literate personnel.
4. *Requirements may overstate performance demands.* Requirements impose level-of-performance demands on data processing transactions. It may be necessary to establish operational models to assess the reasonableness of stringent performance expectations. The availability of software and computer technology to achieve performance expectations must be substantiated by analyzing alternative operational or computational approaches.

14.3.2 Evaluate functional alternatives

Functional models are a means of translating software requirements into logical or behavioral representations that focus on how a data processing transaction can be executed. This results in a functional decomposition from which the software structural configuration will be arranged. There are always multiple approaches to performing data processing transactions and deriving a functional breakdown. The primary reasons for conducting trade studies concerning the functional architecture are:

1. *Evaluating data processing transaction behaviors.* Transactions can become very complex as the number of conditional responses increase. Understanding all of the various discrepancies that may occur and determining the best approach to contend with each variation may necessitate the evaluation of alternatives.
2. *Evaluating resource utilization concentrations.* Certain transactions may consume a disproportionate amount of resources that must be resolved by determining how to adjust the data process burden to stabilize resource utilization.
3. *Evaluating data processing deadlock situations and resolution approaches.* Deadlock can occur any time two data processing transactions compete for resources. Understanding the resource utilization and allocation management strategy associated with design alternatives may provide important insight on how to best avoid deadlock situations.
4. *Evaluating failure modes and possible responses.* Understanding the most appropriate response strategy to failure modes may involve evaluating behavioral alternatives. Failures may arise from a number of sources, and each failure mode will affect the data processing control flow. Alternative approaches to responding to failure conditions should be analyzed and socialized to determine the best response.

14.3.3 Evaluate structural alternatives

The structural configuration represents how the software units are organized into structural components. This involves the assembled and integration tasks that correspond to the high-level conceptual structure of the software product. The preferred structural arrangement and integration strategies must be evaluated to comprehend the performance and physical characteristics associated with configuration alternatives. The primary reasons for conducting trade studies concerning the physical architecture are:

1. *Evaluating the arrangement of structural units.* The arrangement of structural units often imposes restrictions on the accessibility to software functionality. Alternative arrangements or groupings of structural units into structural components should be analyzed to determine the most acceptable structural arrangement.
2. *Evaluating the software integration strategy.* The approach to software integration imposes a workload associated with software integration and testing. The integration strategy may also affect software performance and resource utilization profiles. The consequences associated with the integration strategy can be best understood by evaluating alternative strategic schemes.
3. *Evaluating the integrity of structural solutions.* The structural solution must be evaluated to determine how well it conforms to structural design guidelines and

principles. Deviations from adopted design guidelines should be evaluated to determine if the departure from the guidelines adversely impacts operational performance or structural stability of the structural configuration. Alternative structural solutions may resolve the deviation, but may impose undesirable consequences on product performance and stability.

14.4 Assess project repercussions

Once the alternatives have been analyzed from a technical perspective, they must be evaluated to understand the impacts they may present if they were implemented within the existing project context. The initial assessment of the alternatives delved into the implied software implementation and operational and support challenges. However, the final determination concerning which of the architectural design approaches to advocate must account for the capacity of project resources to accommodate the design scheme.

14.4.1 Assess developmental implications

Each alternative should be evaluated to determine the work involved with implementing the design approach within the project and technical plans. The integrated master plan, schedule, and technical work packages should be reviewed to determine how the alternative corresponds to and complements the anticipated work assignments. The software engineering team must negotiate the adjustment of technical plans, schedules, and work packages with software development organizations. The objective is to ensure that the effort to pursue an architectural solution can be accommodated within established organizational resources.

Elements of architectural solutions may challenge the competencies of development organizations to assimilate a design solution within their plans. Each challenge should be identified as a technical risk to the adoption of a proposed architectural solution. Technical risks should be mitigated in a manner that presents an inconsequential liability to achieving project objectives. Development factors involve the ability to implement, test, and deploy the software product. Associated factors involve software operational stability, usability, user training and education, and software sustainment. This may necessitate the adoption of an innovative or unconventional programming paradigm, language, or computing platform. It is important to ensure that the full range of software product life-cycle factors is addressed before adopting an architectural design solution. The integrated product and process (IPPD) philosophy embraces considering the complete life-cycle set of factors when evaluating architectural design alternatives.

14.4.2 Assess project implications

The project team should evaluate the developmental implications and risks associated with the execution of competing alternatives. The project plan, schedule, and work breakdown structure (WBS) should be reviewed to determine how well each alternative corresponds to and complements the achievement of project objectives. The intent is to ensure that the effort to pursue an architectural solution can be accommodated within established project resources. The project team may propose the application of project reserve resources to accommodate uncertainty and protect against technical risks. The challenges associated with incorporating an architectural solution into the project structure must be evaluated to provide an adequate scheduling margin to account for potential complications.

14.4.3 Identify project execution strategies

A strategy should be developed for each architectural alternative to address how each solution would be assimilated into the current project situation. This involves the evaluation of project plans, schedules, and budgets that must be realigned to accommodate the architectural solution. Each execution strategy must account for the rework necessary to assimilate the design solution into the product configuration. This involves incorporating the solution into software product specifications, diagrams, and drawings to reflect the solution, as well as adjusting any of the software post-development process definitions and associated documentation.

Project plans and schedules must provide the flexibility to accommodate deviations caused by technical complications that may arise. Risks should be closely monitored and contingency tactics must be prepared to facilitate course correction maneuvers should a risk manifest itself and threaten the achievement of project objectives.

14.5 Evaluate trade-study results

The competing alternatives must be prioritized against the trade-study success criteria. The alternative that is regarded worthy of embracing should be the alternative that affords the most balanced solution. The course of action must be determined concerning how to proceed with the execution strategy throughout the project and technical echelons of the development organization. The results of the trade study must be documented to maintain a history of architectural design decisions. These records provide a basis for improving the maturity software engineering practices within the enterprise.

14.5.1 Prioritize architectural alternatives

The alternatives should be prioritized in a manner that optimizes the probability of success. Because each trade-off analysis is different, it is not possible to provide a standard algorithm for computing the probability of success approximation. However, the factors noted in Table 14.2 should be considered when weighting success criteria in terms of project and product success.

Table 14.2 Project Success Factors

Project Success Factors	Description
Timeliness	Probability of completing the project within schedule constraints.
Cost reasonableness	Probability of completing the project within allocated resources (staffing, facilities, equipment, funding, etc.).
Level of confidence	Probability of avoiding risks and completing the project in a timely and cost-effective manner.
Stakeholder satisfaction	Compliance with stakeholders' needs and expectations.
Architectural integrity	Compliance with architectural guidelines.
Architectural stability	Robustness of the product architecture to endure future changes and enhancements.
Value proposition	The perceived value of the product in delivering a return on investment in terms of product effectiveness versus acquisition (purchase price, training and education, operational costs) and support (customer and product support services) costs.

The prioritized set of alternatives should reveal the preferred solution. The remaining alternatives should be evaluated to identify the technical, programmatic, and project differences between each alternative and the preferred solution. This differentiation should provide a summary that substantiates the beneficial characteristics of the preferred solution. This set of prioritized alternatives should be presented to a committee of stakeholders along with the execution strategy for the preferred solution. This provides the stakeholders an opportunity to raise any final concerns with results and conclusions being drawn from the trade study.

14.5.2 Determine the preferred course of action

The execution strategy must be adjusted to contend with the work associated with the selected architectural design alternative. The final course of action must describe the tasks that address the assimilation of the design alternative into the software architecture. Architectural decisions must provide clear direction on how the software architecture will be brought into compliance with each architectural decision. Decisions represent the result of investigating the problem space in depth, which results in a better understanding of the characteristics that must be embodied by an architectural solution. The execution must determine how the selected solution will be integrated into the current state of the software architecture, its documentation, and its work plans.

Each technical organization must update their technical plans, schedule, and work packages to reflect the new understanding of the work ahead. Previous plans, schedules, and work packages provide placeholders for detailed tasks in the form of abstract assignments. These abstract assignments may now be embellished with additional details resulting from an improved understanding of the design solution. Previous prepared drawings, diagrams, specifications, and other design artifacts may need to be refined to incorporate the design solution. This action improves the design representations and incrementally progresses the software architecture toward completion.

14.5.3 Document the trade-study decision

The decision on a preferred course of action must be documented to preserve the rationale for the decision, the representative of the technical organizations involved in the trade study, and stakeholder representatives informed of the decision-making process. The significance of each trade study will vary from minor architectural challenges to a strategic convergence among stakeholder needs, software requirements, functional architecture, and structural configuration. The level of documentation for a decision must reflect its significance to the software architecture.

A trade-study report should be prepared to summarize the following aspects of the trade-study methods, alternatives considered, and outcomes:

1. *Technical challenge*—the engineering enigma thath was investigated and the significance of the problem within the software architecture context.
2. *Trade-study methodology*—the approach to evaluating the architectural design alternatives.
3. *Alternatives*—a descriptive list of candidate alternatives that were evaluated within the scope of the trade study.
4. *Success criteria*—the definition of the success factors and their relative weight in the final determination of a preferred solution.
5. *Analysis results*—the final measures of effectiveness, developmental and project costs, and schedule implications associated with the alternatives and the comparative ranking among the alternatives.
6. *Decision*—the selected design solution and the rational for its selection.
7. *Execution strategy*—the identification of the course of actions to be taken to incorporate the design solution into the software architecture and rework of existing work products (e.g., software programmatic design, coded software units, integrated software components) and documentation items.

14.5.4 Promote the execution strategy

The trade-study execution strategy must be enacted to facilitate the incorporation of the architectural solution into the software architecture, as well as adjustments to technical and project plans, schedules, and work packages. Each technical organization should periodically report its progress toward executing each authorized change package into its work products. Problems or issues that arise during the course of assimilating a change package must be elevated to the software engineering team for deliberation. The change execution strategy may need to be adjusted to accommodate unexpected complications encountered during the integration of the change package into the software architecture or other work products.

Software Verification and Validation Practice

15

CHAPTER OUTLINE

The software verification and validation (V&V) practice confirms the consistency among elements of the software architecture. This implies the determination that the software design, as expressed by the architecture, has been properly formulated and configured to satisfy stakeholder needs. Software verification and validation practices are sometimes confused with testing and quality assurance. However, within the software engineering discipline, V&V involve assessments of the software architecture to determine its fitness to transition to the software implementation stage of development. The software architecture must be continually verified to be internally consistent and validated against stakeholder needs. V&V must substantiate that the software design will fulfill its intended purpose and, consequently, justifies further investment in the development project. Figure 15.1 demonstrates how software engineering V&V confirmations contribute to negotiating the preliminary design review (PDR), critical design review (CDR) and test readiness review (TRR) milestones.

Verification ensures that each element of the architecture is consistent with the preceding element from which it was conceived. In the case of software requirements, verification ensures that the software baseline was properly derived from authenticated stakeholder needs. Verification provides an incremental assessment of the adequacy of the software architecture to fulfill stakeholder needs and project

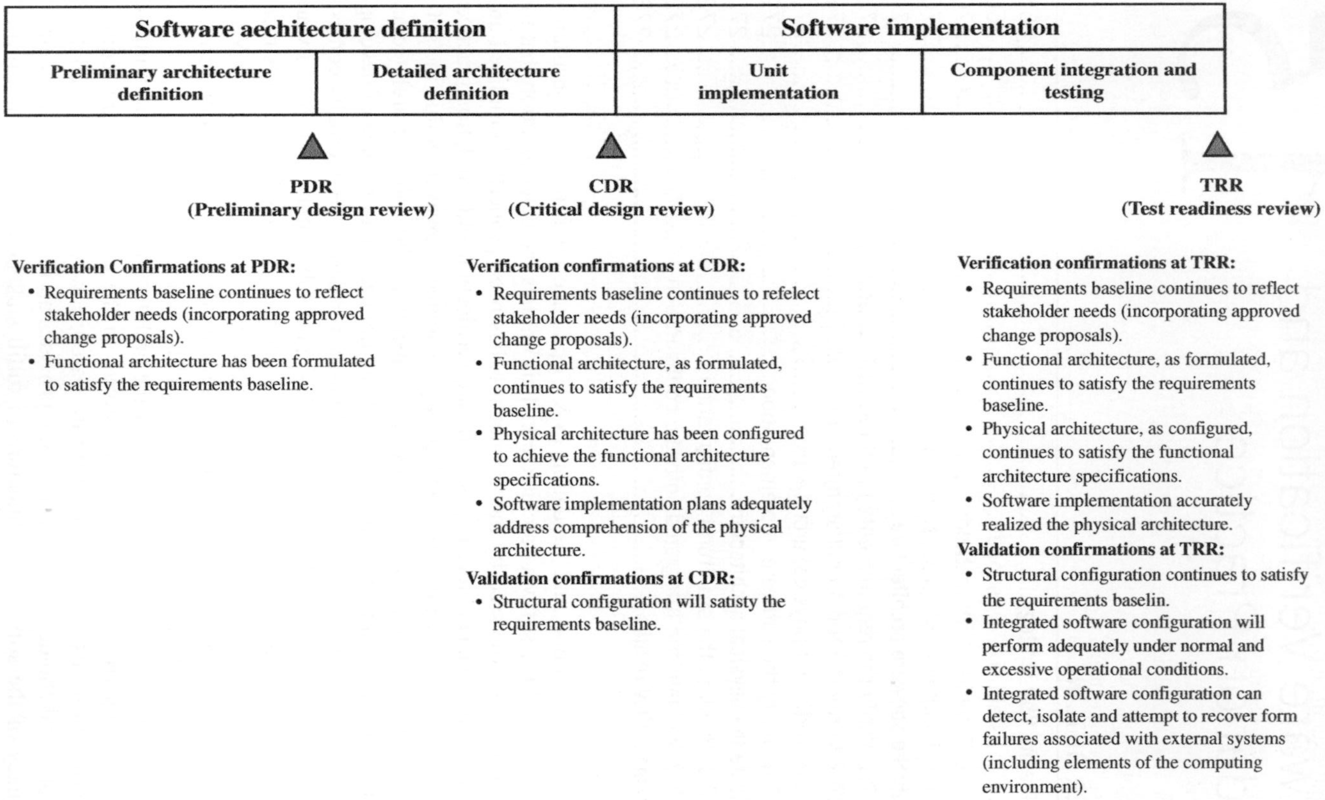

Software aechitecture definition		Software implementation	
Preliminary architecture definition	Detailed architecture definition	Unit implementation	Component integration and testing

▲ PDR
(Preliminary design review)

▲ CDR
(Critical design review)

▲ TRR
(Test readiness review)

Verification Confirmations at PDR:

- Requirements baseline continues to reflect stakeholder needs (incorporating approved change proposals).
- Functional architecture has been formulated to satisfy the requirements baseline.

Verification confirmations at CDR:

- Requirements baseline continues to refelct stakeholder needs (incorporating approved change proposals).
- Functional architecture, as formulated, continues to satisfy the requirements baseline.
- Physical architecture has been configured to achieve the functional architecture specifications.
- Software implementation plans adequately address comprehension of the physical architecture.

Validation confirmations at CDR:

- Structural configuration will satisfy the requirements baseline.

Verification confirmations at TRR:

- Requirements baseline continues to reflect stakeholder needs (incorporating approved change proposals).
- Functional architecture, as formulated, continues to satisfy the requirements baseline.
- Physical architecture, as configured, continues to satisfy the functional architecture specifications.
- Software implementation accurately realized the physical architecture.

Validation confirmations at TRR:

- Structural configuration continues to satisfy the requirements baselin.
- Integrated software configuration will perform adequately under normal and excessive operational conditions.
- Integrated software configuration can detect, isolate and attempt to recover form failures associated with external systems (including elements of the computing environment).

FIGURE 15.1

V&V influence at milestone reviews.

constraints. Verification also confirms the compliance of software implementation plans and execution against the physical architecture.

Validation confirms that the structural configuration will fulfill its intended use. This involves confirming that the integrated structural design will adequately perform data processing transactions under normal and extreme operational conditions. Validation assesses the physical architecture robustness to satisfy the requirements baseline, stakeholder needs, and operational workloads, and provides a stable framework for anticipated product evolution. This involves assessing the software response to end-user or external system failures, including failures associated with elements of the computing environment.

V&V tasks may be considered elements of a software quality assurance or test and evaluation effort. However, software quality assurance focuses on ensuring that policies and procedures are complied with, such as software design and coding standards. Test and evaluation often are focused on qualifying a software product or process against specifications and determining the readiness of the product for deployment. Therefore, the tasks identified within this chapter address V&V from a software engineering context. Figure 15.2 provides an overview of the software V&V tasks.

These V&V tasks provide a comprehensive scope of verification and validation as they apply to establishing a meticulous, consistent, and achievable software product architecture. While there may be other software-related tasks that overlap these responsibilities, they are adjunct assignments that typically support associated software development concerns. V&V tasks are intended to legitimize the effectiveness of the engineering merits of the software architecture. Therefore, the tasks identified within this chapter form the basis for discussing V&V within the software engineering context.

V&V tasks are formulated to ensure that the software architecture is complete and internally coherent. The emphasis is on ensuring the structural integrity, durability, and simplicity of the software architecture. The V&V tasks are grouped into four primary activities, as follows:

1. Define the V&V strategy.
2. Verify the software architecture.
3. Validate the physical architecture.
4. Document the results of V&V.

15.1 Define the V&V strategy

The V&V activities and tasks must be incorporated into the software engineering plans. V&V tasks are intended to review completed work products and ensure their adequacy. This involves examining the assumptions made concerning the operational scenarios each architectural design mechanism was meant to tolerate. V&V tasks should be conducted by members of the software engineering team who

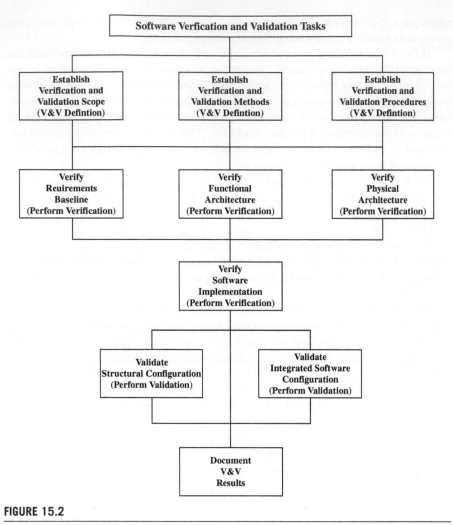

FIGURE 15.2

V&V tasks.

possess the skills and understanding to assess the technical features of the design mechanism being assessed.

15.1.1 Establish V&V scope

The software engineering work products should be reviewed to identify V&V opportunities. Tasks should be established to interrogate each work product in terms of its contribution to the software architecture. The software engineering plan should incorporate V&V tasks by applying resources commensurate with the significance of each work product. Table 15.1 identifies a proposed set of V&V task elements that should be considered when developing the scope of V&V activities.

Table 15.1 Software V&V Task Elements

Practice	Description	Importance
Requirements Baseline Verification Tasks		
Verify software requirements specifications	Confirm that every software requirement can be traced to a legitimate stakeholder need or expectation.	Essential (mandatory)
	Confirm that every requirement is unique, quantifiable, and testable.	
	Confirm that the set of requirements are collectively consistent and nonrepetitive.	
	Confirm that software requirements have been stated in a manner consistent with requirements trade-study records.	
Verify software interface specifications	Confirm that every external interface is specified in a manner that is beneficial to the data processing transactions.	Essential (mandatory)
	Confirm that interfaces provide the data or information necessary to support data processing transactions.	
	Confirm that interfaces do not detract or interfere with effective or efficient data processing transactions.	
Verify operational models	Confirm that operational models accurately represent the operational or business process they are intended to portray.	Essential (mandatory)
	Confirm that every element of the operational model is properly defined to prevent erroneous interpretations.	
	Confirm that operational behaviors establish the software measures of effectiveness and performance.	
Verify requirements pedigree	Confirm that every requirement has been sanctioned by key stakeholders, including the project manager and software engineering team.	Important (advisable)
	Confirm that the source of the requirement has been properly documented in the requirements traceability mechanism.	
	Confirm that every requirement is substantiated by the operational models.	
Functional Architecture Verification Tasks		
Verify functional decompositions	Confirm that the manner by which software requirements have been decomposed functionally is consistent with functional trade-study records.	Important (advisable)
	Confirm that the functional complexity has been evaluated and the functional decomposition is consistent with trade-study complexity resolutions.	

(Continued)

Table 15.1 Software V&V Task Elements (*Continued*)

Practice	Description	Importance
Verify behavioral models	Confirm that the functional behavior models are consistent with the higher-level operational models. Confirm that external interfaces are consistent with the interface specifications. Confirm that the resource availability is consistent with the computing environment specifications. Confirm that the functional timeline is consistent with the operational timeline.	Essential (mandatory)
Verify functional specifications	Confirm that functional unit and component specifications properly assimilate to satisfy higher-level specifications. Confirm that functional unit and component specifications properly reflect the performance characteristics derived from the behavioral models.	Essential (mandatory)
Verify requirements traceability throughout the functional architecture	Confirm that the requirements traceability mechanism is current and provides traceability among elements of the functional architecture.	Important (advisable)
Verify requirements traceability to the requirements baseline	Confirm that the requirements traceability mechanism is current and provides traceability among top-level elements of the functional architecture and the requirements baseline.	Essential (mandatory)
Physical Architecture Verification Tasks		
Verify structural unit specifications	Confirm that the structural unit specifications properly assimilate the functional unit specification characteristics.	Essential (mandatory)
Verify the conceptual design	Confirm that the elements of the conceptual design coherently represent the dominant data processing transactions.	Important (advisable)
Verify the software integration strategy	Confirm that the software integration strategy resourcefully bridges the software design chasm. Confirm that software integration testing properly exercises the integrated structural components.	Essential (mandatory)
Verify structural component specifications	Confirm that each structural component specification establishes the compound behaviors of integrated structural elements and design mechanisms (e.g. graphical user interface elements).	Essential (mandatory)

(*Continued*)

Table 15.1 Software V&V Task Elements (*Continued*)

Practice	Description	Importance
Verify requirements traceability throughout the physical architecture	Confirm that the requirements traceability mechanism is current and provides traceability among elements of the physical architecture.	Important (advisable)
Verify traceability to the functional architecture	Confirm that the requirements traceability mechanism is current and provides traceability among functional units and structural units.	Essential (mandatory)
Software Implementation Verification Tasks		
Verify software implementation plans—implementation of structural units	Confirm that software implementation plans adequately account for the effort necessary to design, code, and test each structural unit.	Informative (useful)
Verify software implementation plans—integration strategy compliance	Confirm that software implementation plans adequately account for the effort necessary to assemble, integrate, and test each structural component.	Informative (useful)
Verify software unit conformance	Confirm that the implementation of each software unit conforms to its structural specification.	Essential (mandatory)
Verify software component conformance	Confirm that the implementation of each software component conforms to its structural specification.	Essential (mandatory)
Configuration Validation Tasks		
Validate achievement of specified data processing transactions	Confirm that the physical architecture accurately facilitates the specified data processing transactions. Confirm that the physical architecture involves design mechanisms that deal with the full ranges of appropriate and inappropriate user inputs. Confirm that the physical architecture involves design mechanisms that deal with the full ranges of appropriate and inappropriate interfaces with external systems.	Essential (mandatory)
Validate achievement of specified performance requirements	Confirm that the physical architecture is adequately configured to achieve specified performance requirements. Confirm that the physical architecture is adequately configured to stabilize resource utilization requirements.	Essential (mandatory)

(*Continued*)

Table 15.1 Software V&V Task Elements (*Continued*)

Practice	Description	Importance
Validate recovery from injected fault conditions	Confirm that the physical architecture is adequately configured to detect, isolate, and recover (return to a previous state of health) from anticipated faults or degraded modes of operation (computing environment or external systems).	Important (advisable)
Validate execution under demanding work loads	Confirm that the physical architecture is adequately configured to conduct data processing transactions during periods of stressful workloads.	Important (advisable)
Validate the adequacy of the computing environment	Confirm that the computing environment is adequately specified to preserve software product operational performance.	Essential (mandatory)

V&V tasks should be performed by a team of senior software personnel lead by a member of the software engineering team. This V&V team must be staffed by knowledgeable, experienced individuals since they are responsible for ensuring the completeness and accuracy of the primary architectural artifacts.

15.1.2 Establish V&V methods

For each V&V task the methods of conducting the assessment must be identified. Verification is intended to establish the accuracy and thoroughness of the architectural design. Validation is intended to confirm the software product exhibits the proper operational transactions, features, and quality characteristics. There are a variety of techniques that can be applied to V&V tasks that fall into four categories of V&V methods:

1. *Documentation evaluation.* A technical evaluation of architectural diagrams, drawings, and specifications to achieve V&V objectives.
2. *Peer review.* A technical appraisal of the fitness of an architectural element by competent colleagues to achieve V &V objectives.
3. *Static analysis.* The application of mathematical or scientific estimation of software behaviors, performance, resource utilization, etc., to evaluate the achievement of V&V objectives.
4. *Dynamic analysis.* The employment of computed statistical measures to quantify the expected levels of performance, resource utilization, and data processing effectiveness to evaluate the achievement of V&V objectives.

15.1.3 Establish V&V procedures

The procedures for conducting V&V tasks must be prepared to establish the intended approach for accomplishing a sequence of actions. Procedures provide detailed instructions pertaining to how a task will be performed, the item(s) under investigation, and the manner in which findings will be reported. V&V procedures must clearly identify the item being verified, the project task and work package the procedure corresponds to, and the recipient(s) of the V&V report.

The V&V procedures must identify the material necessary to be available to enable the verification task to be performed. The organization that is responsible for providing an architectural artifact for evaluation must be identified. The schedule date for each V&V task should not be set before the artifact is scheduled to be completed. Verification tasks can be performed on incomplete products, but this represents an interim or preliminary verification effort. It is necessary to verify a completed architectural element before it is transitioned to the next phase of development. Therefore, the technical and project plans must account for the V&V tasks and any corrective actions to be performed before conducting a technical review.

15.2 Verify the software architecture

The software engineering verification tasks address confirming that the software product architecture is complete, internally consistent, and ready to be transitioned to the software implementation stage of development. This involves verifying the elements of the software architecture (requirements baseline, functional and physical architectures) and confirming that the software implementation has complied with the structural configuration specifications.

15.2.1 Verify the requirements baseline

The requirements baseline must be verified to ensure that every requirement can be traced to a stakeholder need and that the baseline represents a complete set of congruent requirements for the software product. The requirements baseline consists of the software requirements and interface specifications and the operational models from which they were derived.

15.2.2 Verify the functional architecture

The functional architecture must be verified to ensure that the functional decomposition is noncomplex, and efficiently allocates performance measures among subfunctions. The top-level functions must be traceable to the software requirements baseline and operational model. The behavioral models must be verified to accurately express the data processing transactions and control scenarios. The functional specifications must be evaluated to verify that they accurately comply with the functional decomposition and express the allocated performance measures.

15.2.3 Verify the physical architecture

The physical architecture must be verified to ensure that the structural configuration provides a noncomplex framework for software implementation, integration, and testing. The structural unit specifications must be verified to have adequately assimilated the allocated functional unit specifications and provide traceability back to the originating functional unit specifications. The conceptual components must be verified to ensure that they properly reflect the primary data processing transactions. Structural component specifications must be verified to address the integrative functional and performance characteristics resulting from the assimilation of lower-level elements of the structural configuration. The requirements traceability within the structural configuration must be confirmed.

15.2.4 Verify the software implementation

Verify that software implementation plans, schedules, and work packages properly conform to the structural configuration. This involves the effort to design, code, and test structural units, and perform software integration and testing. Structural assembly work packages must be reviewed to ensure that sufficient resources are allocated to the preparation and verification of software test stubs. Software unit design peer reviews should provide evidence that verifies compliance with structural unit specifications. Component integration peer reviews should provide evidence that verifies compliance with structural unit specifications.

15.3 Validate the physical architecture

The software engineering validation tasks address confirming that the physical architecture is complete, will satisfy the software requirements baseline, and is ready to transition to the software implementation stage of development.

15.3.1 Validate the structural configuration

The structural configuration must be validated to ensure that it satisfies the specified performance measures. This involves engineering analysis and mathematical determination of data processing transaction time intervals and resource utilization profiles. Additionally, the performance of the structural configuration must establish projected operational performance measurements that account for the performance of the specified computing environment and interfaces to external systems and applications. These determinations must ensure that the structural configuration will satisfy the performance measures specified in the requirements baseline.

15.3.2 Validate the integrated software configuration

The integrated software configuration must be validated to ensure that is satisfies the specified performance measurements. The software configuration may involve two or more software configuration items that must be validated to operate efficiently and effectively as an integrated product. This involves engineering analysis of the integrated software configuration, taking into account the performance of the specified computing environment and interfaces to external systems and applications. The integrated software configuration validation must establish projected operational performance measurements for data processing work loads that denote normal, severe, and excessive conditions. This determination must establish the data processing work load that causes the software configuration to begin to degrade and become unresponsive. This validation may need to utilize software integration and testing records and computing environment benchmarks to extrapolate performance measurements.

The ability of the software configuration to detect and respond to hardware failures must be validated using engineering analysis or confirmed utilizing software integration and testing records. The ability of the software configuration to continue to operate in the specified degraded modes—fail-safe, fail-secure, or fail-soft—must be corroborated.

15.4 **Document V&V results**

The V&V findings must be reported. Software design defects must be identified and isolated to the offending structural configuration elements. These defects must be analyzed to establish a corrective action plan. Each V&V task must be recorded and summarized in V&V reports. The record of each V&V task should provide sufficiently detailed information to enable the refurbishment of the defective design elements. V&V reports should include the following information, at a minimum:

- Identification of the architectural elements being evaluated.
- Identification of the relationships among the participating elements.
- The approach to conducting the V&V task.
- The findings that resulted from the investigation.
- Recommendations of the V&V participants.

The final report for each V&V task should be uniquely identified and entered into a logbook to record the V&V task identifier, title, time of task conduct, and the identifier and date of the report that summarized the findings. The V&V findings must be published and distributed to the software organizations affected by the results. The findings must clearly identify the defective elements of the software architecture, the defect uncovered, and the recommended course of action to be taken to resolve the defect. The course of action to refurbish a defective design element must be consistent with the state of the software development effort, the severity of the defect, and the ability of the defect to be resolved within the current project schedule. Defects that cannot be resolved before the release of the software product must be avoided with a workaround that prevents inadvertent user encounters. Workarounds must be sanctioned by the approval of a waiver to the requirement not being fulfilled at the time of software release.

Software Control Practice

16

CHAPTER OUTLINE

The software control practice involves a set of tasks intended to provide stability of the software engineering effort, product configuration, and change processing. These tasks represent the technical version of configuration management and project control tasks. This includes the assessment of the potential impact a change request or proposal may have on the software architecture, technical plans, and architectural design artifacts.

Software control tasks must maintain configuration records to provide traceability among elements of the software architecture, design decision, change requests and proposals with stakeholder needs (Figure 16.1). Project-level configuration control is typically enforced at the software configuration item level of the software product configuration. Software control provides the configuration management oversight of the evolving software architecture. Therefore, software control tasks

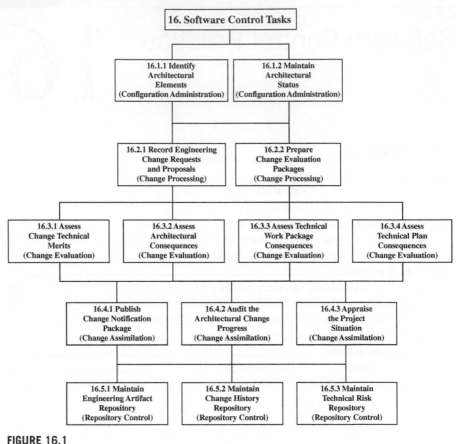

FIGURE 16.1

Software control tasks.

provide a more detailed accounting of the evolving software architecture, trade studies, risks, and the adjudication and assimilation of change requests and proposals. The evolution of the software architecture continues until the structural configuration is submitted for project-level configuration control. This submission signifies that the software architecture has been judged to be relatively stable, durable to change, and methodically detailed and specified.

Typical project-level configuration management (CM) practices apply to the software product configuration and its associated configuration items. Technical configuration control oversees the complete software architecture to manage the allocation and traceability of specified software requirements throughout the functional and physical architecture. This includes the identification and specification of structural units, components, and internal interfaces.

Change requests and proposals must be distinguished between those that affect the project or contract scope and those that only affect the technical effort. Change requests and proposals that affect the project or contract scope may include aspects that impact the technical effort. However, such changes involve a more substantial impact to the project than the technical or engineering consequences. Therefore, they must be processed formally within the project configuration management system. Change proposals or requests that do not impact the project scope should be processed within the technical configuration control system.

16.1 Configuration administration

Software configuration administration provides the day-to-day supervision for the configuration of the evolving software architecture. This involves identifying each element of the software architecture with a project-unique identifier and maintaining the configuration status records for each element.

16.1.1 Identify architectural elements

Each element of the software architecture must be uniquely identified to associate current and historical information with each element of the architecture. Technical configuration identification applies to elements of the architecture that emerge during the definition of the software architecture. Early in this definition, the architectural configuration will experience iterative changes as engineering analysis promotes a credible solution. During this period, it may be prudent to resist assigning configuration identifiers until the design is stabilized.

Identification of architectural elements involves software requirements; functional design hierarchies, behavioral models, and functional specifications; and structural hierarchies, engineering assemblies, integration strategy, models, prototypes, and structural specifications. In addition, architectural configuration identification must establish product versions and baselines that represent the evolution of the architectural configuration. Architectural versioning practices should be established that provide a common reference point for incorporating design alterations, modifications, and variations within an individual architectural partition.[1] Architectural baselining practices provide a reference point when the three architectural partitions have been coalesced and represent a unified software architecture.

Architectural element identification facilitates the following actions to:

- Track architectural elements to the design artifacts in which they are characterized.

---

[1] *Partition*, as used herein, refers to a subdivision of the software architectural representation. Each partition involves one of the following subdivisions: (1) the requirements baseline, (2) the functional architecture, or (3) the physical architecture. *Allocate* means to assign, apportion, or distribute among constituent parts. It can imply an allocation within a partition of the architecture (among elements within the boundaries of a single partition) or between partitions of the software architecture.

- Present a coherent representation of the software architecture throughout the software product's life cycle.
- Establish and maintain engineering records for every element of the software architecture.
- Provide the status of proposed and authorized changes addressing the assimilation of each change package into each architectural element definitions and architectural documentation.

16.1.2 Maintain architectural status

The software architecture status must be maintained to provide a progress indicator of the readiness of the architecture to migrate to the next stage of software development or deployment. The software architecture as a unified product representation involves three partitions that may be at different maturity levels. When all three partitions of the software architecture have been stabilized and unified, their configuration should be placed under configuration control, and the software architectural definition should be considered complete.

Within each architectural partition, every element of the software architecture must be monitored to establish its current status. A suggested set of element status classifications includes:

1. *Draft*—the element has been identified as a necessary item within the partition of which the longevity has yet to be determined.
2. *Primitive*—the element has been determined to be a fundamental ingredient within the partition in which it plays a role.
3. *Alternate*—the element has been conceived as an alternate to a drafted element, or plays a role in a competing design solution.
4. *Controlled*—the element has been fully defined and specified as part of a partition that has been placed under technical configuration control.
5. *Expired*—the element has been excluded as part of a partition, but remains within the element repository for historical significance. Architectural elements drafted as a primitive or alternate to a design concept and later determined to be unnecessary may be removed from status-keeping and retained in the repository for future consideration.

It is important to maintain a record of the architectural status to support progress reporting; track the assimilation of authorized changes into software architecture documentation, models, and design artifacts; and ensure that design decisions have been properly integrated throughout the architecture. The focus must be placed on the architectural elements that make up the architecture, not its documentation, model, or artifacts. Requirements, functions, structural units and components, data items, etc. represent configuration elements at various levels within the architecture that comprise the software product. Therefore, it is necessary to understand the status of the architectural element definitions to derive the status of the overall development effort.

16.2 **Process engineering change packages**

Engineering change requests and proposals must be formally processed to ensure that enhancements suggested by stakeholders or software development team members are properly considered. An engineering change request represents a suggested modification to the software architecture that is within the scope of the existing project. This means that the change, if adopted, should not impact the project workload or schedule. A change proposal represents a modification that is outside the current scope of the development effort and would require an adjustment to project funding and/or schedule deadlines. A proposed modification that is determined to clarify a stakeholder need or correct a faulty assumption should not be considered a change that requires change control.

16.2.1 **Record engineering change requests and proposals**

Every change request or proposal should be recorded in a change-tracking logbook or repository. This record of requested modifications to the software architecture provides a measurement of the stability of the software architecture.

The number of changes registered against each partition of the architecture should become more infrequent as the architecture evolves and matures. Ideally, the number of modifications requested against a partition of the architecture will cease prior to the technical review where the partition is to be presented.

An engineering change record should include the following information to permit tracking and status reporting:

- Change request or proposal number
- Date initiated
- Organization that initiated the change
- Class of change
- Priority
- Primary architecture partition impacted (requirements baseline, functional or physical architectures)
- Disposition
- Disposition date
- Assimilation status

16.2.2 **Prepare change evaluation packages**

A change evaluation package must be assembled to provide a consistent basis for evaluation of a requested architectural modification. The change evaluation package should consist of the principle architectural artifacts that are affected by the change. A change evaluation package should include sufficient information, documentation, and architectural artifacts to enable evaluators to assess the suitability of a requested change to be incorporated into the software architecture, technical and project plans. Therefore, a change evaluation package should include the content noted in Table 16.1.

Table 16.1 Suggested Content for Change Evaluation Package

Content	Description
Change origin and tracking	Provide the source information pertaining to the: • Origins of the requested change • Registered identification number • Originating entity or source of the request • Date the request was recorded into the change-tracking system
Change description	Provide a vigilant description of the requested architectural modification, including: • Architectural element(s) and the partitions to which they are incorporated within which will be affected by the requested modification • The modification to be employed in place of the current architectural element(s) • The anticipated benefits resulting from the architectural modification (e.g., operational improvements, customer or consumer acceptance, expanded market penetration, ease of use, reduced training and education support required for software employment)
Architectural artifacts pertaining to the evaluation	Identification of the architectural drawings, documentation, etc. that are provided as an attachment to the package or their digital library locations. Instructions for locating and accessing the artifacts should also be provided.
Evaluation instructions	Provides the instructions for evaluators on how the requested modification should be assessed and emphasizes the areas of concern with the proposed change adoption. Should focus on determining the: • Technical merits of the change • Architectural design consequences imposed by the modification (e.g., architectural complexity) • Technical plan and schedule consequences, if any • Technical work package consequences, if any, resulting in the need for rework, artifact revisions, software implementation, and testing implications
Evaluation milestones	Identifies the milestones associated with: • Consolidating individual evaluations into a unified determination for the change request • Presenting the determination to the software engineering integrated product team (SWE-IPT) • Presenting the determination to the software change control board (CCB)

Assembled change evaluation packages should be provided to change evaluation team members for consideration. The change control administrator should confirm that each member of the change evaluation team has received the package and can accommodate the change evaluation effort within their work assignments and budget constraints.

16.3 Change evaluation

The change evaluation team members should assess the proposed architectural modification to determine the merits and consequences of adopting the change. The evaluation team must substantiate the value proposition inherent with a change, involving:

- Technical merits of the proposed modification (improvements in functionality, performance, usability, supportability, and operational suitability).
- Consequences implied with adopting the proposed modification to the software architecture (increased complexity, scope (depth and breadth) of the change, and the ripple effect to other architectural elements by adopting the modification).
- Consequences of adopting the modification to the technical plans and schedule.
- Consequences to the technical work packages and resource allocations.
- Additional resources that accompany a change proposal.
- That each technical organization can accommodate the change assimilation effort within their workload capacity, budget constraints, and proposed work package reallocations.

Change proposals may represent a burden for the software development effort to contemplate given the availability of resources within the current structure of the project. Additional resources may accompany a proposed change to offset the rework and realignment of architectural design characteristics. The additional resources needed to assimilate a change must be determined to be sufficient to counteract the amplified workload involved with incorporating the change within the software development agenda.

16.3.1 Assess change technical merits

The change package must be evaluated to determine the technical merits associated with adopting the proposed modification. The business case should have been presented in the change description with the identification of the anticipated benefits to making the change. The technical merits of a proposed modification to the software architecture should address how the modification contributes to improving the product performance, usability, and supportability. Technical merit implies identifying the architectural strengths and weaknesses accompanying the modification. These technical merits should address how the modification would contribute to achieving the architectural guidelines and performance requirements.

Technical merit implies attributes that cannot be directly measured or scientifically substantiated. It suggests the opinions or applied competencies by members of the evaluation team after sufficient investigation and open debate concerning the proposed modification. The assessment of change package technical merits is intended to determine if a proposed change would enhance the operational performance and architectural integrity of the software product. The following influences should be considered when assessing the technical merits of a proposed modification to the software architecture:

1. How will the modification affect the *effectiveness* of data processing transactions?
2. How will the modification affect the *structural stability* (ability to resist disturbances caused by changes in the operational or computational environments)?
3. How will the modification affect the product *scalability* (ability to adjust to load changes in the operational environment)?
4. How will the modification affect the *efficient utilization* of computing resources?
5. How will the modification affect the *complexity* of the software architecture?

16.3.2 Assess architectural consequences

Every proposed change will affect the stability of the architecture by the introduction of new design elements or mechanisms into an existing architectural framework. Changes promoted early in the software engineering effort may not experience as significant repercussions as those considered later in the development schedule. Determining the architectural consequences of adopting a proposed change involves comprehending the pervasiveness of the change in terms of the architectural elements affected by the modification. Every architectural element associated with or tightly coupled with elements directly impacted by modification must be discerned. Elements that may be disturbed by the change will require attention to comprehend the far-reaching impact of the proposed alteration.

The following arguments should be considered when assessing the technical merits of a proposed modification to the software architecture:

1. How *invasively* will the change extend throughout the software architecture?
2. What is the *collective magnitude* of the architectural modifications?
3. What are the architectural *ramifications* associated with the proposed modifications?

16.3.3 Assess technical work package consequences

The current technical effort to complete the software development project must be reassessed taking into account the strenuous effort associated with incorporating a change into the prevailing software architecture and its artifacts. This involves the rework of existing documentation, models, and diagrams (artifacts) to reflect the alterations stimulated by the change. This involves the effort necessary to:

- Update specifications, diagrams, drawings, documentation citations, and models.
- Revise software implementation work assignments and plans, including the necessity to rework previously coded and tested software units or components.

- Revise software test and evaluation work assignments, plans, and procedures.
- Accommodate the impact of the change, if any, into software post-development processes.

The anticipated rework and alterations to software development tasks must be estimated to provide a complete understanding of the magnitude of the proposed change on the technical work packages. Task dependencies must be considered when adjusting work package definitions. It is important to recognize any delays in subsequent tasks incurred by work package alterations. Task resource budgets must be reassessed to ensure that they are adequately provisioned to support the remaining technical efforts. This assessment must account for the work remaining to complete the software development effort and the resources (funding, labor, equipment items, etc.) appropriate for effective task execution.

16.3.4 Assess technical plan consequences

The set of revised technical work packages should be hypothetically incorporated into technical plans and schedules to identify any potential impact to achieving technical objectives. The impact of revised work packages must be projected upon the integrated master plan and schedule to identify conflicts, shortages, or inefficiencies that may emerge. The various technical plans should be reexamined to determine if the workload and resources can be revamped to choreograph a proper execution scheme.

16.4 Change assimilation

Change assimilation addresses the software control tasks responsible for ensuring that authorized changes are properly engineered and integrated into the software architecture. Change assimilation begins when the change request or proposal is approved by the chairperson of the technical or project-level CCB. The change notification package should be prepared before the CCB convenes to approve the change.

If the business case, technical merits, and consequences corroborate that a proposed change is advantageous and achievable, then the evaluation team should advocate for the change to be undertaken. The final authorization of a change request or proposal resides with either the technical or project-level CCB. While the software architecture is controlled by the technical CCB, the chief software engineer or chairperson of the technical CCB can ratify the change to be undertaken. However, if a change proposal involves the provisioning of additional resources for the project to accommodate the proposal, then only the chairperson of the project CCB or project manager can ratify the proposal.

16.4.1 Publish change notification package

The change notification package must be prepared to identify the architectural elements and design material that will be impacted by the change approval. The preliminary software design solution may have been submitted with the change request. However, the actual software design solution must be prepared before and incorporated into the architecture definition, models, diagrams, specifications, documentation and artifact repository. The change notification package should identify the responsible organization for each item to be changed, and the date the change is to be completed. The completed change notification package must be published and made available to the responsible organizations to initiate the assimilation of the change.

16.4.2 Audit the architectural change progress

The software organizations participating in the assimilation of a change package must be periodically queried to appreciate the progress of each change assimilation effort. The architectural change audit must track the status of change inclusion in the software architecture, specifications, diagrams, drawings, documentation, technical plans, and models. The status of the change assimilation is not to be considered complete until the change of all affected artifacts and technical plans reflects the modification.

16.4.3 Appraise the project situation

The status of change assimilation must be evaluated within the total project situation. The status of software engineering tasks that involve the assimilation of a change package should be given special attention due to their volatile circumstances. When all of the tasks for a given change assimilation are completed, a final audit of the change integration into the software architecture should be accomplished. When the final audit has been satisfied, then the change can be classified as satisfied and transitioned to the change history repository.

Architectural versioning should identify the set of change requests and proposals that are addressed by each engineering version of the software architecture and its artifacts. This implies that the evolution of the software architecture definition must be under technical version control. All engineering artifacts must be aligned with some version of the architecture. This enables all software specifications, diagrams, drawings, documents, and models to be associated with one or more versions of the software product architecture. The synchronization of the software engineering tasks and the architecture definition and its artifacts must be a fundamental software engineering practice. It is necessary to understand the engineering evolution of the software architecture to account for the changes that promoted each version of the software product.

16.5 Software repository control

There is a prerequisite for maintaining repositories for capturing and preserving historical information concerning the evolution of the software architecture definition throughout the execution of the software engineering effort. The primary repositories are addressed in the following sections.

16.5.1 Maintain engineering artifact repository

The engineering artifact repository is intended to capture the wide range of engineering artifacts generated throughout the software engineering effort. This involves establishing repository petitions and folders for analytical, design, and documentation artifacts once their need is recognized. Once an artifact has been completed it should be promoted to a controlled folder associated with each version of the software architecture. A subfolder should be established within an architectural element folder to capture trade-study material, reports, and decision rationale.

16.5.2 Maintain change history repository

The software change history repository is intended to capture the history of every change request and proposal entertained by the software engineering team. It should capture the change request or proposal content, change evaluation material, CCB determination results, change notification package, and change assimilation audits.

16.5.3 Maintain technical risk repository

The technical risk repository is intended to capture every risk acknowledged by the software engineering team. This includes risks associated with the software architecture definition, computing environment definition, software implementation, software test and evaluation, and post-development processes. The risk repository should capture the initial risk identification memoranda, assessment reports, abatement strategy, and risk monitoring reports.

SECTION

Stages of Software Engineering Application

3

This section addresses the software engineering and related organizational tasks that should be accomplished for each stage of the software life cycle. These tasks are arranged by the functional organizations involved in the software development effort, including software engineering, computing environment preparation, software implementation, post-development process preparation, and software test and evaluation.

A representation of the software life cycle is shown in Figure 1. This set of life-cycle stages is used to describe how a software product should be developed, distributed, and supported. The software life cycle begins with the identification of requirements for the software product and the computing environment. The product then is designed during architectural definition, which develops the specifications for each of the functional and physical units and components. Once all of the physical units and components have been specified the product and computing environment implementation can commence. Once the software units and components have been integrated into the complete product configuration the product acceptance

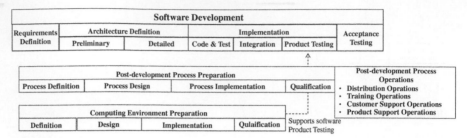

FIGURE 1

Software life-cycle stages.

testing can be conducted. Successful completion of product acceptance testing leads to the post-development stage, which involves software distribution, training, and sustainment. The post-development stage continues until the software product no longer requires sustainment. These life-cycle processes need to be developed concurrently so they are ready to support product distribution and support.

Within each stage of the software life cycle the software engineering process is executed, as necessary, to evolve the product from a concept to a complete, tested product. The software engineering process provides a basis for dealing with complexity, understanding the risks associated with design alternatives, while deriving a design approach that can be implemented within program cost and schedule objectives. Whenever the product is being designed during development, implementation, or support, the software engineering process should be employed. The software engineering process provides the disciplined approach to understanding alternative design concepts, their risks, and the potential impacts on program objectives. This enables a software engineering team to make better decisions concerning the best architectural design configuration.

During this discussion of integrated product and process development the software project hierarchy shown in Figure 2 is used. It addresses an integrated product and process context view of the organizational roles and responsibilities.

> *Software:* The integrated system that is comprised of the software product, its operational computing environment definition, and associated post-development software support processes.
>
> *Product:* The software that is defined, designed, implemented, and tested to satisfy stakeholder needs and expectations.
>
> *Computing environment:* The computing hardware (mainframes, servers, workstations, desktop computing systems, etc.), operating systems, database management systems, and other products, communication access, and networks that provide the operational environment for the product.
>
> *Post-development processes:* The processes that must be established to distribute the software product to customers or consumers, supply training resources and material, and support and evolve the software product throughout its useful life.
>
> *Replication:* The process by which the software product and user documentation is reproduced for digital distribution. Replication is also responsible for

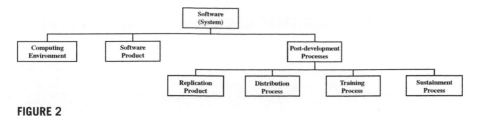

FIGURE 2

Software integrated product and process hierarchy.

packaging the resulting digital and printed material for distribution to vendors, customers, or consumers.

Distribution: The process by which the packaged product is transferred from its originating source to distributors, retail sales stores, customers, or consumers.

Training: The process of transferring to end users knowledge on how to operate the software product in support of business concerns, personal duties, and educational or entertainment purposes.

Sustainment: The process that resolves product deficiencies and enhances the product throughout the post-development stage of the product life cycle. Software sustainment is the process by which software problem reports are documented, investigated, and resolved, and fixes are distributed. Software sustainment may be discussed as two primary activities: customer support and software support. Customer support involves the operations necessary to provide online or phone support associated with a help desk. It involves providing assistance to customers in need of experienced software product installation, configuration, or problem reporting. Software support involves the recreation of reported problems and the isolation of the source of the problem within the software structural configuration. This enables the problem to be corrected and a patch to be issued to revise the executable files. If a patch can not be distributed in an acceptable amount of time, then operational workarounds should be devised and provided to customers experiencing the problem. Enhancement to the software product may involve a series of secondary projects to develop new versions or releases of the software product.

The following four chapters present the tasks associated with each of the stages of the software life cycle. They identify the products that are produced and the tasks by which the products are generated. In addition, they describe the technical reviews that are to be conducted near the conclusion of each stage. Within these chapters the tasks associated with each software organization are identified and described. Each software organization participates in the software engineering integrated product team (SWE-IPT) to bring their unique perspectives to the engineering of the product. The software organizations that are addressed include:

- Software engineering integrated product team
- Software implementation
- Computing environment preparation
- Post-development process preparation
- Software test and evaluation

Software Requirements Definition

CHAPTER OUTLINE

The purpose of the software requirements definition stage of development is to translate stakeholder needs, expectations, and constraints into a balanced and achievable set of software requirements. This involves developing the specifications for the software product, computing environment, and the post-development processes. A key artifact of this stage is a model of the business or embedded systems process it is intended to enable. The operational model forms the basis for deriving the software product, computing environment, and software interface requirements. The computing environment imposes constraints on how the software product operates to support data transaction processes. The software requirements definition stage is focused on understanding the full range of data processing functions the software product must perform.

The operational model provides a basis for assessing the overall software performance under a wide range of situations and workloads. The computing hardware, workstations, networks, and related technologies all contribute to the performance of the software solution. The computational environment should not be prematurely selected until the operational requirements are analyzed. Analysis of the operational environment establishes the integrated software performance requirements constrained by the computing equipment that comprises the computing environment. The software product may be designed to perform more efficiently with certain computing equipment. The analysis conducted during this stage of development should result in architectural decisions that allocate requirements among the computing environment and the software product.

The software requirements definition stage occurs one time during the software development effort unless an incremental or evolutionary development strategy has been chosen. This stage generates the requirements specifications against which the computing environment and software product will be developed. The software requirements analysis practice will be conducted throughout the software engineering effort to resolve challenges or risks associated with the software product or post-development process requirements.

During this stage of development the focus is to ensure that the requirements specified for the software product and post-development processes are complete, feasible to achieve within project objectives and constraints, and introduce minimal risks to the project. Functional analysis and allocation should be performed to decompose software product requirements and allocate them among the software configuration items and elements of the computing environment. At this stage of development, the software product physical architecture should identify the software configuration items and the elements of the computing environment. This results in specifications for the software configuration items, the software external interfaces, and the computing environment.

Staffing for the software implementation, computing environment implementation, post-development, and test and evaluation organizations should be limited to the personnel qualified to support the software engineering effort. There are no benefits to be secured by excessively staffing these organizations until the state of the software architecture warrants workforce escalation.

The software requirements baseline must be established to control the requirements against which the product is to be developed. This is a technical baseline that is to be managed by the software engineering integrated product team (SWE-IPT) until the formal functional requirements baseline is established. The software requirements baseline should not be established until the software architecture has been verified to be adequately specified, congruent, and amenable to all stakeholders. Once the software requirements baseline has been established, the technical change control board (CCB) must approve changes to this baseline. Once the functional requirements baseline is established, the project-level CCB must approve changes to it.

Whenever there is a proposed change to the requirements the SWE-IPT should evaluate the impact of the change on the requirements baseline. The software requirements analysis tasks should be performed to identify alternative requirements assertions that satisfy the proposed change. The software analysis practice should be performed to determine the best requirements statement to be specified.

17.1 Products of software requirements definition

The following products must be generated during this stage of software development:

1. *Operational model*. The operational model is intended to depict how the product will be utilized to facilitate a business or embedded system process. The operational model should treat the software product as a "black box"

and should not attempt to identify any aspect of the product design or inner-workings. The operational model should depict how the software product works cooperatively with operators and elements of the computing environment to accomplish its intended purpose. The operational model should address the functional sequences (including concurrent data processing transactions), the duration of each task, and the exchange of data (interfaces) with elements of the computing environment, other systems or applications, and operators. The resources that are necessary to conduct each function should be identified and whether these resources are temporarily seized, consumable, or shared. The operational model must address the level of data processing necessary to establish the test threads that will be used to determine the acceptability of the product.

2. *Initial software behavioral model.* The software behavior model is intended to depict how the software product works cooperatively with operators, and the computing environment to accomplish data processing transactions. The behavior model represents a decomposition of the operational model with an emphasis on understanding how the operational functions allocated to the software product will be performed. The software behaviors describe the functional flow, control flow, and data flows associated with the accomplishment of each transaction. The behavioral model should address each data processing transaction, as necessary, to adequately specify the software behaviors at the software configuration item or product level. The model represents *what* data processing functions must be performed, and should not represent *how* it is physically or structurally accomplished.

3. *Software requirements specifications (SRS).* The functional and performance requirements that have been allocated to the software product must be documented in the SRS. The requirements may be allocated among multiple software configuration item specifications. It should capture the functional behaviors, data exchange requirements, and interface requirements including the human–machine interface requirements identified by the operational model. These interface requirements may be documented in separate software interface specifications (see item 5). The software distribution, training, and sustainment requirements must also be specified. These post-development requirements may be documented in separate post-development concept documents (see item 7). The software requirements specification should establish a matrix that identifies the software qualification method (analysis, demonstration, inspection, or extrapolation) that applies to determining success of a test.

4. *Computing environment requirements specifications.* The operational requirements that have been allocated to the computing environment should be documented in the computing environment requirements specification. It should identify the computational processing resource requirements, including communication and network bandwidth, the minimally acceptable and objective number of concurrent transactions to be processed, and other transaction quality

metrics[1] , such as: interoperability, portability, scalability, security, maintainability, complexity, and throughput. If the software product is expected to operate on more than one computing platform, then more than one computing environment specification may be prepared to account for the different characteristics of each platform.

5. *Software interface requirements specifications*. The operational data exchange requirements should be documented to address all interfaces, including human–machine interfaces. The software interface requirements specification should identify each interface among the product, other systems, applications, and elements of the computing environment. Each interface requirement must be specified in terms of the informational content of the exchange, as well as the means of transmitting data among the participating configuration items.

6. *Software test and evaluation plan*. The software test and evaluation plan should be prepared to address the software acceptance testing strategy and how and when software quality assurance inspections will be conducted. The software test strategy should address the software qualification methods as they apply to each requirement specified by the SRS. Software quality assurance inspections should ensure that the software development tasks are being performed according to established procedures and that the product requirements, architecture, and implementation are converging toward a complete and consistent product solution.

7. *Software post-development process concept documents*. The preliminary concepts for how the product will be replicated, distributed, and supported, and how training will be conducted should be prepared. These concept documents should be allowed to evolve as the product architecture is developed so that they will reflect the product architectural decisions made during the architecture definition. During software implementation, there should be a parallel effort to implement and test these post-development processes so that they are available when the product has successfully completed acceptance testing.

8. *Software requirements traceability matrix*. The requirements traceability matrix should initially identify the source of each requirement and its dependencies to the computational environment requirements. The source of a software requirement may include, for example, a stakeholder, legal regulation, standard practice, company policies or guidelines, operational model, or derived by analysis. This matrix is intended to be evolved throughout the software post-development (distribution, training, and sustainment) efforts. During this requirements definition stage, the requirements specified for the software product and interfaces should be traced back to their source, for example, customer needs statements, statements of work, project authorization documents, market surveys, trade-study results, recommendations, and decisions. This matrix can be maintained as a single product or separated into two or more individual matrices for each of the identified software configuration items.

---

[1]Distributed Computing Environment, Software Technology Roadmap, *http://www.sei.cmu.edu/str/descriptions/dce.html*

17.2 Software engineering integrated product team (software requirements definition stage)

The lead software engineer should establish and chair the SWE-IPT. The SWE-IPT represents the technical working group of software specialists and subject-matter experts who will contribute to the software engineering tasks. The SWE-IPT should be a multidisciplinary team whose membership represents the various software disciplines, including software engineering, software implementation, computing environment implementation, software post-development process implementation, software test and evaluation, software development management, safety, security, and human–system integration, as applicable.

1. *Develop the operational model.* The SWE-IPT should conduct software requirements analysis tasks to capture stakeholder requirements and constraints as they relate to the business or embedded system processes for which the software is being developed. Stakeholders[2] typically include customers, marketing, business management, partners, suppliers, and subcontractors. An operational model should be developed to depict the various threads through the business processes, including the business rules that govern how the process is conducted and how the process responds to the various situations that may be encountered.

2. *Develop the initial functional behavioral model.* The SWE-IPT should conduct functional analysis and allocation to decompose the abstract or challenging operational tasks allocated to the software product. Functional analysis establishes a more detailed model or representation of how the software product and elements of the computing environment should collaboratively enable the operational processes. Functional analysis accomplishes this by decomposing high-level functions into lower-level functions, arranging functions in logical sequences, and allocating performance requirements from higher- to lower-level functions. Data flows among functions should be derived from the data flows identified in the operational model. Abstract operational data should be decomposed into a set of software data elements and each assigned a unique identifier.

3. *Synthesize conceptual design alternatives.* The SWE-IPT should conduct software design synthesis to establish initial concepts for the structure of the physical architecture.* The initial structural concepts should identify primary structural components and their interfaces. Each element of a structural concept should be traceable to the functional architecture allowing for some consolidation of similar or common functionality to be assigned to a structural component. The structural concepts may be presented as a product hierarchy or as a product block diagram. The product block diagram should describe the product structural layout, internal interfaces among the structural components, and external interfaces with elements of the computing environment.

---

[2] Stakeholders also include each of the software development organizations and representatives from the project management team.

The initial structure concepts may establish, if determined necessary, more than one software configuration item to provide a satisfactory solution. Alternative structural concepts should be considered and viable structures evaluated via trade studies and risk assessments during systems analysis. If multiple software configuration items are identified, then the project plan, work breakdown structure (WBS), and specification tree must be revised to reflect this architectural decision. As the physical architecture matures, it may challenge the validity or correctness of the functional architecture or operational model. In addition, the physical structure of the product may affect the design of or requirements for the computational environment. These conflicts must be captured in problem reports, viable alternatives identified, and the alternatives evaluated against project objectives, product quality metrics, and risks.

*Note: *This is where the process described in this book disregards the design of the computing environment and focuses on the design of the software product. Until this time, there were trade-offs between the computing environment and the software product that needed to be considered to achieve a proper balance between the computing environment and software product requirements and performance. It makes sense that the computing environment implementation team would undertake a similar approach to synthesizing and analyzing computing environment design alternatives. Since this book is about software engineering, computing environment design and implementation have not been addressed in detail.*

4. *Analyze product alternatives, conflicts, and trade-offs.* The SWE-IPT must evaluate identified conflicts between the software requirements and functional and physical architectures to determine a preferred architectural solution. The architectural alternatives must be analyzed to determine if they can be achieved within project cost and schedule objectives and to identify conflicts with stakeholder needs and expectations. The architectural alternatives should be prioritized and a preferred solution recommended to the SWE-IPT. The preferred design alternative should be analyzed to ensure that it represents a congruent combination of software requirements and functional and physical architectures.

   The preferred design alternative should be analyzed and evaluated to understand the implementation challenges and to identify any risk inherent with its adoption. Identified risks must be assessed to devise approaches for eliminating, avoiding, or reducing risks to an acceptable level. It is imperative that risks be identified, quantified, and mitigated before adopting a design alternative. Adopting architectural decisions with inherent risks places the software development project in jeopardy. Architectural modifications later in the project will incur greater cost and potential schedule delays. Risk assessment reports must be prepared to capture the results of the risk appraisal including the probability of occurrence and the consequences to the project should the risk be realized. If the preferred architectural alternative does not impact project and technical plans, it can be adopted as an architectural design decision. Architectural alternatives that negatively impact the scope of technical plans must be documented in a software change proposal. Change proposals must be submitted to the technical CCB for authorization. If a change proposal impacts project plans beyond the authority of the technical CCB, it must be submitted to the project CCB for authorization. These software change proposals represent project-level adjustments that require additional resources and modification of project plans, schedules, and resource allocations.

5. *Establish the software requirements allocations.* As the operational model matures, the functional and physical architectures should reinforce that the product requirements are achievable within project objectives. The operational model should be utilized to allocate requirements among the software configuration items, the computing environment, and the software product interfaces. The SWE-IPT should prepare requirements specifications for these elements of the software architecture. The SWE-IPT should prepare the requirement traceability matrix to associate stakeholder needs and expectations, project objectives, and facets of the operational process to the requirements allocated among the architectural elements.

6. *Prepare software post-development process concepts.* The SWE-IPT should evaluate the requirements for each of the software post-development processes. The SWE-IPT should apply the systems engineering practices to establish an initial concept of operation for each of the software post-development processes. Each of the software post-development process concept documents should address the scope of the process, its operational behaviors, and initial functional and physical architectures.

7. *Prepare and document risk mitigation plans.* The SWE-IPT must prepare risk mitigation plans for each identified risk. Risks must be continually monitored until the risk is eliminated. Risk mitigation plans should identify the approach to monitoring a risk, the criteria that would activate contingency plans, and the course of action that would be executed if the risk were deemed unavoidable.

8. *Revise the work breakdown structure.* The SWE-IPT must review and update the work breakdown structure to reflect the impact of architectural decisions and adopted change proposals. The work packages, associated tasks, and resource allocations should be adjusted to reflect the enhanced understanding of the effort that will be necessary to architect, implement, and test the software product and post-development processes. Some tasks may be eliminated or reduced in scope, others will demand more time and resources, and new tasks might be created. The WBS must be a flexible mechanism that can be adjusted from initial planning estimates to reflect architectural decisions and adopted change proposals.

9. *Refine the product specification tree.* As a result of identifying the software configuration items, the requirements for software documentation must be revisited to align the specification tree with the adopted architectural structure of configuration items. The specification tree should reflect the software hierarchy of documentation required for each identified configuration item. It must be extended and updated to reflect the software plans, specifications, documents,

models, drawings, or other forms of documentation necessary to manage the development of each configuration item.

10. *Refine project and technical plans*. The plans for the remaining stages of the software development project should be revisited to reflect the enriched understanding of the scope of the development effort. The project and technical plans have to be dynamic documents that are continually updated to reflect architectural decisions and authorized change proposals. Project plans must illuminate the scope of work remaining to be performed and amplify the probability of successful execution.

11. *Prepare the software nomenclature register*. The SWE-IPT should prepare the software nomenclature register[3] to designate unique identifiers, names, and definitions for the elements of the software architecture. Registry entries should include the elements identified by the operational model, and the initial functional and physical architectures. Data items should be defined in terms of their purpose, type (e.g., constant, variable, string, integer, Boolean, or date), security classification (if applicable), units of measurement, and acceptable range of values. The nomenclature register is intended to ensure that the entire software development team has knowledge of the authorized architectural element names, identifiers, and definitions. This is to ensure that architectural elements are properly exploited and that duplicate names or identifiers are not assigned.

12. *Prepare for the software requirements review (SRR)*. The SWE-IPT should prepare for the SRR, which is a formal project-level review performed to exhibit the status of the software architecture to project management personnel, customers, and other stakeholders. The identified risks and their abatement plans must be reviewed. Finally, the modifications to the WBS, specification tree, and project plans should be promoted. The architectural decisions that drove the major changes to the project plans should be identified and traced to the impact on the WBS, specification tree, and project plans. The software updated technical plans and outcome of software quality inspections and audits should be reported.

17.3 Software implementation (software requirements definition stage)

1. *Participate in the SWE-IPT*. Senior representatives of the software implementation organization should participate in the SWE-IPT to contribute to making constructive software requirements specification and allocation decisions. Representatives from software implementation contribute their knowledge of

---

[3]Originally referred to as a data dictionary. However, it is necessary to address the full range of architectural elements in a nomenclature registry.

the computing languages, design patterns, and implementation challenges to software engineering tasks.

2. *Identify software implementation challenges, constraints, feasibility, and risks.* The representatives of the software implementation organization should identify implementation challenges, constraints, and risks associated with the specified software requirements. These representatives are essential to ensuring that the requirements specified for the software product are achievable.

3. *Identify the software development environment.* The software implementation organization should identify elements of the software development environment that will be necessary to implement, test, and debug the evolving software architecture.

17.4 Computing environment preparation (software requirements definition stage)

1. *Participate in the SWE-IPT.* Senior representatives of the computing environment organization should participate in the SWE-IPT to contribute to making constructive software requirements specifications decisions. Representatives of the computing environment organization bring their knowledge of computing hardware, networking, communications, operating systems, middleware, and computing technology challenges to software engineering tasks.

2. *Identify computing environment implementation challenges, constraints, feasibility, and risks.* The representatives of the computing environment organization should identify computing technology challenges, constraints, and risks associated with specified computing environment requirements. Representatives of the computing environment organization are essential to ensuring that the requirements specified for the computing environment are achievable.

17.5 Post-development process implementation (software requirements definition stage)

1. *Participate in the SWE-IPT.* Senior representatives of the software post-development process organization should participate in the SWE-IPT to contribute to making constructive software requirements specifications decisions. Representatives from software post-development process areas bring their knowledge of the software replication, distribution, training and sustainment technologies, procedures, and challenges to the SWE-IPT.

2. *Identify software post-development process implementation challenges, constraints, feasibility, and risks.* Representatives of the software post-development process organization should identify challenges, constraints, and risks associated with the post-development process concepts. Representatives of the software post-development process organization are essential to ensuring that the

requirements specified for the software product and sustainment environment do not constrain the post-development processes.

3. Prepare the software post-development process concepts. Representatives of the software post-development process organization should develop the concept of operations (CONOPs) documents, which must be prepared to express the initial scope and requirements for each of the process areas. The CONOPs should identify any unique tools, equipment, facilities, or materials necessary to support these processes.

17.6 Software test and evaluation (software requirements definition stage)

1. *Participate in the SWE-IPT.* The senior representatives of the software test and evaluation organization should participate in the SWE-IPT to contribute to making constructive software requirements specifications decisions. These representatives bring their knowledge of techniques for replicating stressful computational loads, measurement of resource utilization, and other challenges associated with software testing to the SWE-IPT.

2. *Identify software test and evaluation feasibility, challenges, constraints, and risks.* Lead representatives of software test and evaluation should identify challenges, constraints, and risks associated with the software test and evaluation effort. Representatives of software test and evaluation are essential to ensuring that the software requirements, as specified, are testable within allocated resources and constraints.

3. *Prepare the software test plan.* The software test and evaluation organization should prepare the software test plan to describe the strategy for conducting software acceptance testing. This plan should identify the preliminary test strategy and test cases, the elements of the software test environment, and establish the test schedules based on the software specifications.

4. *Revise the software quality assurance plan.* The software test and evaluation team should prepare the software quality assurance plan to describe the strategy for conducting software inspections and audits during software preliminary architecture definition.

5. *Conduct software quality assurance inspection and audits.* Software quality inspections should be conducted periodically (during the software requirements definition stage) to evaluate the software requirements specifications and architectural artifacts. The following inspections should be conducted:
   - Inspection of the operational model
   - Inspection of the functional architecture
   - Inspection of the physical architecture
   - Inspection of the product requirements specification(s)
   - Inspection of the computing environment specification(s)
   - Inspection of the software interface specification(s)

- Inspection of the software test plan
- Inspection of the requirements traceability matrix
- Inspection of the post-development process concept documents
- Inspection of the nomenclature register

Software quality inspections should be conducted to ensure that organizations are complying with established policies and procedures. Software audits should be conducted prior to the SRR to ensure the available software specifications provide a consistent and traceable framework for evaluating software requirements against project and technical plans and stakeholder needs and expectations. The following audits should be conducted:

1. *Software requirements audit*—traces stakeholder needs to the specified requirements in the software specifications through the operational model to the preliminary functional and physical architectures. The source for derived requirements should be associated with the engineering analysis or trade study that recognized the implied need. Derived requirements must be included within the requirements traceability matrix.
2. *Software test audit*—traces software test cases or scenarios to the operational model data processing transactions and software requirements each scenario will exercise. The test cases should be properly reflected in the requirements traceability matrix.
3. *Corrective action audit*—traces each software problem report, change request, or proposal to its trade-study report and corrective action plan. Ensures that the corrective action is properly reflected in the operational model, software requirements specifications, functional and physical architectures, and associated architectural artifacts affected by the action.

17.7 Reviews, milestones, and baselines (software requirements definition stage)

1. *Conduct the SRR.* The software requirements review should be conducted for the purpose of substantiating the adequacy of the software specification(s) and post-development process concepts to the stakeholders. The SRR should focus on the state of the requirements allocation to the software product, and its configuration items, external interfaces, and elements of the computing environment. The review should focus on the architectural decisions that were made during the software requirements definition and any risks that have been identified. The purpose is not to provide a forum for nonparticipants in the software engineering effort to approve or comprehend the software requirements; rather, the purpose is to confirm that the software requirements are complete and consistent with stakeholder needs and project objectives. To accomplish this, it is necessary to demonstrate that the operational problem and solution spaces have been adequately explored, alternative solutions have been analyzed, and

architectural decisions made with credible technical rationale. A typical agenda for the software requirements review should address the following topics:

1. Software Requirements Definition Stage—Objectives
   1.1. Products of Requirements Analysis
      1.1.1. Stakeholder Needs and Constraints
      1.1.2. Operational Model Composition
      1.1.3. Preliminary Functional Architecture Formation (Behavioral Model and Hierarchy)
      1.1.4. Conceptual Physical Architecture
      1.1.5. Key Trade-off Analysis, Alternatives, Results, Decisions, and Rationale
      1.1.6. Software Requirements Specifications Status
      1.1.7. Computing Environment Specifications Status
   1.2. Post-development Process Concepts
      1.2.1. Replication Process
      1.2.2. Distribution Process
      1.2.3. Training Process
      1.2.4. Support Process
      1.2.5. Post-development Processes Development
         1.2.5.1. Schedule and Milestones
         1.2.5.2. Resource Requirements
   1.3. Software Engineering Plan, Schedule, and Milestones (Preliminary Architecture Definition Stage)
2. Software Implementation Strategy
   2.1. Software Implementation Challenges, Constraints, and Risks
   2.2. Software Development Environment
   2.3. Software Implementation Schedule and Milestones (Overview)
3. Computing Environment Definition
   3.1. Computing Environment Implementation Challenges, Constraints, and Risks
   3.2. Computing Environment Implementation Schedule and Milestones (Overview)
4. Software Test and Evaluation
   4.1. Software Test and Evaluation Challenges, Constraints, and Risks
   4.2. Software Test Plan (Overview)
      4.2.1. Software Test Strategy
      4.2.2. Software Test Environment
      4.2.3. Software Test Cases
      4.2.4. Test and evaluation Schedule and Milestones
   4.3. Software Quality Assurance Plan
      4.3.1. Software Quality Inspections
      4.3.2. Software Quality Audits
      4.3.3. Software Quality Schedule and Milestones

5. Software Control
   - **5.1.** Updated Project Plans and Schedule
   - **5.2.** Updated Specification Tree
   - **5.3.** Updated Work Breakdown Structure
   - **5.4.** Engineering Artifact Repository
   - **5.5.** Change History Repository
   - **5.6.** Technical Risk Repository
   - **5.7.** Software Nomenclature Registry

2. *Establish the requirements baseline.* The SWE-IPT should place the software requirements specifications under technical configuration control upon successful completion of the software requirements review. These specifications form the architectural requirements baseline and establish the foundation for developing the product functional and physical architectures. The functional baseline is comprised of the software product, interface, and computing environment specifications. Once the requirements baseline is established it requires technical CCB approval of a change request or proposal to make any changes to these specifications.

The operational model should be captured in the software engineering artifact repository since it was the basis for deriving the software requirements. The preliminary functional and physical architectures should not be controlled at this time. The functional and physical architectures will continue to evolve during the preliminary architecture definition stage and provide the technical infrastructure for expanding the software architectural solution.

Software Architecture Definition

CHAPTER OUTLINE

The purpose of the software architecture definition stage of development is to establish the software product functional and physical architectures, as well as initiate the development of the software post-development processes. The architecture definition stage is divided into two substages as depicted in Figure 18.1. The first stage, preliminary architecture definition, is focused on decomposing top-level functions

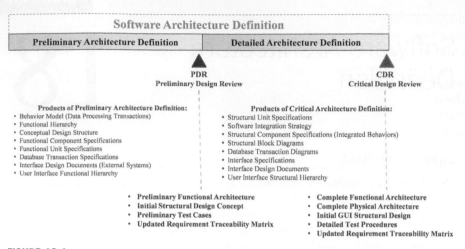

FIGURE 18.1

The architecture definition stage.

into a complete functional hierarchy. It also derives the preliminary physical architecture that defines the conceptual components of the structural configuration. The second stage, detailed architecture definition, finalizes the physical architecture by establishing the specifications for structural units and components while establishing the software integration strategy. During the software architecture definition stage, the computing environment definition should be established to devise a unified software product architecture.

During the preliminary stage of architectural definition, the top-level functions are analyzed and decomposed into a complete functional hierarchy of components and units. There is no set number of levels for this decomposition. However, the decomposition should continue until the functional solution is well understood, complete, and noncomplex. When a functional element is recognized to represent an uncomplicated data processing action, then no further decomposition is necessary. Uncomplicated elements should be labeled functional units, which represent the foundational piece of the architecture. Functional unit specifications should be prepared to reflect the functional characteristics established by the behavior model. The physical architecture definition is instigated by conceiving a conceptual structural solution. This structural solution represents an arrangement of conceptual components that coalesce principal data processing functionality that is ultimately provided by a set of underlying structural elements. This stage of development concludes with the preliminary design review (PDR). The PDR is intended to demonstrate that the functional decomposition and behavioral models are complete and in compliance with the software requirements.

During the detailed architecture definition stage, the lowest-level structural units must be conceived by aligning and grouping functional units around coherent themes. Structural units must be specified in terms of their behavior, data elements, algorithms, conditional control mechanisms, interfaces, and fault detection and recovery procedures. This is accomplished by coalescing functional unit specifications while resolving conflicting or duplicative functional characteristics. A structural unit inheritance hierarchy should be developed to formulate how object-oriented characteristics will be transmitted from parent units to offspring. The software integration strategy must be established to bridge the design chasm between structural units and conceptual components. The structural user interface hierarchy must be established to identify the mechanism involving information displays, navigational controls, data formatting, and data entry mechanisms. Database queries must be specified that satisfy identified functional database transaction behaviors. Software test procedures and the plans for software implementation must be finalized.

The detailed architecture definition stage concludes with the critical design review (CDR). The CDR is intended to demonstrate that the physical architecture is complete, verified, and validated. The physical architecture must be verified against the functional architecture and against the software requirements baseline. The distilled structural unit specifications will guide the software implementation team in the design, coding, and testing of each software unit. The arrangement of structural units and components must be reviewed to ensure that the structural configuration is not unreasonably complex and will facilitate problem resolution and preplanned product improvements (P^3I).

18.1 Preliminary architecture definition

The preliminary architecture definition effort is focused on establishing the functional architecture and conceptual structural solution. The purpose of this stage is to fully understand the software challenge as defined by stakeholder needs, software specifications, and computer technology capabilities. The functional architecture provides an analytical solution to the software product operational essentials. The initial software product structural configuration will be established as a conceptual representation of the dominant, topmost structural components. The initial structural configuration involves the arrangement of, and interconnections among, abstract components and user interface design mechanisms.

18.1.1 Products of preliminary architecture definition

The following products should be generated during the preliminary architecture definition stage of the software development project:

1. *Functional behavior model.* The functional behavioral model provides the functional flow, control flow, data flow, timing, error detection and handling procedures, and resource utilization characteristics of the software solution. The behavior model is derived from the operational model and decomposes operational activities into the deliberate behaviors the software product will be fabricated to possess.

2. *Functional hierarchy.* The functional hierarchy stipulates the layered breakdown of functional complexity to elementary, uncomplicated functions. Topmost functional components are decomposed into lower-level components to provide a logical framework for deriving software behaviors. Lower-level functional components must be further decomposed until functional units are perceived. Functional units represent elementary functions that can no longer be decomposed or of which the effective and efficient formulation does not warrant further exploration or decomposition.

3. *Database transaction behavior diagrams.* Provides a behavioral representation of each database transaction the software product must support. These diagrams should identify the database tables accessed, the expected responses to transaction queries, and transaction rollback procedures.

4. *User interface functional hierarchy.* This hierarchy depicts how common user interface functional mechanisms have been grouped into functional components, subcomponents, and finally to functional units.

5. *Conceptual component block diagram.* This diagram provides a layout of conceptual components, the interfaces among components, and interfaces with operators and elements of the computing environment.

6. *Software test cases.* The software test cases should be identified by tracing operational threads of behavior in the operational model. Each operational thread represents a unique test case. Each test case should identify the set of conditions under which a data processing transaction is exercised and the criteria for determining that the transaction has been satisfied.

7. *Updated requirements traceability matrix.* The requirements traceability matrix must be updated to reflect the evolving elements of the functional and physical architectures and software test cases.

8. *Updated nomenclature register.* The software architecture dictionary must be updated to reflect the elements of the functional and physical architectures.

9. *Preliminary software implementation plan.* The software implementation plan should be drafted to establish the level of effort and resources that will be necessary to accomplish the implementation stage of the software development effort. The implementation plan should provide a basis for refining the related work packages to reflect the evolving software architecture and establish the resource allocations among subpackages. In addition, the software implementation plan should identify the staffing requirements for the software implementation organization including the types of skills that will be necessary to properly implement the software architecture.

10. *Preliminary computing environment implementation plan.* The computing environment implementation plan should be drafted to establish the level of effort and resources that will be necessary to establish the computing environment. The computing environment implementation plan will provide the basis for refining the related work packages to reflect the resource requirements for the computing environment implementation organization.

11. *Revised software test plan.* The software test and evaluation team must revise the software test plan to reflect the effort associated with preparing and conducting software acceptance testing. The software test plan should provide the basis for refining the work packages to establish the resource requirements for the software test and evaluation organization.

12. *Preliminary post-development process implementation plan.* The post-development implementation team must prepare the preliminary post-development process implementation plan to reflect the effort associated with implementing the post-development processes. The post-development process implementation plan will provide the basis for refining the work packages to establish the resource requirements for the post-development process implementation organization.

18.1.2 Software engineering integrated product team (preliminary architecture definition stage)

1. *Refine the operational model.* The software engineering integrated product team (SWE-IPT) should analyze each of the top-level functional components derived from the operational model to determine how to break down functional complexity. The behavior of complex functional components should be analyzed to provide more insight into the software functional behaviors that must be formulated to support the operational process. Functional behavior models should be prepared to facilitate functional analysis of complex functions. Derived functions should be identified that are necessary to enable a functional component to behave properly and to detect and respond to failure conditions.

2. *Refine the functional hierarchy.* The SWE-IPT should conduct functional analysis to decompose functional components to establish a more detailed functional hierarchy. Functional components should be decomposed into functional subcomponents until functional units are recognized. Functional decomposition alternatives should be evaluated and trade studies conducted to determine the performance, interfaces, and risks associated with each alternative. The preferred functional solution should be integrated into the functional hierarchy and reflected in the other artifacts of the functional architecture.

3. *Synthesize conceptual configuration alternatives.* The SWE-IPT should conduct software design synthesis to identify top-level conceptual components. Conceptual configuration alternatives should be identified and evaluated to narrow the solution space to one or more practical alternatives.

4. *Analyze functional alternatives, conflicts, and trade-offs.* The SWE-IPT should evaluate identified functional decomposition, grouping, and allocation alternatives to determine the best solution set. The risks associated with each alternative should be identified and assessed to distinguish architectural design schemes that eliminate, avoid, or reduce risks to an acceptable level. The preferred solution, in terms of a coherent set of functional behaviors and decomposition, should be selected that provides the best performance, satisfaction of

stakeholder needs and expectations, and opportunity to achieve program cost and schedule objectives. The SWE-IPT should evaluate identified conflicts between the functional and initial physical architectures to determine potential courses of corrective action. Viable approaches to resolving architectural conflicts should be explored and evaluated against program objectives and stakeholder needs. The software implementation and testing challenges and risks associated with each approach must be identified. The alternative approaches should be prioritized to facilitate architectural decision making.

5. *Specify the functional architecture.* The SWE-IPT should conduct software requirements analysis to coherently specify functional component and unit requirements. The internal software interface or data exchange requirement must be stipulated for the transmitting and receiving functional element. The control, error handling, and resource regulation mechanisms must be designated to preclude ineffective solution.

6. *Verify the functional architecture.* As the functional architecture matures it must be verified to ensure that it reflects a solution that satisfies the requirements baseline and is achievable within program objectives. When the requirements baseline and functional architecture are aligned, the requirements traceability matrix must be updated to reflect how the software requirements have been allocated among the elements of the functional architecture. The requirements traceability matrix should associate the elements of the functional architecture to elements of the requirements baseline and test cases.

7. *Update risk mitigation plans.* Risk mitigation plans should be prepared for those risks that could not be eliminated or avoided and still threaten the achievement of program objectives. Risk assessment reports should capture the results of each risk assessment, including the probability of occurrence, and the consequences should the risk be realized. Risk mitigation plans should identify the course of action being taken to monitor and prevent the risk from occurring, the criteria that would make the risk unacceptable to proceed as planned, and the contingency actions that would be executed should the risk deviation criteria be encountered.

8. *Revise technical plans.* The tasks identified in the work packages need to be reexamined and refined to accurately reflect the work remaining to be performed. The technical plans should be revised and the program work breakdown structure (WBS), work package, and resource allocations must be adjusted to reflect the improved understanding of the remaining scope of the development effort.

9. *Refine project plans.* The program plans for the remaining stages of the software development project should be updated to reflect the remaining scope of the development effort. The program plans must be living documents and reflect the design decisions that have been made on the scope of work remaining to be performed.

10. *Update the software nomenclature register.* The software nomenclature register should be updated and expanded to reflect the elements of the functional architecture.

11. *Prepare for the PDR.* The SWE-IPT should prepare for the PDR. The purpose of the PDR is to present the consistent software requirements, functional architecture, and conceptual structural configuration to program management, customers, or other stakeholders. The architectural decisions that guided the formulation of the functional architecture should be identified. Architectural decisions must be traced to their impact on the WBS and program and technical plans. The software quality assurance inspection and audits conducted during the preliminary architecture definition should be reported. The risks identified during this stage of development and their risk abatement plans should be discussed.

18.1.3 Software implementation (preliminary architecture definition stage)

1. *Participate in the SWE-IPT.* The senior representatives of the software implementation organization should participate in the SWE-IPT to contribute to making favorable architectural decisions. Representatives from software implementation bring their knowledge of the implementation languages, design patterns, and software implementation challenges to the SWE-IPT.
2. *Identify software implementation challenges, constraints, feasibility, and risks.* Representatives of the software implementation organization should identify implementation challenges, constraints, and risks associated with their comprehension of the functional architecture and its influence on the software implementation effort.
3. *Prepare the preliminary software implementation plan.* The software implementation organization should prepare the preliminary software implementation plan to reflect the insight obtained during the preliminary architecture definition stage. This plan must identify the software implementation tasks, work packages, and schedule milestones for accomplishing the software implementation effort. This plan will not have the requisite clarity necessary to be executable due to the amorphous state of the structural configuration. However, it should provide a more accurate forecast of the anticipated workload than previous versions of the plan.

18.1.4 Computing environment preparation (preliminary architecture definition stage)

1. *Participate in the SWE-IPT.* The senior representatives of the computing environment organization should participate in the SWE-IPT to contribute to making favorable architectural decisions. Representatives from the computing environment organization bring their knowledge of the computing hardware, networking, communications, operating systems, middleware, and other computational challenges to the SWE-IPT.
2. *Identify computing environment implementation challenges, constraints, and risks.* Representatives of the computing environment organization should

identify computational challenges, constraints, and risks associated with aligning the computing environment implementation workload with the requirements baseline and functional architecture.

3. *Prepare the preliminary computing environment implementation plan.* Representatives of the computing environment organization should prepare the computing environment implementation plan. This plan must identify the computing environment implementation tasks, work packages, and schedule milestones for establishing and qualifying the computational environment. This plan will not have the requisite clarity necessary to be executable due to the amorphous state of the structural configuration. However, it should provide a more accurate forecast of the anticipated workload than previous versions of the plan.

18.1.5 Post-development process preparation (preliminary architecture definition stage)

1. *Participate in the SWE-IPT.* The senior representatives of the post-development process organization should participate in the SWE-IPT to contribute to making favorable architectural decisions. The representatives from the post-development process organization bring their knowledge of software replication, distribution, training, and customer and software support challenges to the SWE-IPT.

2. *Identify post-development process implementation challenges, constraints, and risks.* Representatives of the post-development process organization should identify implementation challenges, constraints, and risks associated with aligning the post-development processes with the requirement baseline and functional architecture.

3. *Prepare the preliminary post-development process implementation plan.* Representatives of the post-development process organization should prepare the post-development process implementation plan. This plan must identify the post-development implementation tasks, work packages, and schedule milestones for establishing and qualifying the distribution, training, and software sustainment processes. This plan will not have the requisite clarity necessary to be executable due to the amorphous state of the structural configuration. However, it should provide a more accurate forecast of the anticipated workload than previous versions of the plan.

18.1.6 Software test and evaluation (preliminary architecture definition stage)

1. *Participate in the SWE-IPT.* The senior representatives of the software test and evaluation organization should participate in the SWE-IPT to contribute to making favorable software architecture decisions. The representatives from software test and evaluation bring their knowledge of the testing demands and challenges to the SWE-IPT.

2. *Identify software test and evaluation challenges, constraints, and risks.* As the component architecture is derived via the software engineering process, senior representatives of the software test and evaluation team should identify implementation challenges, constraints, feasibility, and risks associated with the requirements baseline and functional and physical architecture alternatives.

3. *Prepare software test plan.* The software test and evaluation organization must refine the software test plan. The software test cases should be derived by identifying test threads within the operation model. A test case describes the initial test environment state; inputs, actions, or events that occur throughout the test conduct; and the expected software response, or results of data processing transactions. This plan must identify the test and evaluation tasks, work packages, and schedule milestones for establishing the software acceptance test environment and procedures, qualifying the test environment, and performing acceptance testing. This plan will not have the requisite clarity necessary to be executable due to the amorphous state of the structural configuration. However, it should provide a more accurate forecast of the anticipated workload than previous versions of the plan.

4. *Conduct software quality assurance inspections and audits.* Software quality inspections should be conducted periodically to examine software engineering artifacts and products to ensure that they are complete, accurate, and conform to established policies and procedures. Software quality inspections should be conducted to ensure that organizations are complying with established procedures and are observing approved plans. The following software quality inspections should be conducted during the preliminary architecture definition effort:
   - Inspection of the functional hierarchy
   - Inspection of the functional component specifications
   - Inspection of the functional unit specifications
   - Inspection of the conceptual configuration documentation
   - Inspection of organizational technical plans
   - Inspection of the software nomenclature register
   - Inspection of the requirements traceability matrix

Software audits should be conducted prior to the PDR to ensure the software products and architectural artifacts are complete and have incorporated approved change proposals and requests. The following audits should be conducted:

1. *Functional architecture audit.* Tracing the functional element requirements from the originating source (stakeholders' needs) through the operational model, requirements baseline, and functional architecture. The source for derived functional elements should be traceable to architectural decisions or the result of engineering analysis.

2. *Acceptance test case audit.* Tracing each test case to the specification requirements it is intended to validate. A test case must be traced from an operational thread (operational model), to the source of the requirements (stakeholder needs), to the specified requirement (specification identifier) it is intended to qualify. A software test may affect one or more of the architectural

specifications (requirements, interface, or functional), and this should be properly reflected in the requirements traceability matrix.

3. *Corrective action audit*. Tracing each authenticated change request or proposal to its corrective action disposition. This audit must ensure that the corrective action was properly accomplished and is reflected in the affected software product and architectural artifacts.

18.1.7 Reviews and milestones (preliminary architecture definition stage)

The PDR should be conducted for the purpose of describing the functional architecture and how architectural decisions were settled. The purpose of the PDR is to substantiate the software architecture as a framework that will enable the software architecture to evolve over time. The rationale for design decisions should be the focus of the review and how they affect program plans and the achievement of program objectives. The agenda for the architecture preliminary design review should address the following topics:

1. Preliminary Design Review—Overview
    1.1. Requirements Baseline and Outstanding Change Proposal Status
    1.2. Functional Architecture Status
    1.3. Physical Architecture Status (Conceptual Structural Configuration)
    1.4. Key Trade-off Analyses, Alternatives, Results, Decisions, and Rationale
    1.5. Requirements Traceability Matrix
2. Software Implementation
    2.1. Preliminary Software Implementation Plan
    2.2. Preliminary Software Implementation Schedule and Milestones
    2.3. Software Implementation Challenges, Constraints, Feasibility, and Risks
3. Computing Environment
    3.1. Computing Environment Implementation Plan
    3.2. Computing Environment Qualification Plan
    3.3. Computing Environment Schedule and Milestones
    3.4. Computing Environment Challenges, Constraints, Feasibility, and Risks
4. Software Test and Evaluation
    4.1. Software Test and Evaluation Plan
    4.2. Software Test Schedule and Milestones
    4.3. Software Quality Assurance Inspections
    4.4. Software Quality Assurance Audits
    4.5. Software Test and Evaluation Challenges, Constraints, Feasibility, and Risks
5. Software Post-development Process
    5.1. Software Post-development Process Plan
    5.2. Software Post-development Process Schedule and Milestones
    5.3. Software Post-development Process Challenges, Constraints, Feasibility, and Risks

18.2 **Detailed architecture definition**

The detailed architecture definition stage is focused on finalizing the software architecture and transitioning to software implementation. The physical architecture is established by bridging the topmost conceptual level with derived physical units by identifying integrating structural components. The physical architecture should be configured in a manner that permits modification, extension, and enhancement to reduce software support costs and facilitate software reuse.

18.2.1 **Products of detailed architecture definition**

The physical architecture should be anchored on the fabrication of structural units. Structural unit specifications are established by synthesizing the assimilated functional unit specifications and resolving conflicting and redundant requirements. The software integration strategy must be derived by synthesizing one or more levels of structural components and assemblies that integrate structural elements to align with the topmost conceptual structure. The following products should be generated during the detailed architecture definition stage:

1. *Structural unit block diagram.* The structural unit block diagram should be prepared to represent how structural units will interact with one another. Block diagrams are a method of explaining complex systems in an uncomplicated manner. They are composed of labeled blocks representing structural units that are joined by arrows that indicate the direction of data flow for inputs to and outputs from the blocks.
2. *Structural unit inheritance hierarchy.* The structural unit inheritance hierarchy should be developed by grouping similar structural units and deriving paternal unit characteristics. It should display how the offspring structural units inherit common functionality and data elements and how each offspring adds additional unique characteristics. This is known as *specialization* within the object-oriented domain.
3. *Software integration hierarchy.* The software integration hierarchy should be developed to provide a depiction of how structural units will be assembled and integrated into larger components. Structural assemblies should be identified that involve an integrated component and the test stubs necessary to support integration testing. This integration hierarchy should depict the sequential levels of integration necessary to result in a complete, integrated software configuration item. The hierarchy should also depict where in the hierarchy integration testing will be conducted.
4. *Physical user interface hierarchy.* The physical user interface hierarchy should be developed by grouping related user interface mechanisms, synthesizing them as structural units and components, and configuring the physical user interface.
5. *Database structure block diagram.* The database structure block diagram provides a graphical representation of the database tables, records, fields, and the relationships that link records within multiple tables together.

6. *Database query specification.* The database query specification should be developed to provide general query instructions for prevalent database transactions. The data persistence functions identified during functional analysis should be the basis for database query specifications. Each data persistence function involves preservation of data in a repository or database management system (DBMS). Structured query language (SQL) instructions provide a standard set of instructions or commands for adding, deleting, updating, and sorting information in a DBMS. The database query specification should establish the set of privileged database queries that provide access to restricted database information.

7. *Structural unit specifications.* Each structural unit must be specified to permit it to be designed with leveraging the selected programming language expressions or constructs. A software development folder (SDF) should be established for each structural unit to provide a repository for all subsequent implementation artifacts. The requirements specification associated with each physical unit should be retained in the appropriate SDF. Structural unit specifications should express the coalesced functional requirements, interfaces, and programmatic design characteristics (e.g., budgeted line of code) to which each unit must conform.

8. *Updated requirements traceability matrix.* The requirements traceability matrix should be updated to reflect the structural unit linkages to the functional architecture, as well as the extended reach of software integration strategy.

9. *Updated software nomenclature register.* The software nomenclature register should be updated to reflect the physical architecture and ensure that each structural unit, component, assembly, and data element name and definition is unique throughout the software architecture.

10. *Finalize the software implementation plan.* The software implementation plan should be finalized to identify the level of effort and resources necessary to accomplish the implementation stage of the software development effort. The implementation plan must refine the work packages to reflect the evolving structural configuration and software integration strategy.

11. *Finalize the computing environment implementation plan.* The computing environment implementation plan should be finalized to identify the level of effort and resources necessary to establish and qualify the computing environment that will be utilized during software acceptance testing. The computing environment implementation plan must refine the work packages to reflect the resource requirements for the computing environment implementation organization.

12. *Software test plan.* The software test and evaluation organization must expand the software test plan to establish test scenarios and procedures. The software test plan must refine work packages to reflect the effort associated with preparing for and conducting software acceptance testing.

13. *Post-development process implementation plan.* The post-development implementation organization must expand the post-development process implementation plan to reflect the effort associated with implementing the post-development processes. The post-development process implementation

plan must refine work packages to reflect the effort associated with defining, designing, assembling, integrating, and qualifying the environment supporting each of the post-development processes.

14. *Software technical data package (TDP).* The technical data package must be prepared to provide a basis for software implementation and acceptance testing. The software TDP should include, at a minimum, the following architectural artifacts:

    • Software requirements baseline (software product and interface specifications and the computing environment specifications)
    • Structural unit specifications
    • Structural component specifications
    • Structural assembly specifications
    • Software integration strategy.

18.2.2 Software engineering integrated product team (detailed architecture definition stage)

1. *Synthesize structural unit alternatives.* The SWE-IPT should conduct software design synthesis to identify and group common functions and allocate them to identified structural units. This includes determining the physical unit inheritance and physical unit user interface hierarchies. Structural unit block diagrams should be develop to identify how the structural units will need to interface. Alternative structural unit configurations should be identified and evaluated to narrow the solution space to the preferred physical design solution.

2. *Develop the software integration hierarchy.* The software integration hierarchy should be developed to depict the software integration strategy. This hierarchy depicts how structural elements will be assembled, integrated, and tested to form a single integrated structural configuration item.

3. *Analyze structural configuration alternatives, conflicts, and trade-offs.* The SWE-IPT should analyze structural design alternatives to identify the preferred architectural solution. Trade-off studies should be conducted for structural design alternatives, as necessary. The risks for structural design alternatives must be identified and assessed to ensure the resulting structural configuration can be implemented within program cost and schedule constraints. The preferred structural design solution should be selected that achieves a balance among performance characteristics, reduced physical architecture complexity, architectural stability, and the satisfaction of stakeholder needs and expectations. The SWE-IPT should evaluate identified conflicts between the functional and physical architectures to determine potential courses of corrective action. Viable approaches to resolving architectural conflict should be explored and evaluated against program objectives and stakeholder needs. The software implementation and test challenges and risks associated with each approach must be identified. The alternative approaches should be prioritized to facilitate architectural decision making.

4. *Update risk mitigation plans.* Risk assessment records should be prepared for those physical unit risks that could not be eliminated or avoided and still threaten the achievement of program objectives. Risk mitigation plans should be identified for each identified risk. Risk assessment records should capture the results of the risk assessment, including the probability of occurrence and the consequences should the risk be realized. Risk mitigation plans should identify the course of action being taken to monitor and prevent the risk from occurring, the criteria that would make the risk unacceptable to proceed as planned, and the contingency plans that would be executed.

5. *Revise the WBS.* Once the physical architecture is complete and the software implementation plan finalized, the program WBS should be adjusted to reflect the improved understanding of the scope of the software implementation and test and evaluation work effort. The software engineering–related work packages, associated tasks, and resource allocations must be assigned to the tasks identified in the software implementation plan.

6. *Refine technical plans.* The technical plans must be revisited for the remaining stages of the software development program to have them reflect the remaining scope of the work effort. The technical plans must be living documents and reflect the design decisions that are made and their impact on the scope of work to be performed. The software engineering–related work packages, associated task descriptions, and resource allocations must be aligned with the tasks identified in the plan. The resulting software engineering plan should identify the tasks to be performed throughout the remaining stages of the software development effort. The SWE-IPT must synthesize organizational plans and refine the integrated technical plan and schedule (ITP/ITS).

7. *Update the software nomenclature register.* The software architecture dictionary should be updated and expanded to reflect the physical architecture. The names of all physical units and components must be added to the software architecture dictionary.

8. *Prepare for the CDR.* The SWE-IPT must prepare for the architecture CDR. The purpose of the CDR is to present the consistent requirements baseline and functional and physical architectures to program management, customers, or other stakeholders. The design decisions that drove the major changes to the program structure and plans should be identified and traced to the impact on the WBS and program plans. The software test planning, including quality assurance inspection and audits conducted during the detailed architecture definition, should be addressed. The risks identified and their risk abatement plans should be reviewed.

18.2.3 Software implementation (detailed architecture definition stage)

1. *Participate in the SWE-IPT.* The senior representatives of the software implementation team should participate in the SWE-IPT to contribute to making favorable functional and physical architectural decisions. The representatives from the software implementation team bring their knowledge of the implementation languages, design patterns, and challenges to the SWE-IPT.

2. *Identify software implementation challenges, constraints, feasibility, and risks.* Representatives of the software implementation team should identify software implementation challenges, constraints, feasibility, and risks associated with physical architecture alternatives.

3. *Finalize the software implementation plan.* The software implementation plan should be finalized to reflect the effort necessary to implement the completed software physical architecture. The software implementation–related work packages, associated task descriptions, and resource allocations must be aligned with the tasks identified in the software implementation plan. This includes the effort to:

   - Design, code, and test each structural unit.
   - Integrate and test structural components.
   - Design, develop, and evaluate prototypes to refine software implementation concepts.
   - Assemble, integrate, and test the fully integrated software product configuration items.

18.2.4 Computing environment preparation (architecture detailed definition)

1. *Participate in the SWE-IPT.* Senior representatives of the computing environment organization should participate in the SWE-IPT to contribute to making favorable physical architectural decisions. Representatives from the computing environment organization bring their knowledge of the computing hardware, networking, communications, operating systems, middleware and software architectures, and challenges to the SWE-IPT.

2. *Identify computing environment implementation challenges, constraints, feasibility, and risks.* Representatives of the computing environment implementation organization should identify computing environment challenges, constraints, feasibility, and risks associated with physical architecture alternatives.

3. *Finalize the computing environment implementation plan.* The computing environment implementation plan should be finalized to reflect the effort necessary to implement the computing environment to support software acceptance testing. This should include facility preparations, equipment acquisition, installation and checkout, workstations, software applications, and test tools. The computing environment implementation-related work packages, associated task descriptions, and resource allocations must be aligned with the tasks identified in the plan.

18.2.5 Post-development process preparation (detailed architecture definition stage)

1. *Participate in the SWE-IPT.* Senior representatives of the post-development process implementation organization should participate in the SWE-IPT to contribute to making favorable physical architectural decisions. The representatives

from the post-development process implementation organization bring their knowledge of the software replication, distribution, training, and support process demands and challenges to the SWE-IPT.

2. *Identify post-development process implementation feasibility, challenges, constraints, and risks.* Representatives of the post-development process implementation organization should identify post-development process challenges, constraints, feasibility, and risks associated with physical architecture alternatives.

3. *Finalize the post-development process implementation plan.* The post-development process implementation plan should be finalized to reflect the effort necessary to implement the post-development processes. This should include facility preparations, equipment acquisition, installation and checkout, workstations, software applications, and support tools. The post-development process implementation-related work packages, associated task descriptions, and resource allocations must be aligned with the tasks identified in the plan.

18.2.6 Software test and evaluation (detailed architecture definition stage)

1. *Participate in the SWE-IPT.* Senior representatives of the software test and evaluation organization should participate in the SWE-IPT to contribute to making favorable architectural decisions. Representatives from software test and evaluation bring their knowledge of testing demands and challenges to the SWE-IPT.

2. *Identify software test and evaluation feasibility, challenges, constraints, and risks.* Representatives of the software test and evaluation organization should identify software testing challenges, constraints, feasibility, and risks associated with the physical architecture.

3. *Finalize the software test plans and procedures.* The software test and evaluation plans and procedures should be finalized to reflect the effort necessary to conduct software acceptance testing. Software test procedures must be established for each software test case and scenario identified during the preliminary architecture definition. Software test procedures should articulate the detailed steps that need to be followed to perform each test, including test setup and post-test analysis actions.

4. *Conduct software quality assurance inspections and audits.* Software quality inspections should be conducted periodically to examine software engineering artifacts and products to ensure that they are complete, accurate, and conform to established policies and procedures. Software quality inspections should be conducted to ensure that organizations are complying with established procedures and are observing approved plans. The following software quality inspections should be conducted during the preliminary architecture definition effort:
   - Inspection of the structural configuration
   - Inspection of the structural unit specifications
   - Inspection of the structural component specifications

- Inspection of the software integration and test strategy
- Inspection of the software nomenclature register
- Inspection of the requirements traceability matrix

Software audits should be conducted prior to the CDR to ensure the software products and architectural artifacts are complete and have incorporated approved change proposals and requests. The following audits should be conducted:

1. *Structural configuration audit.* Tracing structural element requirements to the functional units it assimilated. Ensuring integration tests do not repeat testing conducted at lower levels of the configuration unless warranted. Ensures that all internal software interfaces are adequately addressed throughout the software integration strategy.
2. *Software test audit.* Tracing each test case and procedure to the software specification requirements it is supposed to validate. A software test may affect one or more of the software specifications (software product, computing environment, and interface), and this should be properly reflected in the requirements traceability matrix.
3. *Corrective action audit.* Tracing each authenticated change request or proposal to its corrective action disposition. This audit must ensure that the corrective action was properly accomplished and is reflected in the affected software product and architectural artifacts.

18.2.7 Reviews and milestones (detailed architecture definition stage)

The CDR should be conducted for the purpose of describing the software physical architecture. The purpose of the CDR is to substantiate that the functional and physical architectures are complete, consistent, and will satisfy the specific software requirements. A typical agenda for the CDR should address the following topics:

1. Critical Design Review—Overview
   1.1. Requirements Baseline and Outstanding Change Proposal Status
   1.2. Functional Architecture Status
   1.3. Physical Architecture Status
   1.4. Key Trade-off Analysis, Results, Decisions, and Rationale
   1.5. Structural Unit Requirements Traceability
   1.6. Software Integration Strategy
   1.7. Technical Data Package Status
2. Software Implementation
   2.1. Final Software Implementation Plan
   2.2. Software Implementation Challenges, Constraints, Feasibility, and Risks
3. Computing Environment
   3.1. Computing Environment Implementation Plan
   3.2. Computing Environment Qualification Plan

3.3. Computing Environment Schedule and Milestones
  4. Software Test and Evaluation
    4.1. Software Test and Evaluation Overview
    4.2. Software Test Procedure
    4.3. Software Quality Assurance
        4.3.1. Status of Software Quality Inspections
        4.3.2. Status of Software Quality Audits
        4.3.3. Software Quality Schedule and Milestones
  5. Software Post-development Process
    5.1. Software Post-development Process Implementation Plans
    5.2. Software Post-development Process Qualification Plans
    5.3. Software Post-development Process Schedule and Milestones

18.2.8 Establish the allocated baseline

The allocated baseline should be established to place structural unit, integrating component, and structural component specifications under technical configuration control. The allocated baseline establishes the specifications for each physical unit, their interfaces, and traceability to the software requirements baseline. Physical unit and component specifications form the basis for the design, coding, and testing of software units during the initial software implementation activity. The software integration strategy, integrating component, structural assemblies, and structural component specifications complete the physical architecture. The physical architecture should be placed under technical configuration control since it provides the analytical basis for evaluating proposed changes that may arise during software implementation.

Software Implementation

19

CHAPTER OUTLINE

The software implementation stage involves the transformation of the software technical data package (TDP) into one or more fabricated, integrated, and tested software configuration items that are ready for software acceptance testing. The primary activities of software implementation include the:

- Fabrication of software units to satisfy structural unit specifications.
- Assembly, integration, and testing of software components into a software configuration item.
- Prototyping challenging software components to resolve implementation risks or establish a fabrication proof of concept.
- Dry-run acceptance testing procedures to ensure that the procedures are properly delineated and that the software product (software configuration items (CIs and computing environment) is ready for acceptance testing.

Software implementation begins with the effort of software fabrication. *Fabrication* is an act of making something. Software fabrication involves programmatic design, source code editing or programming, and testing of each software unit. This series of technical tasks represents how software procedures, routines, modules, objects, or graphical models are produced. Each software unit is presumed to be suitable for their intended purpose or role in the overall architectural context. The result of software fabrication should be a documented unit of source code that has been tested against its structural unit specification. This source code (software unit) is then available to be assembled, integrated, and compiled with other fabricated software elements to craft larger software components. These integrated software components are tested against structural component specifications to ensure

Software Implementation		
Unit Fabrication	Component Integration & Testing	Acceptance Testing Dry-run

• Software unit programmatic design
• Unit design peer review
• Unit coding & testing
• Software unit documentation
• Architecture problem reports
	• Software assembly test stub fabrication
	• Software component prototyping
	• Software component assembly and integration
	• Software component testing
	• Architecture problem reports
		• Software CI testing
		• Software test reporting
		  – Test procedure deficiency
		  – Fabrication deficiency
		  – Architecture deficiency
		• Architecture problem reports

FIGURE 19.1

Software implementation stage.

their correctness. This assembly, integration, and testing series of events continues to generate larger, more complex software components. Software integration progresses until a completely integrated and tested software configuration item is realized and available for acceptance testing. The software implementation stage is shown in Figure 19.1.

Software implementation includes the dry-run of the software acceptance testing. This dry-run exercise is intended to ensure that the acceptance test procedures are effective and the software product performs according to software specifications. A dry-run provides a demonstration of the software product's readiness for acceptance testing. Acceptance testing represents a formal demonstration to stakeholders that the software development effort has achieved its objectives. If the tests are successful, the software product is deemed to be ready for distribution and post-development sustainment. The act of declaring the acceptance testing successful is the first step in transitioning from the software development project to deployment and post-development operations. Additional projects may be initiated to provide software post-development process operations and provide preplanned product improvement through an incremental or spiral approach. Alternatively, the software development project may simply transition into the post-development stage of the software life cycle.

Software deficiencies identified within the software implementation stage must be resolved. Those deficiencies that are determined to be the result of architectural flaws must be documented in architectural problem reports. The software engineering integrated product team (SWE-IPT) must be responsible for resolving architectural deficiencies and repairing the architectural artifacts. Other deficiencies may be discovered that stem from programmatic design or coding mistakes. However, those software problem reports are the responsibility of the software implementation organization to resolve. The software implementation team should not be allowed to deviate from the software TDP. Software architectural deficiencies must be resolved by the SWE-IPT. Architectural problem reports should be generated by software implementation personnel to document perceived software deficiencies that stem from the software TDP.

An acceptance testing dry-run is conducted to ensure that the software product can successfully pass acceptance testing while running on the specified computing environment. Upon successful completion of dry-run testing, the resolution of any software problem reports, and regression testing, the software test readiness review (TRR) should be conducted. The TRR is conducted to demonstrate to program management and stakeholder representatives that the software development is complete and the software product is ready for acceptance testing.

If the program chooses to bypass dry-run testing, there are risks that extensive regression testing will be necessary should any defects be uncovered during acceptance testing. Conducting dry-run testing ensures the development team that the software product will successfully pass acceptance testing and no further modifications to the software will be necessary prior to deployment.

19.1 **Products of software implementation**

The products identified in this section do not represent the complete set of products generated during software implementation. The following artifacts identify the software implementation artifacts that concern the software engineering effort:

1. *Software unit programmatic design diagrams.* The programmatic design diagrams provide a representation of the computational logic for each software unit. They should address control, data, and procedural flows necessary to transform inputs into desired outputs. Emphasis should be placed on the algorithmic computation of data items that result in accurate data values, fault handling mechanisms, and procedural calls or interfaces to other software elements. Each software unit must be evaluated to ensure that it satisfies its specification that involves performance and other nonfunctional requirements (e.g., size, resource utilization).

2. *Programmatic design descriptions.* Programmatic design descriptions provide a narrative, procedural explanation of how the software unit design achieves it data processing responsibilities.

3. *Software unit test scenarios.* Unit test scenarios should identify the data sets, procedures, and expected outcomes for each unit test case. Unit test scenarios describe how a software unit will be verified to confirm that it satisfies its structural unit specification. Unit test scenarios should be developed and documented in the software development folders (SDFs).

4. *Software unit source code files.* Source code files represent the computing language-specific data declarations and instructions that constitute a software module, routine, procedure, or class. A source code file is intended to be compiled into an executable binary file that can be run on the target computing system.

5. *Software unit test results.* The results of software unit testing should be documented and captured in the unit SDFs.

6. *Software component assembly, integration, and test procedures.* The software integration strategy should be detailed by establishing the procedures necessary to compile, assemble, and link (integrate) source code files into an executable file to support software component testing. The software component

test scenarios and procedures should be described and captured in a component SDF.

7. *Software integration test results.* The results of software integration testing should be documented and captured in the component SDFs.

8. *Dry-run test report.* The dry-run test report should summarize the test results, problems, and defects encountered. Each software problem or defect should be assigned to the organization responsible for resolving the issue. The associated set of regression tests that need to be conducted on the repaired software product must be identified. This report will be used in determining the readiness of the software product to commence acceptance testing.

9. *Acceptance testing report.* The acceptance testing report should summarize the test results, problems, and defects encountered (*there should be no problems or defects encountered!*). Each software problem or defect should be assigned to the organization responsible for resolving the issue. The associated set of regression tests that need to be conducted on the repaired software product must be identified. This report will be used in determining the readiness of the software product for operational deployment.

10. *Software build procedures.* The software build process should be defined, which establishes the manner by which the source code files are assembled, integrated, and verified to produce executable files for distribution. The build procedures should address the following tasks and automated support to script calls to compiler and link editors:
    - Compiling source code into binary code.
    - Packaging binary code libraries as extractable files.
    - Verifying build integrity.
    - Distribution of extractable executable images.
    - Creating documentation and/or release notes.
    - Release and patch (binary file fixes) coordination.

11. *Software problem reports.* Software problem reports should be generated for problems or deficiencies uncovered during software implementation.

12. *Engineering change requests (ECRs).* ECRs should be generated to capture a desired change to the software architecture. Each ECR should include the necessary specification and documentation change pages that will be used to assimilate the change into the architectural artifacts, and documentation consistent with the proposed change, if approved.

13. *Prepare waivers and deviations (as necessary).* Waivers or deviations to a requirement in one of the baselined software specifications should be prepared and submitted to the project-level change control board (CCB) for approval. Deviations do not relieve the program from achieving the specified requirement, but will permit the initial release of the software product with an understanding that the problem will be corrected in a future patch or release. Waivers relieve the program from the necessity to satisfy a specified requirement.

19.2 **Software engineering tasks (software implementation stage)**

1. *Monitor software implementation progress.* The SWE-IPT monitors the software implementation effort to ensure that the implementation is being accomplished as specified by the physical units. When software engineering proposals are submitted, the SWE-IPT must execute the software engineering process to determine the appropriate corrective action. It is acceptable for the SWE-IPT to reject an ECP and not deviate from the established requirements baseline and functional and physical architectures.
2. *Refine the software architecture.* The SWE-IPT should modify the software architecture to resolve engineering change requests that are necessary for the software implementation effort to be successfully accomplished. The functional and physical architectures may need to be modified and updated to reflect changes required to resolve a requested architectural deficiency. The supporting artifacts, models, and formal documentation should be updated, as necessary, to reflect the change in the software architecture.
3. *Evaluate ECRs.* The SWE-IPT should evaluate each ECR to determine if the desired change can be satisfied within project cost and schedule constraints. The impact of the change on the software architecture must be determined and the level of effort required to implement the change determined. If the functional or allocated baselines need to be changed, the SWE-IPT should prepare an engineering change proposal (ECP) to identify the extent of the change, its impact on the achievement of program objectives and customer satisfaction, and the resources necessary to implement the change proposal.

19.3 **Software implementation tasks (software implementation stage)**

1. *Prepare software unit programmatic designs.* The software implementation team leverages the selected programming language constructs to develop flow charts or other descriptions of the operating principles[1] of each unit's data processing execution. These design descriptions should utilize the structural conventions of a programming language, however they must be comprehendible and verifiable by humans.
2. *Conduct software unit design reviews.* Each software unit must be reviewed before it is transitioned to the coding activity. Software unit designs must be reviewed with senior representatives of the software implementation team to ensure that the software design is consistent with the structural unit specification

---

[1] See *http://en.wikipedia.org/wiki/Pseudocode*

and adheres to software design and coding standards. In addition, each unit design should be evaluated to determine if it provides a noncomplex and well-documented solution that will facilitate post-development sustainment. These design walk-throughs or peer reviews can be performed for individuals or groups of related software units.

3. *Prepare software unit source code files.* The software implementation team edits the source code according to the unit programmatic design documentation. A source-coded editor should be used to facilitate code generation due to its ability to dynamically check the syntactic validity of instructions; it may provide interpretive execution and debugging.

4. *Prepare software problem reports.* Software problem reports should be generated whenever a software unit test procedure uncovers a defect. Software problem reports must be evaluated to determine the proper resolution, and tracked to ensure they are resolved. Software defects that can only be rectified by making adjustments to the software architecture should be submitted to the SWE-IPT as an ECR.

5. *Prepare software unit test scenarios.* The software unit test scenarios and procedures should be developed and documented in the software development folder.

6. *Code software units.* The software implementation team generates the code for each software unit according to the unit programmatic design documentation.

7. *Test software units.* The software implementation team tests each software unit to ensure that it performs as expected, and achieves the software unit specifications. The results should be documented in the software unit test report. Deficiencies identified during unit testing may be resolved, if possible, by modifying the programmatic design and fixing the source code appropriately. Software problem reports must be generated to document identified deficiencies that stem from the structural unit specifications.

8. *Prepare software unit test report.* The results of the software unit testing should be documented in the software unit test report and captured in the software unit SDF. The software unit test report should identify every error encountered during testing, and identify the software problem reports that were generated to document the deficiencies.

9. *Resolve identified deficiencies.* As software unit testing identifies deficiencies, the software unit must be redesigned and its code updated to reflect the corrective action. The software development folder should be updated to preserve test results and properly reflect the "as-implemented" software unit design. The modified software unit is retested to ensure that the modifications did resolve the problem reports and did not introduce any additional problems.

10. *Place software units under configuration control.* Once a software unit has satisfied its unit test procedures the code should be captured in the software library and placed under configuration control.

11. *Prepare software component integration and test procedures.* The software component integration and test procedures should be prepared and captured in the component SDF. Software component test procedures should not repeat

the testing associated with each of the software units. Component test procedures are intended to ensure that the interfaces among software units and components are not broken or damaged as a result of integration. In addition, software components that involve interfaces with external elements should be tested to validate the interfaces.

12. *Integrate and test software components.* The software implementation organization should integrate and test each software component to ensure that it performs as expected. Component integration testing should not reconduct software unit testing but should focus on ensuring that software interfaces work properly and that no problems were introduced by integrating software elements.

13. *Support dry-run testing.* Representatives of the software implementation organization should participate in the dry-run of the acceptance test. Confusion may arise concerning interpretations of test success. Representatives from the computing environment, test and evaluation, and implementation organizations must collaborate to isolate the source of each unsuccessful test. A software problem report should be prepared to identify the cause of each test failure and to recommend a preferred course of corrective action.

14. *Support ECR evaluations.* The software implementation representatives to the SWE-IPT should participate in evaluating ECRs and determining the appropriate architectural resolution.

19.4 Computing environment tasks (software implementation stage)

1. *Define and implement the computing environment.* The computing environment should be designed and implemented in a timely manner that supports software acceptance testing.

2. *Qualify the computing environment.* Computing environment qualification should be performed to ensure that the computing environment satisfies the computing environment specification. The performance of the computing environment should be measured to establish integrated benchmarks necessary to verify software product performance specifications.

3. *Support ECR evaluations.* The computing environment representatives to the SWE-IPT should participate in evaluating ECRs and determining the appropriate architectural resolution.

19.5 Post-development process tasks (software implementation stage)

1. *Define and implement the software replication process.* The software replication process should define the equipment and software applications needed to produce electronic copies of software executables on the desired distribution media. The process and procedures for software replication should be identified

and verified to ensure that the replication process is ready to support software deployment. This should include the packaging of the distribution media, manuals, warranty information, etc., so that it may be distributed to customers or retail/resale outlets, as appropriate.

2. *Define and implement the software distribution process*. The software distribution process and the equipment and software applications needed to package, distribute, or deploy the software product should be defined. Software distribution may involve: (1) establishing an Internet-based distribution approach, (2) employing a dedicated sales team, or (3) establishing distribution and sales channels for packaged merchandise. This may include methods for single-item distribution, mass quantity conveyance to retail or resale outlets, and Internet file download mechanisms. International distribution should be explored and compliance with country-unique regulations concerning the distribution of software products must be investigated. If the software product is being developed for a single customer, then distribution involves delivery, setup, and check-out of the software product.

3. *Define and implement the software training process*. The software training material and mechanisms must be defined and prepared. Training may be in the form of Internet-based instruction, software-based tutorials, or classroom hands-on training. Training materials should be prepared based on the established software configuration and authorized engineering change proposals.

4. *Define and implement the software sustainment processes*. The software and customer support processes should be defined and the equipment and software applications needed to provide product and customer support must be identified. The customer support process may involve phone or online-based help desks or other mechanisms to provide assistance to customers and to record and track software problem reports. Software sustainment processes involve the software development equipment and applications that enable the resolution of software defects within source code files, and the issuance of software patches or service packs. *Note:* The software sustainment process does not involve the effort to provide preplanned product improvement or the advancement of software versions in an iterative or spiral manner. Spiral or incremental efforts involve an intentional software development effort that warrants an organizational commitment and project instantiation.

5. *Support ECR evaluations*. The post-development process representatives to the SWE-IPT should participate in evaluating ECRs and determining the appropriate architectural resolution.

19.6 Software test and evaluation tasks (software implementation stage)

1. *Prepare the software test environment*. The software test environment that will be used to support software acceptance testing must be prepared. Special equipment, test applications, and metric data collection and analysis tools may need

to be acquired or developed to provide the load, stress, scalability testing, software product performance benchmarking, and regressions testing.

2. *Finalize the software acceptance test procedures.* Software acceptance test procedures should be finalized during software implementation in a timely manner that supports dry-run of software product acceptance test procedures.

3. *Conduct dry-run testing.* The software test and evaluation team should execute the acceptance test procedures on the software product executables. The motivations for dry-run testing include:
   - To gain experience with conducting the acceptance test procedures.
   - To identify and correct any defects with the test procedures.
   - To ensure that the computing environment is properly configured to support testing.
   - To ensure that the software product will satisfactorily pass the acceptance testing obstacle.

   Members of the SWE-IPT should monitor the execution of each test to ensure that the test procedures were followed and that the results were accurately captured and recorded.

4. *Generate software problem reports.* When a software test procedure does not generate the expected results, then a software problem report should be generated to identify the problem and explain how it deviated from expected results. Software problem reports that require a modification to the software architecture or TDP should be identified as an ECR. ECRs must be resolved by the SWE-IPT to identify the proper change to be implemented to resolve the architectural design problem.

5. *Revise the software test procedures.* The software test procedures should be revised to correct any errors identified during the dry-run activity. It is possible for a test failure to occur because the software test procedure was improperly defined or its expected results were incorrectly postulated.

6. *Support ECR evaluations.* Test and evaluation representatives to the SWE-IPT should participate in evaluating ECRs and determining the appropriate architectural resolution.

7. *Conduct software quality assurance inspection and audits.* Software quality inspections should be conducted periodically during the software implementation phase to assess the compliance with approved policies and procedures. The following inspections should be conducted:
   - Inspection of the assimilation of change request and proposal resolutions.
   - Inspection of software problem report resolutions.
   - Inspection of the software development folders for software units and components.
   - Inspection of software integration and test records.
   - Inspection of dry-run test records.

   Software audits should be conducted prior to TRR to ensure the software documentation provides a consistent, traceable framework for providing post-development sustainment or incremental/evolutionary development. The software documentation and artifacts must be audited to ensure that they reflect the "as-tested" software product configuration. The following audits should be conducted.

a. *Software development folder audit.* The audit evaluates the software unit detailed design against the physical unit specification to ensure that all of the allocated requirements have been addressed by the software unit design. Audits of software development folders must ensure that the software unit programmatic design and source code comply with established software design and coding standards.

b. *Acceptance test audit.* This audit evaluates the traceability of each test case and procedure to the software specification requirements it is supposed to validate. A software test may affect more than one of the requirement specifications and this should be properly reflected in the requirements traceability matrix.

c. *Computing environment readiness audit.* This audit evaluates the readiness of the computing environment to participate in software dry-run testing. The computing environment is an important element of the software architecture and the software product cannot be tested properly if the computing environment is not available.

d. *Corrective action audit.* This audit traces each approved software engineering request to an approved architectural corrective action plan. The corrective action audit must ensure that the corrective action was properly assimilated into the software architecture and reflected in the affected documentation within the technical data package. The resulting software implementation documentation must be inspected to ensure that the architectural corrective action was properly incorporated.

19.7 Reviews and milestones (software implementation stage)

1. *Software unit design walk-through.* Each software unit should undergo a peer review to ensure that its programmatic design satisfies the unit specification, and that the design documentation has been prepared according to documentation standards. Upon successful completion of a software unit design walk-through the software unit may proceed to the software code and testing effort.

2. *Unit code walk-through.* The software implementation team conducts a code walk-through for each software unit. The purpose of the code walk-through is to ensure that the unit programmatic coding is complete. The unit code and test results should be reviewed to ensure that they properly achieve the specifications, that the source code documentation correctly reflects the "as-implemented" code, and that no Trojan horse[2] or backdoors[3] are present within the code.

---

[2] A *Trojan horse* is in reference to the story of the Trojan horse from a Greek legend. It is a malicious program disguised as a normal application. See *http://netsecurity.about.com/cs/generalsecurity/g/def_trojan.htm*

[3] A *backdoor* is a secret or undocumented means of getting into a computer system. See *http://netsecurity.about.com/cs/generalsecurity/g/def_backdoor.htm*

3. *Conduct test readiness review.* The test readiness review should be conducted to determine the readiness of the software product and computing environment to enter into formal acceptance testing. A typical agenda for the testing readiness review should address the following topics:

1. Test Readiness Review Overview
   1.1. Goals of the Test Readiness Review
   1.2. Review Prerequisites
   1.3. Expected Outcomes
2. Software Readiness Status
   2.1. Software Engineering Status
      2.1.1. Software Architecture Stability
      2.1.2. Outstanding Engineering Change Requests and Proposals
   2.2. Software Implementation Status
      2.2.1. Acceptance Testing Dry-run Results
      2.2.2. Outstanding Software Problem Reports
      2.2.3. Software Development Folder Audit Status
   2.3. Computing Environment Status
      2.3.1. Computing Environment Configuration
      2.3.2. Computing Environment Readiness Status
      2.3.3. Computing Environment Readiness Audit Results
3. Acceptance Testing Readiness
   3.1. Test Plan Overview
   3.2. Test Coverage
   3.3. Test Schedule
   3.4. Outstanding Software Problem Reports
   3.5. Regression Testing Approach
4. Wrap-up
   4.1. Action Items and Assignments
   4.2. Conclusion
   4.3. Final Remarks

Software Acceptance Testing

20

CHAPTER OUTLINE

Acceptance testing is the formal testing activity that involves enterprise, customer, and stakeholder representatives to witness the readiness of the software product to be deployed. If a contract was the genesis for the software development program, then this activity represents a significant step in demonstrating that the software development program has fulfilled its contractual obligations. If the project was funded by internal enterprise resources, then this activity provides proof that the program requirements have been satisfied and the product is ready for deployment. Such products may be distributed internally in support of business processes or they may be marketed as consumer software packages.

Prior to software deployment, the software configuration items must be subjected to a final examination to ensure that the software data packages are complete. The architecture technical data package (TDP) must be audited to ensure that it accurately reflects the "as-built and tested" software configuration. The functional configuration audit (FCA) inspects software test results to ensure that the software product satisfies its specifications, as augmented by change proposals. The physical configuration audit (PCA) inspects the definitive software deployment data package (DDP) to ensure that the as-built and tested software configuration is properly reflected in its documentation set. These configuration audits should be performed to establish the uniformity of the software product configuration to the architectural and configuration DDPs.

A deployment readiness review (DRR) should be conducted to present the results of acceptance testing, software configuration audits, and the status of each of

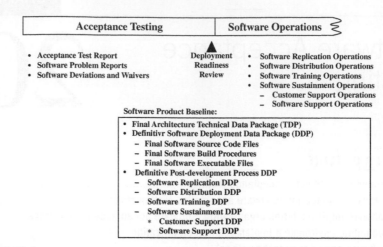

FIGURE 20.1

Acceptance testing stage.

the post-development processes. The DRR is intended to ensure that the processes for software replication, distribution, training, and sustainment are operationally prepared to bolster customer and stakeholder demands to software product training and problem resolution. Figure 20.1 depicts the products of the acceptance testing stage of software development.

20.1 Products of software acceptance testing

1. *Acceptance test report.* This report summarizes the results of software acceptance testing. It should provide the traceability to software problem reports generated to the software components and units of which the behavior did not satisfy the test procedure. Acceptance testing confirms that the software product (software configuration items and computing environment) satisfies the software specifications.
2. *Software problem reports.* Software problem reports should be generated for every discrepancy found during acceptance testing. The priority level, risks, workarounds, and resolution alternatives should be identified so the proper resolution alternative can be identified that will permit software deployment at the soonest opportunity. If dry-run testing was conducted, then there should not be any new software problem reports generated during acceptance testing.
3. *Software deviations and waivers.* Deviations and waivers should be generated for deficiencies in the software product that conflict with the software specifications. Deviations represent nonconformity of the software product with software specifications. Deviations represent acknowledgment of these situations, and request authorization to proceed to deploy the software product in its current

noncompliant state. The deviations provide temporary authorization to deploy the software product with a commitment to resolve the problems with a future patch or release. Waivers are for situations where the software does not satisfy contractual or software requirements, and by waiving the requirement, the software product can be deployed, as is, without a commitment to resolve the deficiency in future patches or releases.

4. *Definitive software DDP.* The software DDP should contain the implementation artifacts that will permit the consideration of future extensions and enhancements to the software architecture. The definitive software DDP should be accompanied with a list of all authorized changes assimilated into the software architecture and its design artifacts. There may be a separate software DDP for each software configuration item that comprise the software product.
   * *Final software executables.* The final software executables should be prepared to establish a baseline for software replication and distribution.
   * *Final software source files.* The final set of source code files should be prepared to be incorporated into the software product baseline. A software bill of material (SBOM) should document each of the source code files that make up the final software product configuration.
   * *Final build procedures.* The final software build procedures should be documented to explain how the software executable files are generated. These procedures will be utilized by the software sustainment organization to generate patches or future releases of the software product.
   * *Final architecture TDP.* The updated software architecture artifacts (requirements baseline, functional and physical architectures, software nomenclature register, models, etc.) should be documented to provide a basis for post-development sustainment and software product and process improvement.

5. *Definitive post-development process DDPs.* The final deployment data packages for each post-development process should reflect the arrangement and layout of the facility, equipment, workstations, communications, networking and equipment connectivity, software tools and databases, etc. involved in facilitating each process. These DDPs provide the detailed design schematics and support documentation necessary to sustain each of the processes.

20.2 Software engineering (software acceptance testing stage)

1. *Witness software acceptance testing.* Representatives of the software engineering integrated product team (SWE-IPT) should witness the conduct of acceptance testing to ensure that the tests are conducted according to the software test procedures.

2. *Witness post-development process qualification.* Representatives of the SWE-IPT should witness the conduct of each post-development process qualification testing to ensure that the tests are conducted according to the test procedures.

3. *Reevaluate the software architecture.* The SWE-IPT should reevaluate the software architecture to understand the impact of software problems and assess potential solutions. The resolution of deficiencies at this late juncture in the software development effort may not be possible. Therefore, the SWE-IPT should prepare software deviation or waivers, as appropriate, to address the resolution of unresolved problem reports.

4. *Support the software configuration audits.* Representatives of the SWE-IPT should participate in the conduct of software FCAs and PCAs.

5. *Prepare the final architecture technical data package.* The SWE-IPT should prepare the updated architecture artifacts to support the software configuration audits. The definitive architecture data package should be accompanied with a list of all authorized changes assimilated into the software architecture and its artifacts (documentation, drawings, models, etc.).

20.3 Software implementation organization (software acceptance testing stage)

1. *Monitor software acceptance testing.* Representatives of the software implementation organization should witness the conduct of acceptance testing to provide insight into software behaviors and responses to test scenarios and conditions.

2. *Evaluate software problem reports.* The software implementation organization must determine the corrective action to be taken to resolve problems that arise during acceptance testing. Software problem reports generated as a result of acceptance testing should be evaluated to determine if they stem from software implementation defects. If necessary, a problem may be elevated to the SWE-IPT to be resolved by modifying the software architecture or pursuing a deviation or waiver.

3. *Deliver the final software executables.* The final software executables should be generated and delivered to the project configuration management organization to support the software replication process and software configuration audits.

4. *Deliver the final software source files.* The final set of source code files should be prepared to provide a basis for software problem isolation and resolution. The source code files also provide a basis for implementing future extensions and enhancement to the software product baseline.

5. *Deliver the software build procedures.* The final software build procedures should be prepared and delivered to the project configuration management organization to facilitate the software replication process. The software build procedures will be utilized by the software replication team to generate distribution media and accommodate patching and releasing future versions of the software product.

6. *Support the software configuration audits.* Representatives of the software implementation organization should participate in the conduct of software FCAs and PCAs.

20.4 Computing environment implementation organization (software acceptance testing stage)

1. *Support the software acceptance testing.* Representatives of the computing environment organization should participate in the conduct of acceptance testing to provide insight into the computing environment implementation behaviors. Confusion may arise among development team members concerning interpretation of requirements or behavior specifications during testing. The computing environment is an element of the software product and is qualified as a result of software acceptance testing.
2. *Deliver the computing environment DDP.* The final computing environment DDP should be prepared to support the software configuration audits. The final computing environment DDP should contain a detailed specification of computing environment physical characteristics and performance benchmarks.
3. *Support the software configuration audits.* Representatives of the computing environment organization should participate in the conduct of the software FCAs and PCAs.

20.5 Post-development process organization (software acceptance testing stage)

1. *Finalize data processing workflow procedures.* The post-development process organization should finalize the data processing workflow procedures for conducting software deployment or sustainment tasks. The workflow procedures should establish guidelines for how to perform typical tasks and contend with atypical situations.
2. *Qualify the post-development processes.* The post-development process organization should prepare test procedures for the software replication, distribution, training, and support processes. Each post-development process should be qualified to ensure that it is ready to conduct software sustainment procedures.
3. *Finalize the post-development process DDPs.* The final deployment data packages for each post-development process should be prepared to provide the detailed design schematics and documentation necessary to sustain each of the processes.

20.6 Software test and evaluation (software acceptance testing stage)

1. *Execute the acceptance test procedures.* The software test and evaluation organization should execute acceptance test procedures to qualify the software configuration and computing environment. Any test failures must be analyzed to identify the source of the failure. Members of the software quality assurance

team should monitor the execution of each test to ensure that the test procedures were followed and that the results were properly captured or recorded.

2. *Generate software problem reports.* When a software test procedure does not generate the expected results, then a software problem report should be generated to identify the problem and how it deviated from the expected results. Software problem reports should document each problem encountered in a manner that enables reconstructing the test results. Each problem report must be assigned to the appropriate software development organization for resolution.

3. *Publish the acceptance test report.* The software test and evaluation organization should prepare the acceptance test report to document the status of software acceptance testing. This report should identify any deficiency identified and establish the regression testing necessary to properly demonstrate that the repaired software configuration or computing environment characteristic adequately resolves the deficiency.

20.7 Reviews and milestones (software acceptance testing stage)

1. *Functional configuration audit.* The software engineering integrated product team leads the audit of the software configuration to ensure that requirements have been properly implemented, tested, and satisfied. Each requirement in the software specifications should be traced to the test results that confirmed the suitability of the software implementation. All authorized engineering change proposals (ECPs) and software problem reports should be evaluated to ensure that they have been resolved and assimilated into the software DDP.

2. *Physical configuration audit.* The software engineering integrated product team leads the audit of the software configuration to ensure that requirements have been properly implemented, tested, and satisfied. The audit should ensure that all authorized ECPs and software problem reports have been resolved.

3. *Deployment readiness review.* The deployment readiness review should be conducted to review the results of acceptance testing and configuration audits. The status of each of the post-development process qualifications must be reviewed to ensure their readiness to support software deployment. Once the deployment readiness review has been successfully completed, the software product is ready to transition to the software deployment stage of its life cycle. The software development project should be considered concluded unless an iterative or spiral development approach is being employed. A typical agenda for the deployment readiness review should address the following topics:

   1. Introduction
      1.1. Agenda
         1.1.1. Goals of the Deployment Readiness Review
         1.1.2. Review Prerequisites
         1.1.3. Expected Outcomes

20.8 Establish the software product baseline

The software product baseline (SPB) should be established at the conclusion of the DRR. The SPB combines the final architecture TDP and software DDP into a complete baseline for the initial release of the software product. This product baseline should be provided to the software sustainment organization as a basis for software problem resolution and deriving engineering solutions for software product extensions and enhancements. If an incremental or evolutionary development concept is utilized, then the software product baseline should be provided to the next program organization taking responsibility for software product enhancements.

Establish the software product baseline

Index

Printed and bound by CPI Group (UK) Ltd, Croydon, CR0 4YY

03/10/2024

01040327-0004